DESPERATE DIPLOMACY

William H. Seward's Foreign Policy, 1861

Diplomacy is "the art of gaining time."
—BARON E. P. BRUNNOW

DESPERATE DIPLOMACY

William H. Seward's Foreign Policy, 1861

BY NORMAN B. FERRIS

THE UNIVERSITY OF TENNESSEE PRESS
KNOXVILLE

Library of Congress Cataloging in Publication Data

Ferris, Norman B   1931–
        Desperate diplomacy.

        Bibliography: p.
        Includes index.
                1.   United States—Foreign relations—1861–1865.
2.   United States—Foreign relations—Great Britain.
3.   Great Britain—Foreign relations—United States.
4.   United States—History—Civil War, 1861–1865—
Foreign public opinion, British.   I.   Title.
E469.F38   973.7'2   75-5509
ISBN 0-87049-170-9

To Paul Whyte Ferris

Preface

Passing through a great library in England . . . , we came upon an alcove, where an author sat, surrounded by great piles of works, on the subject of which he was to write.

"There," said Sir Henry, "is an illustration of the feebleness of all our boasted intellect and invention. That is the way books are made—out of books. Here are eight hundred thousand volumes, on these shelves, slowly and laboriously reproduced out of each other, during successive centuries." And they will continue, for centuries to come, gradually evolving others, in which an original thought, or a novel fact, will be the exception: while the great mass of their facts and ideas will be selected, copied, and rearranged with more or less skill, from their predecessors.

WILLIAM H. SEWARD
February 26, 1872.*

MUCH HISTORY, as Seward suggested, involves an unimaginative rewriting of books. The story of Anglo-American relations during the very important year of 1861 appears in practically all contemporary histories little changed from the way it was told half a century or more ago. Authors of textbooks and scholarly monographs continue to offer readers a tale that is seriously distorted from reality. This traditional account depicts William H. Seward as trying at the outset of the Civil War to plunge the United States into a rousing foreign war, only to be curbed, not once but twice, by Abraham Lincoln, until, under the wise guidance of the president, Seward desisted, and afterwards became one of the nation's ablest secretaries of state.

At the annual meeting of the Southern Historical Association in 1966, I read a paper entitled "To Roll Back the Demoralizing Tide—The Early Foreign Policy of William H. Seward." In this brief essay I tried to correct some commonly held misconceptions regarding the policies and activities of the American secretary of state in 1861. The present work is an extension of that short paper. Before writing it, I completed my examination of practically every book, pamphlet, and scholarly article pertaining to Anglo-American relations during 1861 published in the English language. My narrative, however, is based largely on manuscripts and other archival material, and to a much smaller degree on a very critical approach to contemporary periodicals.

Although my documentation and story development are, I trust, adequate, this book is less thorough than I wanted it to be. The original manuscript was over twice the length of what follows, and much evidence and many illustrations used to support and to illuminate my generalizations have been excised in order to reduce the manuscript to publishable length.

History offers no exact parallels. But time after time, when I have encountered expressions of attitudes toward foreigners emanating from American diplomats or political notables in recent years, I have felt the proverbial "shock of recognition," as I compared those statements with similar declarations of British diplomats or governmental leaders of the 1860s. Could it be that a diplomatic crisis like the *Trent* affair, born of unwarranted suspicion and misunderstanding of foreign leaders, lies just beyond our current horizon? The Americans and Englishmen of 1861 were fortunate; in the end they escaped war against each other. Will we, in our generation, fare as well?

The people who have aided me in this undertaking are so numerous that merely to list their names would take many pages. I have thanked them all in person. Hence, apprehending that if I should attempt here to acknowledge all the assistance I have received during the past decade in writing this book I might inadvertently omit some well-deserved expression of gratitude, I have confined my formal acknowledgments to the appropriate portions of my bibliography.

Norman B. Ferris

Murfreesboro, Tennessee
January, 1975

Contents

	Preface	*Page*	vii
I	Europe Interferes		3
II	Warnings of War from Washington		15
III	Rebels Become "Belligerents"		33
IV	Misunderstandings Proliferate		55
V	The Declaration of Paris Negotiation		73
VI	The Blockade as a Dangerous Issue		85
VII	The Pressure from London Increases		91
VIII	The Bunch Affair Begins		97
IX	The Bunch Affair Reaches Crisis Proportions		104
X	Seward Jails British Subjects		117
XI	England Edges Toward Intervention		126
XII	European Intervention Averted		138
XIII	Europeans Invade North America		154
XIV	England Becomes the Armory of the Confederacy		171
XV	American "Amorality" and British Aggravation		180
XVI	A Historical Misunderstanding		194
	Abbreviations		208
	Notes		210
	Sources		250
	Index		261

DESPERATE DIPLOMACY

William H. Seward's Foreign Policy, 1861

I

Europe Interferes

We are dealing with an insurrection within our own country. . . . We do not desire . . . foreign interference; . . . we do not hesitate, in case of necessity, to resist it to the uttermost. . . . A contest between Great Britain and the United States would wrap the world in fire.

WILLIAM H. SEWARD TO WILLIAM H. RUSSELL,
Washington, D. C., July 4, 1861.

WHEN HE BECAME Abraham Lincoln's secretary of state, William Henry Seward was almost sixty years old. He had already served his native state of New York for four years as governor and for more than a decade as a United States senator. Having traveled extensively abroad, as well as in his own country, and having served actively as a member of the Foreign Relations Committee of the United States Senate, he was probably as well suited by experience for the State Department portfolio in the administration of Abraham Lincoln as any man likely to be considered for the position. Most of those then living who had more significant diplomatic experience than Seward had opposed Lincoln in the presidential election and had thus made themselves politically ineligible for further service after he took office.[1]

The task confronting Seward when he began his tenure at the State Department was a formidable one. Somehow, with few resources initially other than an agile mind and a facile pen, he had to find the means of preventing foreign intervention in behalf of the Southern secessionists from permanently fragmenting the Union. The man in the White House seemed unlikely to give him much help. As Lincoln himself declared to a foreign diplomat two days prior to his inauguration: "I don't know anything about diplomacy. I will be very apt to make blunders."[2]

Foreign meddling in the quarrel between North and South was

almost a certainty. No one was better aware than Seward of the historic proclivities of the great European powers for intervening in the internal conflicts of weaker nations, especially when such conflicts presented an opportunity to strike a blow against the democratic ideals of the American and French revolutions. The hereditary aristocracies clinging to dominance in Europe during the nineteenth century were determined to eradicate these ideals whenever and wherever possible.[3] From the perspective of the leading men of Europe, the United States had not only become during its short period of national existence a dangerous center of ideological subversion, but also a significant threat to the carefully constructed balance-of-power system whereby a select group of Europeans monopolized the resources, markets, and commerce of most of the world. Hence the gusto with which Sir John Ramsden, in May of 1861, announced to the British House of Commons that they "were now witnessing the bursting of the great republican bubble which had been so often held up to us as the model on which to recast our own English Constitution"; hence the joyful shouts of "Hear! Hear!" from his auditors.[4]

As the year 1861 began, no segment of British commercial intercourse was more important than the cotton trade with the Southern United States. Seward could not have been unaware that the leading men in the English ministry placed the highest importance on the preservation of that prosperous import trade, without which the industrial economy of Lancashire could not long continue to flourish. The British prime minister, Henry John Temple, Lord Palmerston, was himself a freetrader of many years' standing, unlikely to look with friendly favor at the Republican party's Morrill tariff of March, 1861, which doubled the general level of duties on imports from England into the United States and reestablished a policy of protection, as opposed to free trade.[5]

It was natural that the Washington cabinet should contemplate choking off the nascent slaveholders' rebellion by blockading the coastline of the Southern states. Should this course of action be taken, however, the British were likely to consider the ensuing injury to their trade to be a provocation calling for some commensurate step in response. Out of such abrasions war might come. And the United States, torn by insurrection, with a government unable to enforce its laws within its own territorial jurisdiction, and with the national capital itself in danger of capture by seditious forces, was poorly equipped to combat mighty Great Britain.

By the time Seward took office as secretary of state, the American Union was shattering. As the New Yorker began his labors in his State Department cubicle, surrounded by insistent callers and piles of papers, seven seceding states, having formed a Southern slave confederacy, had expelled most traces of Federal sovereignty from within their borders and had threatened by taking in both Virginia and Maryland to engulf the national capital as well. Abroad, hundreds of American émigrés and tourists thronged through Europe, testifying "continually," as Seward knew from personal observation, about widespread "demoralization of public spirit and virtue at home."[6] Nor had American diplomats abroad patriotically supported their country. Rather were some sympathetic to the slaveholders' revolt,[7] while others were disposed because of political ambitions to tread cautiously in opposing the Southern disunion movement.[8] Consuls stationed abroad by the Buchanan administration were likewise unreliable.[9]

All over Europe, then, Americans had spread the impression, over a period of many months, that the United States was on the verge of dissolution.[10] Leaders of foreign governments saw no sign up to the time of Lincoln's inauguration that the Federal authority would be brought forcibly to bear against the rebellion. And even though American diplomats in Europe had received instructions in mid-March both to inform the governments to which they were accredited that the United States government had "not relinquished its constitutional jurisdiction" in the South, and to request that no foreign power take any steps "which may tend to encourage the revolutionary movement of the seceding States," these instructions were generally acted upon with a decided lack of fervor. During his first week as secretary of state, Seward renewed the injunction to stand firm, in circular instructions delivered in Europe before the end of March. But the force of his initial communication was diminished not only by the heavy burden of doubt in the stability of the Union already created in Europe, but also by the manifest weakness and confusion in Washington, the hesitancy and vacillation exhibited by Lincoln hardly less than by former President James Buchanan, and the almost unanimous declaration of opinion by foreign diplomats stationed in the United States that the Union was already permanently destroyed.[11]

As Seward feared, threats of foreign intervention in western hemispheric affairs, in contravention of the Monroe Doctrine, and even signs of a disposition to meddle in the internal disorders of the United States itself, began to emanate from Europe. News was received in Washington on March 31 that the Spanish had invaded San Domingo and that the French were contemplating a similar movement against Haiti.[12] Early next day word arrived from Paris that the French government was sending warships to the American coast, whether to emulate the Spanish in some Latin American venture, whether to aid the Southern insurrectionists, or whether merely to protect French commerce should war follow an attempt by Lincoln to repress secession, Seward's diplomatic informant did not know. But the newspapers of the North, having obtained the same information through their European correspondents, or from each other, reflected widespread apprehension that the Old World, in some way, was commencing a concerted invasion of the New World, taking advantage of the incipient rebellion of the American slave states.[13]

Meanwhile, it was well known in Washington that the French minister there had drafted a memorandum to his government arguing in favor of European recognition of Confederate sovereignty in case of civil war in America, and that he had invited the diplomatic representatives of the other great powers to support him by sending similar recommendations to their governments.[14] At the same time, the Russian minister in Washington, a gentleman long intimate socially with the slaveholding leaders in Congress, had attempted to assist the efforts of the Confederate commissioners in the capital to obtain peaceful recognition of Southern independence by the Lincoln administration. This failing, he had said, he would recommend that the czar not be far behind England and France in opening diplomatic relations with the Confederacy.[15]

Although these occurrences foreshadowed hostile action against the United States by the governments of Spain, France, and Russia, comprising together a potential threat to the American Union of massive proportions, an even greater menace came from England. There, as early as February, and again at the beginning of March, the British foreign minister, Lord John Russell, had called in the American plenipotentiary to warn him that if the United States, while trying to suppress the rebellion, interfered with British trade at Southern ports, the British government would strongly object and might as a result recognize the independence of the Southern Confederacy.[16] Russell also instructed his envoy at Washington "above all things" to endeavor to prevent a blockade of the Southern coast.[17]

Lord Richard B. P. Lyons had moved at once to carry out these orders. By mid-March he had begun "preaching" in his diplomatic conversations that any interference with foreign commerce by the partisans of either North or South "would in all probability be a fatal step to the party which first adopted it, by bringing the Powers of Europe into the quarrel, and throwing their weight into the other scale."[18] Anticipating this development, Seward, even before he left the Senate to enter Lincoln's cabinet, began to formulate a policy for meeting the expected challenge from Europe. This policy required the adoption of a firm—even a contentious—attitude toward any European threats to the integrity of the American Union. Unfortunately, words would have to take the place of deeds, at least until the new Republican administration could organize the resources of the nation to create a military machine as useful in backing up foreign policy declarations as in putting down the Southern insurrection. Seward began to tell members of the foreign diplomatic corps in Washington, and others who might repeat the message to them, that the European governments could not legitimately intervene in the dispute in America, "and that the Southern Commissioners who had been sent abroad could not be received . . . without incurring the risk of breaking off relations with the

Government of the United States."[19] When confronted by European envoys with the threat that their governments might break a Northern blockade to get cotton, Senator Seward replied defiantly, according to the minister from Bremen, that a war with a European power might be one way to re-establish internal peace.[20]

Seward and Lord Francis Napier, the previous British minister in Washington, had been close friends. But Lyons, Napier's replacement, was cold and distant, convinced from the outset of his mission that most Americans were easily swayed by "violent feelings," and that they tended to be a boastful, boorish lot. In Lyons's opinion, the acts of the United States government would usually reflect "what will sway the mob." The way to deal with Americans was with "firmness on our side. If they thought they could attain their ends by threats and bluster, there would be no limit to their pretentions." In all relationships with Americans where "British interests and British rights" were involved, Lyons advised that spokesmen for the British government should "be clear and distinct in our language, and firm and decided in our conduct," indeed absolutely "unyielding." By such means might the mother country ensure a proper subservience on the part of her "irritable, excitable, . . . 'bumptious' " trans-Atlantic offspring.[21]

A British minister with these preconceptions was likely to believe that Lincoln's choice for secretary of state, a man who had himself long been a beneficiary of the native "mob-rule" political system, would reflect the typical American "administration of bullying and violent proceedings, . . . universal among the populace here." Lyons was therefore the last person to be surprised when Seward bluntly rejected the demands of European envoys in Washington that nothing be done to injure the trade of their citizens with the Southern slaveholders involved in an insurrection against the United States government.

Early in February, Lyons reported to the Foreign Office in London that he was afraid Senator Seward "would not be very reluctant to provide excitement for the public mind by raising questions with Foreign Powers." For the man who was soon to become secretary of state, Lyons said, had told him personally that

8

if European governments intervened to protect their commerce, a foreign war in order to resist such interference would reunite the American nation.[22] Within a short period of time, Seward had implanted the idea in the mind of the British minister that he was likely to be "arrogant and . . . reckless towards Foreign Powers," whose leaders should act with great caution in dealing with the nation for which Seward, as secretary of state, would speak. Men like Charles Sumner, chairman of the Senate Foreign Relations Committee, who envied and hated the secretary of state-designate and hoped to discredit him politically, were happy to reinforce this impression.[23] By February 12, Lyons was expressing fear that "some of the leaders of the party which is about to come into power are on the look-out for a foreign dispute in the hope that they should thus be able to divert the public mind from home quarrels, and to rekindle the fire of patriotism both in the North and in the South."[24]

The men in London who directed British foreign policy were hoary and shrewd; they were not easily bluffed. Instructions to stand firm against interference by the American government with British trade in Southern ports continued throughout the month of March to appear in Lyons's mail pouches. On March 20, therefore, the British minister told Secretary Seward that he "could not answer for what might happen" if the United States authorities tried to stop "so important a commerce as that of Great Britain with the cotton-growing States." If British shipping should be excluded from Southern ports, "an immense pressure would be put upon H. M's. Government to use all the means in their power to open those ports. . . . the most simple, if not the only way, would be to recognize the Southern Confederacy."[25] Less than one week later, in front of the French and Russian ministers, Lyons repeated his threat that any plan to blockade the Southern coast "placed Foreign Powers in the dilemma of recognizing the Southern Confederation, or of submitting to the interruption of their commerce."[26]

By March 30, Lyons had reached the point of telling Henri Mercier, the French minister at Washington, that in his judgment the "position of the European Powers would become intolerable" if hostilities broke out between North and South, for both England and France depended greatly on imports of Southern cotton, which would be cut off whenever the Federal government imposed an effective blockade on the Southern coast. Lyons had "hoped that the fear that such measures would lead to an immediate recognition of the South by Europe would suffice to prevent their being taken." He advised the Foreign Office that the Southern commissioners seeking recognition of their government in Europe should not be rebuffed there. Finally, echoing a recommendation which Mercier had written to his government the previous day, Lyons emphasized his conviction of "the importance of England and France acting together and securing, if possible, the cooperation of the other Great Powers in whatever course might be taken."[27]

The danger that Lyons's threats and proposals presented to the American Union was formidable. They indicated, as Seward told the Washington correspondent of the London *Times*, that some foreign statesmen might have been "led to imagine the Federal government was too weak to defend its rights, and that the attempt to destroy the Union and to set up a Southern Confederacy was successful."[28]

Against this background of French, Spanish, Russian, and especially British threats to the integrity of the Union, which appeared during a period of about forty-eight hours from March 30 to early April 1 to be leading to tangible activity, Seward produced a hasty exposition of his thoughts about what seemed a desperate situation. While conversing with the president about such matters as the re-supply of Federal forts in the South, the slavery and secession problems, and appointments to office, Seward appears to have broached the topic of the developing intervention crisis, but without arousing Lincoln's interest in the urgency of the problem. The secretary of state then returned to his office, "full of occupation, and more anxieties," as he wrote his wife that day, with "dangers and breakers . . . before us."[29] Under great emotional stress he wrote a terse summary of what he had earlier told the president orally. The resultant memorandum, "Some Thoughts for the President's Consideration," suggested that the United States government "demand explanations from Spain and France, categorically, at once," and "seek explanations from Great Britain and Russia," while replacing the traitorous or lackadaisical diplomatic and consular representatives in Canada, Mexico, and Central America with men who would attempt "to rouse a vigorous . . . *spirit of independence* on this continent against European intervention."[30]

"And, if satisfactory explanations are not received from Spain and France," Seward continued, "would convene Congress and declare war against them."[31] For the deliberate dispatch of French and Spanish military expeditions; the threats, particularly from Lyons, to employ warlike force to prevent the United States government from putting down a rebellion of its own citizens; and the apparent hunger on the part of European representatives in Washington for a settlement based on separation, which *they*, speaking in concert for the Great Powers of Europe, would dictate—all this, taken together, portended a premeditated movement against the United States, which, if unopposed, would probably lead to outright military intervention in behalf of the Southern rebellion. Although it would take weeks, even months, to gather all the members of Congress in Washington, and to present the facts of the foreign policy crisis to them for their consideration, Seward hoped that by initiating steps in that direction he and the president might slow down the growing movement toward European intervention and, in the end, fend it off altogether.

Seward continued:

> But whatever policy we adopt, there must be an energetic prosecution of it.
>
> For this purpose it must be somebody's business to pursue and direct it incessantly.
>
> Either the President must do it himself, and be all the while active in it; or
>
> Devolve it on some member of his Cabinet. Once adopted, debates on it must end, and all agree and abide.
>
> It is not in my especial province.
>
> But I neither seek to evade nor assume responsibility.[32]

This memorandum, with its insistence that incessant and energetic attention be devoted at once to foreign policy, its assertion that when a policy had been agreed upon and adopted the cabinet must thereafter present a united front to avoid conveying further impressions of discord and disarray to Europe, and its offer by Seward to assume exclusive responsibility for putting the new policy into effect, brought forth a reply from Lincoln which showed that the president still misunderstood both the seriousness of the emergency and Seward's purposes in writing his memorandum. Declaring that if it should be necessary to adopt and prosecute a new foreign policy, "*I* must do it," the president indicated that he saw no need for precipitate action, and that he wished to postpone any decision on the matter until he had leisure further to consider the secretary of state's proposals.[33]

Two weeks later, Southern shells burst over the American flag at Charleston, South Carolina; whereupon, notwithstanding the British minister's repeated threats of intervention should the American government hinder trade with the cotton states, the president followed Seward's advice and proclaimed a naval blockade of the Confederate coastline.[34] Lyons's rather tame reaction was to write the Foreign Office grudgingly that if the blockade was carried out in accordance with international law, "I suppose it must be recognized," and momentarily to abandon his threats of British interference, confining his official representations to a mild request for "assurances" that the blockade would be carried out "with a liberal consideration for the interests of foreign nations." These Seward gladly gave him.[35]

Along with his diplomatic colleagues, Lyons had "exhausted every possible means of opposition" to the blockade and failed. Seward's "arrogant spirit and disregard of the rights and feelings of Foreign Nations" had not been shaken by British menace. The British minister in Washington remained "in constant apprehension of some foolish and violent proceeding of the Government with regard to foreign Powers." For the president and his cabinet, inexperienced in foreign affairs, were all inclined to be over-confident of American strength in relation to that of other nations.

Seward was "now the fiercest of the lot," so it had been asserted by one of the secretary of state's "colleagues."[36]

Continuously during the month of May, Lyons sent warnings to Foreign Secretary Russell about Seward's "high-handed conduct and violent language towards us." The British minister offered no specific examples of this behavior. Rather, contemporary newspaper accounts depict Lyons as a frequent and apparently contented guest in the Seward home during this same month, without a hint of friction between the two men. Yet, asserting that he could "perceive little or no understanding in Mr. Seward" of the "power of the Great Countries of Europe," or of the importance to the Washington government "of conciliating the European Powers," he declared that it was still "conceivable" that Seward believed in the absurd notion of a foreign war to reunite North and South. To prevent him from causing such a war, Lyons again advised, Great Britain should "act in entire concert with France" in regard to America, for "even Mr. Seward could hardly be violent against England and France united."[37]

Meanwhile, the French minister at Washington urged that Great Britain and France jointly declare that they would not recognize the blockade of the Southern ports after the 1861 cotton crop was ready for export in September. Mercier agreed with Lyons that no hope remained of "a reconstruction of the Union." The British minister, however, was by this time convinced also of the lack of "prudence" of Lincoln's councillors and believed it possible that such an announcement as the French envoy proposed would "lead them, with a view to keeping up public excitement here, to resort to some violent proceeding with regard to England and France." Lyons refused to approve Mercier's project.[38] At last, Seward's firmness, coupled with the British minister's own natural caution, had begun to show dividends.

But there was still great danger that at any moment—as the disruptions and temptations born of the cotton growers' rebellion proliferated—some sudden diplomatic misunderstanding (or miscalculation) would ignite a terrible war of two continents. Such a world conflict would bury the unique American democratic experiment in the ruins of the Federal Union, even as it might, in Seward's words, reopen the same "fountains of discontent" in European society that gave birth to "the memorable French revolution," and bring on "a general carnival of the adventurous and the reckless of all countries, at the cost of the existing commerce of the world."[39]

II

Warnings of War from Washington

My mind is naturally occupied almost unremittingly in considering the means best adapted to remove the erroneous ideas, and check the reckless conduct, which are tending to results so disastrous.

Lord Lyons to Lord John Russell,
Washington, D. C., May 20, 1861.

In london, Seward's warnings were received in the spirit with which Lyons transmitted them, more as the rantings of a demagogue than as pleas for restraint and vision to preserve world peace. British aristocrats understandably accepted Lyons's evaluation of Seward's policy and attitude. After more than a generation of dealing with Americans who were coarse, bellicose, and often maladroit, Englishmen were inclined to be supercilious and irritable about infringements by their trans-Atlantic cousins upon what they fancied as their rights and interests. Prime Minister Palmerston, who was himself older than the American Constitution, had spent half a century in public office resisting and resenting American impudence through one war and countless provocative incidents related to Canadian border violations, boundary disputes, and especially the African slave trade, which Palmerston bitterly hated and which, after about 1840, was carried on mostly under the protection of the American flag. Twenty years earlier, the old man had suggested the most effective tactic to employ in dealing with the Americans. "With such cunning fellows as these Yankees," he wrote, "it never answers to give way, because they always keep pushing on their encroachments as far as they are permitted to do so; and what we dignify by the names of moderation and conciliation, they naturally enough call fear." However, he added, like all bullies Americans would yield "when in the wrong, if they are firmly and perseveringly pressed."[1] To ensure that England's "diplomatic voice" would be taken seriously by foreigners, Palmerston

believed, it was the duty of the cabinet to provide military reinforcements at times and places of tension and pressure, for "if once
we were palpably inferior we should meet with nothing but insult
and contempt."[2]

As early as February 18, in view of "Lyons's account of Seward's
language," Palmerston suggested that a British regiment and mod-
ern artillery ought to be sent at once to Vancouver Island, where a
boundary dispute still existed between the United States and
Canada. The paltry number of regular troops, about 4,300
stationed in Canada and Nova Scotia, and the disorganized and
poorly equipped state of the militia there were obviously inadequate to put up even a token defense against invasion across the
border. The cabinet members all agreed with the premier that
reinforcements should be sent. Later, discussing the Vancouver–
San Juan boundary question, the foreign secretary cautioned
Lyons: "If it can possibly be helped Mr. Seward must not be
allowed to get us into a quarrel." Although he was not yet convinced that "while the Southern cauldron is boiling over Seward
will indulge the insolence of his nature & nation," Russell added
that he expected his representative at Washington to be watchful
and exercise "wisdom, patience, & prudence to steer us through the
dangers of this crisis."[3]

As warnings of Seward's apparent belligerence continued to
arrive from Washington, Russell wrote back reassuringly that the
Cabinet had great confidence in Lyons's "discretion & firmness,"
and that he could count on aid both from the French government,
whose envoy in the United States was expected soon to "receive
instructions analagous to yours," and from the admiral of the
British West Indian fleet, a man of "sound judgment," whose
"powers of argument," however, were not to be used "without
absolute necessity." Moreover, Seward's newly appointed minister
to Great Britain, Charles Francis Adams, "made a very favourable
impression" as a "calm & judicious man" who could be expected to
try to preserve peace and amity. It was unfortunate that the American secretary of state had turned out to be "so reckless & ruthless,"
but Russell still found it difficult to believe "that Mr. Seward's

colleagues will encourage him in a game of brag with England. The times are too serious, & the U. S. which used to be reckoned secure of neutrality in all wars has now enemies more than enough."[4]

Despite Russell's skepticism of the prospect of Seward's going beyond mere brag against England, however, Lyons's premonitions were accepted as essentially well founded by Palmerston. The premier assessed the American secretary of state as "a vapouring blustering ignorant man." The communications from Washington, he wrote, were "very unpleasant. . . . It is not at all unlikely that either from foolish and uncalculating arrogance and self-sufficiency or from political calculation Mr. Seward may bring on a quarrel with us." The American secretary of state "would be tempted to do so" if Canada were defenseless; hence it seemed to the prime minister desirable that at least three regiments should be sent "without parade" to Canada, as a "foundation for an irregular army." This might be "a useful hint to Seward and Lincoln and their associates."[5]

Palmerston's desire to hurry off troops to Canada was produced by more than "the conclusion which Lyons very urgently impresses upon us that there is great danger that Seward may create some serious difference between the two governments." For, even if Seward and Lincoln had "sense enough to respect us," other administration leaders had joined them in "rousing the military spirit of the people, and have been telling them that their national dignity & power & position among the nations of the earth will be greatly damaged by the separation of the Southern States." Should this military ardor be frustrated by lack of success against the slaveholders, whom Palmerston thought Seward might find "too hard a morsel for his teeth," the excited people of the North might well "seek a vent against what they may think a weaker antagonist in our provinces." Or, finding it beyond their power to restore the Union, the Republican leaders might "then think of indemnifying themselves in the North for what they have irrecoverably lost in the South." For all these reasons the British West Indian and North Atlantic naval squadrons should be reinforced, and regular troops "with arms as good as those of the people whom they may have to meet" should be sent to Canada as a nucleus to which local militia might be added to form an army "sufficient to make head against a large United States force."[6]

While the British cabinet was working out the details of sending military forces to Canada as a means of deterring Seward from provoking an Anglo-American quarrel, the American secretary of state was receiving vexatious dispatches from his envoys in Europe. On April 27 he learned from the American representative at Paris that the French foreign minister had insisted on "the right of *de facto* governments to recognition when a proper case was made out for the decision of foreign powers."[7] The United States minister at London had reported a week or so earlier that Russell had refused to discuss Seward's objections to recognition of the Southern Confederacy, saying only that the question was "not ripe for decision one way or the other." The same dispatch also mentioned that English public opinion seemed to favor "a peaceful separation" of North and South.[8]

Seward quickly sent off instructions to London and Paris ordering his new ministers there to object to these indications of "a policy that the government would be obliged to deem injurious to its rights and derogating from its dignity," and suggesting that they say, "with the highest consideration and good feeling," that European statesmen ought to dismiss thoughts "of a dissolution of this Union, peaceably or by force," from their minds. Having permitted newspaper publication of the instruction to William L. Dayton, his representative at Paris, the secretary of state handed Lyons a copy of the instruction to Adams, to make doubly sure that the British government received the message.[9]

Then, on May 17, Seward learned that Great Britain and France had agreed to act together in dealing with the "American question." The only logical reason for the existence of such an arrangement was that some form of intervention was contemplated by the two great powers. A motion to recognize the Confederacy had already been placed on the calendar of the British House of Commons, and Russell had called in the American minister to tell him that the Southern commissioners were in London and that although he had not seen them he "was not unwilling to do so, unofficially." Moreover, the London correspondent of the *New York Times* had warned that "in the highest of official circles" in England, a war with the United States to get cotton was "already regarded as all but unavoidable, and such being the case, it may not be difficult to provoke." Should British ships be seized in any blockade of Southern ports, "a collision will not easily be warded off."[10]

In Paris, meanwhile, where the Virginia secessionist, Charles Faulkner, continued to preach in favor of the permanent dissolution of the Union which employed him as its envoy to the French court, Henry S. Sanford, newly appointed United States minister to Belgium, arrived with special instructions from Seward. Prevented by Faulkner and by French protocol from seeing the French foreign minister, Edouard Thouvenel, officially for seven frustrating days, he finally arranged an interview for April 24. On that occasion he presented Thouvenel with a plea from Seward neither to receive the secessionist commissioners, even unofficially, nor to allow ships from the rebel states access to French ports. He also requested that the French disavow any intention of granting diplomatic recognition to the Southern insurrectionists. Thouvenel replied, according to Sanford, that although he regretted the disruption of the American Union, he planned nevertheless to receive the Southern commissioners unofficially to hear what they had to say. Moreover, French ports would remain open to Southern ships on the same basis as to vessels flying the United States flag, although this would not imply diplomatic recognition of the Confederate government. Finally, Thouvenel asserted, he was obliged to say frankly, what he had told Faulkner slightly more than one week earlier, that if the South was able to establish a *de facto* independence, France would acknowledge it as an independent nation, as soon as it was to her interest to do so.[11]

When Thouvenel's account of the interview with Sanford reached Washington, Mercier proudly showed it to his Russian, British, and Belgian colleagues, and probably to other foreign envoys as well, as an example, in Edouard Stoeckl's words, of how the wise Old World diplomat had put Seward "in a false position."

The Russian minister, who had earlier praised the New Yorker as "an indispensable man" and "the ablest American statesman, . . . who above all others should be President of the United States," had become disillusioned when Seward had tactfully rejected Stoeckl's hints that he, individually or in concert with Lyons and Mercier, should mediate the North-South quarrel on the basis of separation. Seward had declared in a letter which he had avoided sending directly to any foreign representative, but had rather published in the newspapers as addressed to the governor of Maryland, that foreign mediation, unasked, would be foreign intervention and would be vigorously resisted by the United States government. Thus rebuffed, Stoeckl decided that Seward had exhibited "complete ignorance of all that which concerns international affairs" and that the secretary of state was personally so arrogant and vain "that he will not listen to any advice." Lyons, too, agreed that the "insolent" Seward, whose "ridiculous pretensions to a knowledge of Europe" were totally unfounded, hoped to "excite the American mob" against European powers by "blustering words," which might well lead to "violent deeds." Hence he strongly recommended that Mercier acquaint the secretary of state with Thouvenel's categorical account of what he had told Sanford, as a means of preventing, "if anything could have that effect, Mr. Seward's making any further violent communications to England or France."[12]

Accompanied by Stoeckl, the French minister went to Seward's home with Thouvenel's dispatch, but when the American secretary of state seemed to be in an unreceptive mood, Mercier decided "to postpone the conversation to a moment when he would be more docile." That moment seemed never to come, however, and after waiting several days more, the Frenchman changed his mind about delivering the unpleasant message personally to Seward; instead he made a lengthy extract from Thouvenel's dispatch, which he handed "confidentially" to Frederick Seward, for transmittal to his father. The appearance of this missive in the State Department, almost simultaneously with the receipt of Sanford's dispatch repeating Thouvenel's politely worded threats to aid and possibly to recognize the slaveholders' Confederacy, only seemed to reinforce the earlier indications of forthcoming intervention by the French and the British in favor of the Southern rebels.[13]

Seward was greatly depressed. He wrote his wife: "They have misunderstood things fearfully in Europe." Great Britain was in "danger of sympathizing so much with the South," for the sake of cotton, that she seemed to contemplate making herself "the ally of the traitors." And Great Britain was the key to the whole problem of European intervention, for Thouvenel had admitted to Sanford that since England "was more deeply interested than France" in the cotton trade, the French "should look rather to her course to guide them in their policy." Seward was determined "to get a bold remonstrance through the Cabinet" before it was too late to stop the war that would almost inevitably ensue if Great Britain and France attempted to "save cotton, at the cost of the Union."[14] He wrote a friend that he hoped his earlier "demonstrations" had come "in time for France and England," for those nations appeared "to have been in danger of getting committed" to the idea that the Union was permanently divided. He intended to send Adams more instructions, "bold and decisive," to meet the latest threats from London.[15]

To another friend who suggested that he might be acting *too* decisively, he answered: "Will you . . . advise us to consent that Adams and Dayton have audiences and compliments in the Minister's Audience Chamber, and [the Southern] emissaries have access to his bedroom?" Private recognition would soon lead to public recognition. A string of concessions granted to the rebels by European governments would lead inevitably to recognition of their cause; such intervention would signify the permanent destruction of the Union and would probably also precipitate a general trans-Atlantic war.[16]

The "bold remonstrance" which Seward finally got the president to approve was incorporated into an instruction to Adams dated May 21. Seward's intent in writing it was to preserve trans-Atlantic peace by preventing British intervention in the American Civil War. The instruction began with a résumé of the latest information received from England—that the British foreign minister had re-

21

fused thus far to hear American protests against European recognition of the Confederacy, that he had said he would see the Southern commissioners unofficially, that Great Britain and France had an "understanding" with regard to the United States, and that a debate in Parliament on the question of recognition had been announced. Seward pointed out that "Intercourse of any kind with the so-called commissioners is liable to be construed as a recognition of the authority which appointed them. . . . Moreover, unofficial intercourse is useless and meaningless, if it is not expected to ripen into official intercourse and direct recognition." If Russell insisted on carrying on discussions with the Southern envoys, Adams was instructed to "desist from all intercourse whatever" himself with the British government and to refer to Washington for further instructions.[17]

In the light of reports from the Continent that Great Britain and France had asked other European nations "to follow them in whatever measures they adopt on the subject of recognition," it appeared likely that the "understanding" between the two great powers had an intent that might not be friendly to the United States. Should this alliance later be announced as being for some specific purpose, Seward declared, those involved might expect the United States government to be "frank and explicit in our reply." That government intended to carry on its blockade of the Southern ports in accordance with the rules of international law, and it anticipated, therefore, that foreign powers would respect the blockade. Should any foreign agent disobey federal laws or disown federal authority, he would be asked to leave the country. And although the United States would not treat recognition of the rebel government as a matter of technical definition, it would not let a public acknowledgment of Confederate sovereignty, an official reception of Confederate diplomats, or a concession of belligerent rights to the insurgents pass unquestioned.[18]

"British recognition," Seward warned, "would be British intervention to create within our own territory a hostile state by overthrowing this Republic itself. (When this act of intervention is distinctly performed, we from that hour, shall cease to be friends and become once more, as we have twice before been forced to be, enemies of Great Britain.)" If, as Lyons had already suggested she might, Great Britain should shelter "privateers in the insurgent service" from Federal "pursuit and punishment," the United States would avail itself of "the law of nations" for its remedy. It had already accepted the rule of the Declaration of Paris of 1856 "abolishing privateering everywhere in all cases and for ever." If Great Britain, as an original signer of that agreement, should now object to American adherence to it, the reason could "only be because she is willing to become the patron of privateering when aimed at our destruction."[19]

Seward recognized, he said, "the grave importance of the occasion." For it appeared that, to defend its own sovereignty and independence, the United States might be forced to fight "one, two, or even more European nations." The idea of war was "revolting"; yet if Great Britain decided to make common cause with the Southern insurgents, the United States would have no choice other than to defend itself. Such a dispute between two branches of the same race, Seward said, ought to be considered unthinkable. Europe had "atoned by forty years of suffering for the error that Great Britain committed in provoking" the wars of the American and French revolutions. If the same great error were repeated, even wider "social convulsions" would follow. The United States would survive, because its cause would be that of men everywhere— simply that of the preservation of "the independence of nations and the rights of human nature." But what would happen to European powers whose aristocracies fomented a war of aggression against democracy in the New World? Their own populations would rise in revolution. Before intervening in the American disturbance, Great Britain ought to "calculate for herself the ultimate as well as the immediate" consequences of such an act.[20]

During the period of time, probably lasting several days, that it took Seward to obtain the president's approval for his instruction of May 21, Lyons apparently discovered that such a communication was being prepared. Alluding to "an eminent Senator, well acquainted with Europe," as his source of information, Lyons warned

23

that "it might be impossible to deter this government from offering provocations to Great Britain, which neither our honour nor our interest will allow us to brook." Senator Charles Sumner, the British minister's unnamed informant, claimed to have urged Seward to ensure that any measures taken against the South "should injure the manufacturing body in Great Britain as little as possible," but the secretary of state had allegedly shown "little disposition," Lyons reported, "to listen to counsels of this kind. His notion appeared to be that the United States should take any measures that suited them, and England might interfere if she dared."[21]

For the United States government to refuse to let British commercial considerations weaken its determination to subdue the Southern rebellion was described by Lyons as "naughty" conduct. According to the British minister, Seward had "ever regarded the Foreign Relations of the country as safe materials from which to make . . . political capital at home." His "arrogant language and high handed conduct towards the Powers of Europe" were common among party politicans in the North. Seward's obsessive anxiety for personal popularity, Lyons wrote, "disposes him to pander to these cravings." His intemperate boasting was probably based on "a conviction that under no provocation will England or France really go to war with the United States." The secretary of state apparently thought that in Europe "the sacrifice of the supply of cotton may be regarded as less grievous than that of the trade with the North," that as longstanding rivals England and France were incapable of acting together in dealing with third parties, that neither would dare fight the United States alone, and, finally, "that apprehension for Canada will induce us to avoid a contest." Indeed, Lyons asserted (incorrectly), Seward had publicly "advocated, during the Presidential Canvass, the annexation of Canada, as a compensation for any loss which might be occasioned by the disaffection of the South." Considering that Seward's "future Despatches, and his future conduct towards Foreign Powers will be regulated by the same design to obtain personal popularity," Lyons wrote: "My mind is naturally occupied almost unremittingly in considering the means best adapted to remove the erroneous ideas, and check the reckless conduct, which are tending to results so disastrous." To convince Seward and other leading Americans that "there is a point beyond which forbearance cannot be carried," Great Britain should show "absolute inflexibility of purpose" in putting "Canada at once in a complete state of defence," reinforcing British naval squadrons in the West Indies and along the American seacoasts, and acting in complete concert with France to prevent the "unhappy contest" in the United States from "interfering with the supply of cotton from the South, until other sources of supply may be opened," which would take years to accomplish. The "appalling" prospect of being deprived by the Northern blockade of a single year's supply of cotton, Lyons asserted, was enough in "itself to alienate the sympathy of England & France," and the "threats and vexations" sure to arise out of that blockade would only increase the "possibility of a war between Great Britain and the United States."[22]

He had "reason to know," Lyons wrote Russell, that the president and some members of the cabinet had been awakened "in some degree to a sense of the danger" into which Seward was "leading them by his treatment of the Great Powers of Europe." For when the secretary of state, upon learning that Great Britain had granted belligerent rights to the Southern Confederacy, had drawn "up a Despatch to Mr. Adams to be communicated to Y.L. in terms still stronger than any he had before used," Lincoln and the rest of the cabinet had refused "to sanction it" at a meeting called to discuss the document. "I believe however," Lyons continued, "that Mr. Seward insisted upon its being adopted without change, and I fear that the President has consented to its being sent, on condition however that it is to be left to Mr. Adams's discretion to communicate it or not as he may think advisable." The British minister thought that "whether the President and Cabinet will exercise a due control" over Seward; "or whether by the aid of the violent war party, he will domineer over them, are matters, I fear, very uncertain." He reiterated his belief that "the most effectual check to these dangerous proceedings" would be to make no concessions to "violent

25

language and conduct," but to proceed inflexibly to prepare for a war with the United States as a means of attempting to prevent one.[23]

Lyons's warnings that an entire series of offensive instructions written by Seward had been so belligerently worded that they portended a policy of war against England were supported by letters from the governor general of Canada, in which that gentleman visualized the American secretary of state reasoning that the South was lost, irrevocably; so that, even though the North might fight on for a while, the Southerners would eventually establish their independence.

> Then will be our time to indemnify ourselves in the North [Head visualized Seward as brooding] by annexing British North America & the moment we have come to terms with the South we can turn against Canada all the warlike ardour & warlike preparations which were got up for other purposes.
>
> In order to do this with effect we must make our people think that England has injured us by recognizing the existence of the Southern Confederacy. It is our interest therefore to keep on those terms with England which will enable us at any moment without warning to declare war & march into Canada.

Head could "attribute Seward's tone towards Lord Lyons to nothing but some speculation of this kind," and apparently his superiors in London gave full credit to his analysis, as well as to Lyons's warnings.[24]

On June 3, Palmerston informed the secretary for war "that the bullying and arrogant tone and proceedings of Seward and his colleagues who think to make political capital by insulting England may bring on a serious quarrel between us and the Northern States. It is therefore of great importance that our reinforcements should go out as soon as they can be sent, and that they should be accompanied by a strong detachment of artillery with a sufficient number of Armstrong guns."[25] Moreover, no time should be wasted in transferring large warships to the American station. "Their going could produce no bad impression here," Palmerston wrote the duke of Somerset, "and depend upon it that as to impression in the

United States the yankees will be violent & threatening in proportion to our local weakness and civil & pacific in proportion to our increasing local strength."[26] Thus the premier echoed the sentiments of his minister at Washington, who had declared that "the best way to maintain the peace . . . will be found in being evidently prepared for war. Nothing is so likely to prevent an attack as manifest readiness to prevent one."[27]

Queen Victoria strongly endorsed Palmerston's proposal to send reinforcements, especially more warships, to the Western Hemisphere. For she thought "it of great importance that we should be strong in Canada" and that both artillery and infantry should be rushed there, even though it appeared "less likely that the remnant of the United States could send expeditions by land to the North while quarreling with the South, than that they should commit acts of violence at sea."[28]

Most members of the British cabinet likewise favored strengthening the Canadian garrisons.[29] Even Lord Sidney Herbert, the secretary for war, who believed that the "American effervescence will pass away," endorsed a plan which resulted in the departure from England during May of an infantry regiment bound for Canada, followed in June by two more regiments, along with a field battery of new Armstrong guns, and arms, ammunition, and other supplies for the Canadian militia. The June shipment was sent on the huge iron steamship, the *Great Eastern*, which made a dramatic dash across the Atlantic in the record time of eight days and six hours and disembarked its cargo and passengers in Quebec to the accompaniment of great publicity. To dispatch these military reinforcements with such élan, in a manner openly calculated to overawe the Americans, however, touched off sporadic splatters of criticism in England, even in the cabinet. For example, the home secretary, Sir George Cornewall Lewis, wrote the governor general of Canada that it seemed to him "incredible that any Government of ordinary prudence should at a moment of civil war gratuitously increase the number of its enemies, and moreover incur the hostility of so formidable a power as England." Therefore, should Seward and Lincoln *not* intend mischief to British possessions in North

America, they might be irritated, rather than subdued in ardor, by the flamboyant gesture of the *Great Eastern*'s voyage.[30]

Doubts about the wisdom of the venture were likewise expressed by the editors of the London *Times*, who claimed to be unable to discern why so many more troops were going to Canada. The expedition appeared to have resulted from "a rash and ill-considered policy." There appeared to exist little reason for apprehending an attack by the United States upon Canada. For a quarrel with England could hardly be expected to bring about an early end to the American Civil War; rather would it prolong the war, "by giving the South a powerful, though a very unwilling ally. . . . If the presence of our troops in America has a tendency to preserve peace it may well be submitted to, but we fear," the *Times* editors declared, "that in her present state of mind America is more likely to regard it as a challenge than as a precaution."[31]

Indeed, Her Majesty's loyal opposition found the *Great Eastern* episode culpable. Sir James Fergusson told the House of Commons that "so decided and conspicuous a measure" as the sending of 3,000 troops to Canada, "in hot haste in a very ostentatious manner, in the largest and fastest vessel which this country had ever possessed," had certainly been inadvisable. This criticism brought Palmerston himself to his feet to defend the step. It had been merely "an ordinary precaution," he asserted, of the kind taken by all governments whenever war broke out in states adjoining their own territories, and it signified "no intention whatever to take any part in the unfortunate differences now prevailing . . . in the United States." The *Great Eastern* was used, instead of other, smaller ships, in order to inflict upon the troops the minimum of "inconveniences which a sea passage too often produces."[32]

The prime minister's defense of the government's action was weak enough to prompt a further Tory sally. Benjamin Disraeli quickly rose to announce his dissatisfaction with what he termed an "ingenious" rejoinder, but one which had failed to meet the real point of Fergusson's question: "What is the object of the despatch of these troops?" Disraeli considered

it a very serious measure, and that the Government have incurred a very grave responsibility indeed. . . . Dismissing from our minds the disturbances in the United States, I do not see the necessity of this operation; and if those disturbances are its cause, then we have to consider it an act of very grave policy on the part of the Government. . . . [The only inference that the Americans could draw] will be that there is on the part of the English Cabinet suspicion and fear, and a preparation for hostilities which may be contingent with the United States. . . . it seems to me that this movement has a fretful and feverish character.[33]

Little of the fret and fever detected by Disraeli in the ministry found its way into Russell's replies to Lyons. The foreign secretary confined himself to reiterating a former admonition that Lyons should "be both forbearing and firm," continuing steadily to express his government's desire to remain on terms of "peace and amity with the United States," but also warning against "blustering demonstrations" that might try British patience too far. The language and conduct of the American minister in London remained highly satisfactory, Russell wrote. He did not believe, he said, "that the American Republic will seek a quarrel with a nation sprung from the same parents, and united by language as well as by ties of kindred, and a long period of friendly intercourse."[34]

Soon, however, more war-scare missives from Lyons arrived at the Foreign Office. Following a telegram in which he abruptly warned against "a sudden declaration of war by the U.S. against Great Britain, . . . so long as Canada seems open to invasion," Lyons wrote that the "dominant" party in Washington was "in a state of mind so utterly unreasonable as to border upon frenzy. . . . The cry was, 'We will conquer the South with one hand and chastise Europe with the other.' " When Congress resumed its deliberations on July 4, Lyons predicted, it was "easy to see how soon a struggle between different members to obtain the palm for strong words and strong measures will lead to the strongest proposal of all—that of an immediate declaration of war against Great Britain." The secretary of state seemed himself to share in the mass delusion that the naval and military might of the North was sufficient "for carrying on simultaneously a war with the South and with a great European Power." Indeed, Lyons asserted, Seward encouraged this palpably absurd notion in others, as shown by the language of that portion of the press "directly under the influence of the government," which seemed to be purposely intending "to prepare the public mind for violent proceedings against Great Britain as soon as Congress meets."[35]

Even if the present crisis should subside, Lyons continued, the necessity of acquiescing in the division of the Union between North and South sooner or later would render it "almost necessary . . . for the personal safety of President Lincoln and his Cabinet to divert the popular wrath from themselves to a Foreign Foe." With a large new army "ready and eager for an invasion of British North America," the Northern people would "rush eagerly into any contest, which would relieve the feeling of humiliation that an acquiescence in the separation of the Southern States must bring with it." Lyons, however, was personally "making every effort" to avert "so great a calamity as a war with the United States," by "studiously avoiding everything which may increase popular irritation, or give occasion to the government for intemperate language or conduct towards Great Britain."[36]

As part of his effort to help avert war by "avoiding everything which may increase popular irritation," Lyons forwarded, in a dispatch marked with the rarely used "Secret" designation of the British Foreign Service, a juicy piece of gossip received from the British consul at New York. The rumor was that certain Irish residents of that state were planning an "insurrection in and an invasion of Canada." Although he was later forced by a disclaimer from the governor general of Canada to concede that this particular rumor was false, Lyons nevertheless staunchly maintained that "vigilance for designs against the peace of Canada should at the moment be kept high." Three weeks later he wrote Russell that he had discovered another threat to Canada. A plot allegedly existed to negotiate an armistice between the combatants in the American Civil War and then to embark on a joint conquest of all the rest of North America, as well as Central America, and the West Indies. This project had been "day after day seriously recommended" by the *New York Herald*, the newspaper "having the largest circulation in the United States," a fact which Lyons found "not without significance." He neglected, however, later to mention an attack on the "absurdity" of these articles which soon appeared in the *New York Times*, whose editor was well known to be a close friend of Seward, and which frequently published official news understood to have been "leaked" from the State Department. Nor did Lyons bother to point out that the *Herald* had a long history of bitter attacks against Seward and his policies, and that it had also been notorious for many years for its Anglophobia.[37]

The British foreign minister's unruffled comment on these communications was: "These are not very respectable maneuvers. You will do well to continue calm, & let Mr. Seward take his own course." Russell observed to Palmerston that he thought he perceived, amid all the conflicting reports from America, some "signs that the Northerns are calming down from their frenzy." But when Lyons's dispatches were passed on to the prime minister, the old man nevertheless complained that the prospect which they all seemed to portend of the

> manner in which our Relations with the Northern States of America are liable to be affected by the character & conduct of Seward is very disagreeable; and the question . . . of communication with the Southern States may also lead to serious difficulties.
>
> My opinion therefore is that we ought before winter at all events, and sooner, if possible, to add to our Military Force in Canada which should not be less than Ten Thousand Troops of the Line, with proportionable artillery. . . .[38]

Five months previously the prime minister had considered a single regiment of reinforcements enough for Canada; then he had decided as a result of Lyons's recommendations to send three regiments; finally, after a spate of warnings from Washington, he had concluded that a total force of ten thousand regulars, necessitating the transport of three more regiments, would be required to maintain the security of Great Britain's North American colony against invasion from the United States. Based on a grievous misconception of the motives and policies of the American secretary of state, this movement of troops only enhanced apprehensions in Washington that the British government contemplated active measures to ensure the success of the Southern rebellion. Meanwhile, this suspicion was being reinforced, and the atmosphere of hostility thickened, by the equally unfortunate assumption by Lyons and his superiors that the division of the Union was necessarily permanent, which led to a premature concession by the British government of belligerent rights to the Southern insurrectionists, thus pronouncing "the parties to the contest equal in its sight."[39]

Rebels Become "Belligerents"

It did not rest with you to "allow" belligerent rights, and it was also a departure from your profession of neutrality. To be neutral you had to be silent.
ISSAC IRONSIDE TO LORD RUSSELL,
6 June 1861.[1]

As THE YEAR 1861 BEGAN, British public opinion had favored the Northern cause. The South, asserted the editors of the London *Times*, could expect no aid or sympathy from England. That nation's antislavery policy of over half a century could not be abandoned "for the sake of an extended cotton trade." When news reached England early in January, 1861, that South Carolina had seceded from the American Union and that other states were expected to follow her lead, the *Times* castigated the Southern political leaders as "a proud, lazy, excitable and violent class, ever ready with the knife and revolver," and added that "South Carolina has as much right to secede from the . . . United States as Lancashire from England." *Punch* expressed similar sentiments, praising Lincoln for upholding "the necessity of acquiescence by minorities in the decision of majorities" and labeling the secession leaders "lunatics. . . , fools and madmen." At the end of February a leading English statesman wrote that the South's conduct had "disgusted everybody." The Southern politicians had "shown a measure of passionate haste and unreasoning arrogance which has astonished and alienated all lookers-on."[2]

The English press generally expressed a hope that the North would permit the South to go in peace—that the inhabitants of the North would gain by thus disassociating themselves from the odium of Negro slavery. But, little by little, British sympathy for the North, based initially on a mistaken belief that the election of Lincoln represented the advent in office of a party committed to abolition of slavery in the United States, was undermined by the efforts of Republican leaders like Seward to hold the Union to-gether by reaching a compromise with the slaveholders. Lincoln himself, while promising in his inaugural address to "preserve, protect and defend" the Union, reiterated what he had said many times previously—that he did not mean "directly or indirectly, to interfere with the institution of slavery in the States where it exists."[3]

Gradually, Englishmen became aware that the election of Abra-ham Lincoln did not mean, as they had vaguely surmised for many weeks, the peaceful abolition of Negro slavery in America. They also began to see that the danger of civil war in the United States over the issue of disunion was increasing every day. Next followed the realization that if war came to the United States, British com-mercial interests there must surely suffer.[4]

On January 22 the editors of the London *Times* exhibited their first sign of trepidation over the harm an American civil war might do to British trade. England had "enormous interests at stake," they warned. "Lancashire depends on South Carolina." Over one-sixth of the population of Great Britain and one-third of her exports were dependent on cotton manufacturing, and over three-fourths of England's cotton originated in the Southern United States. The suspension of cotton production in the slave states of North America and an interruption of supplies from that quarter were growing more probable. A *Times* editor asked whether any Eng-lishman could contemplate that prospect without terror.[5]

Charles Greville, nearing the end of his forty-year tenure as clerk of the Privy Council, frequently reflected the prevalent view of the English oligarchy. An American civil war, he wrote, would

> be almost sure to interfere with the cotton crops, and this is really what affects us and what we care about. With all our virulent abuse of slavery and slave-owners, . . . we are just as anxious for, and as much interested in, the prosperity of the slavery interest in the Southern States as the Carolinian and Georgian planters themselves.[6]

As early as January 10, Russell had written Lyons that he did not see how the United States could be "cobbled together again." He had added that in his opinion "the right to secede should be acknowledged, and that there should be a separation" into two republics. Lyons, too, though claiming to be "sincerely interested in the welfare" of the United States, nevertheless wished the Lincoln administration would not fight to keep the slave states in the Union. For war, he asserted, could "lead only to the exhaustion of the North [and] . . . the utter devastation of the South. It would at all events occasion a suspension of Southern cultivation which would be calamitous . . . even more to England than to the Northern States themselves."[7]

Nor did the British foreign secretary in London receive any intelligence from his consuls in America during the early months of 1861 to contradict his own supposition that the Union was irrevocably divided. In Charleston, British Consul Robert Bunch took it for granted that the South had established its independence. A. T. Lynn, British consul at Galveston, Texas, wrote the Foreign Office that "the separation of the seven Confederate States is final & that any endeavour of the Free States to effect a reunion by concessions to the demands of the Slave States or by coercion would be alike ineffectual." The London press echoed these beliefs: Northern conquest of the seceding states, asserted the editors of the *Illustrated London News*, "is just an impossibility. . . . The world must henceforth expect to see two moderate Republics established on that continent where for many years it has been accustomed to contemplate the growth of a nation which bade fair to be stupendous in its greatness." Meanwhile the editor of the London *Times* responsible for its American news columns maintained that to try to preserve the Union would be "mad." And the British chancellor of the exchequer declared: "I think the whole notion of 20 millions of Republicans making war upon 10 other millions, to compel them, irrespective of all differences of climate, interests, spaces, and circumstances, to continue in free voluntary & equal union with them, which taints and infects their very freedom, [is] one of the most strange paradoxes, and one of the most lamentable pictures, that has lately been presented to the eye of humanity."[8]

As the Russian ambassador to London wrote home: the privileged class of men who ruled England at the bottom of its heart, desires the separation of North America into two Republics, which will watch each other jealously and counterbalance one the other. Then England, on terms of peace and commerce with both, would have nothing to fear from either; for she would dominate them, restraining them by their rival ambitions.[9]

Faced thus with an "American crisis," the Palmerston ministry adopted a policy of caution, based on the premier's own dictum that "Nothing could be more unadvisable than for us to interfere in the dispute" in America. Or, put more picturesquely: "They who in quarrels interpose, will often get a bloody nose," and "If you would keep out of strife, step not in 'twixt man and wife." When asked what the British government's policy would be in regard to the Southern secession crisis, the foreign minister replied that the cabinet was "in no hurry to recognize the separation as complete and final." It would wait to see what the future brought.[10]

This policy of vacillation, as we have seen, was considered unsavory by the American secretary of state, who realized that behind it lay an unspoken wish for the fragmentation of the Union, if only it could be accomplished without disruption of British trade.[11] At any moment, once the Northern blockade of the Southern coast became onerous, British restraint would gradually diminish, and intervention to further the cause of separation might well follow. Hence Seward applied all the pressure he could in the opposite direction, designed to increase British fears that intervention would harm their economic interests more than it could help them.

Meanwhile, English supporters of the Southern cause were working hard for British intervention in favor of separation. Early in April, William H. Gregory, an ambitious Irish politician who represented Galway in Parliament, let it be known in the House of Commons that he intended to offer a formal motion favoring the recognition of the Confederacy. But British governmental leaders remained wary, and both Russell and Palmerston informed Gregory that the government would oppose his motion. They persuaded him to postpone it, first from April 16 to April 30, and then until the end of May. As the prime minister sagely observed, "all the Americans will say that the British Parliament has no business to meddle with American Affairs." Gregory's friends, he said, would praise the South and condemn the North; others would do the reverse; and in America "each party will be offended by what is said against them, and will care but little for what is said for them." Therefore, England should continue to stand "aloof" and maintain its future freedom of action.[12]

The advisability of caution in dealing with what had now become the "American question" was also implied in dispatches from Washington received in London on April 30. In these messages, Lyons warned that "some foolish and violent proceedings" could be expected from the United States government. For Fort Sumter had just been attacked by South Carolinians, and war was now a reality. Already Confederate President Jefferson Davis had approved the issuance to privateers of letters of marque and reprisal. Russell had scarcely digested this bad news for British maritime commerce when, on May 5, he received word of Lincoln's proclamation of April 19 declaring a blockade of the Southern coast from South Carolina to Texas, and proclaiming the intention of the United States government to treat any privateers acting under Southern letters of marque as pirates.[13]

Russell had thus far remained steady in his avowed purpose of awaiting the turn of events in America before taking any irrevocable action in behalf of his government. But with civil war in the United States a fact and with each side threatening to sweep the seas of the other's maritime trade, the preservation of British commercial interests and the safety of British subjects appeared to demand a statement of governmental policy respecting the fratricidal conflict so rapidly developing in America. Russell apparently was unaware that Davis did not currently have the ships to make good his threat to send out privateers, nor did he seem to recall that Lyons had written him earlier that the Federal navy, most of whose vessels were still scattered on various assignments all around the globe, could not possibly put all of its ships on station in an effective blockade of Confederate ports for months to come. The British foreign minister took the words of Lincoln and Davis at face value.

Consequently, he envisioned the dangers of British vessels barred by blockade from entry into Southern ports and threatened with capture or destruction by lurking Confederate corsairs if they continued trading in Northern ports.[14]

With news of the outbreak of war and Davis's proclamation in his possession, but before he had received anything more than vague speculations about a possible Northern blockade, Russell told the American minister in London, in effect, that he reserved the right to open diplomatic relations with Jefferson Davis's government should the expected Northern blockade be found injurious to England. The warning was clear that British commercial interests in the South must remain unharmed. Russell also told George M. Dallas "that there existed an understanding between this government and that of France which would lead both to take the same course as to recognition, whatever that course might be." But as Adams was supposed to be on his way to London, presumably with the latest official information and fresh instructions from his government, Russell added that no action would be taken in regard to any recognition of Southern independence until the arrival of the new American minister.[15]

Apparently, nothing was said in the conversation between Dallas and the British foreign minister about a possible proclamation of neutrality. Such a proclamation was looked upon by the British government as a domestic measure, and therefore Russell felt no need, even had the rapid course of events allowed him time, to consult with a representative of the United States government about it. From the British point of view, a realistic policy had to take official notice of the war that had already broken out in America, in order that British subjects might be informed of their rights, obligations, and liabilities in the new situation. On May 1, Russell directed that the British fleet in American waters be reinforced, with the object of protecting British shipping and British property on board American ships against Southern privateers. The following day, when Lincoln's proclamation of blockade became known unofficially in London, and it now appeared that both sides in America had announced the immediate institution of maritime warfare, Russell inquired of the crown law officers whether, in view of the danger to British interests growing out of these developments, the belligerency of the South should be recognized and the neutrality of Great Britain proclaimed. That night, his question as yet unanswered, he told the House of Commons that the only justification Great Britain would have for interfering in the "lamentable contest now raging in the American States" would be if British interests should be attacked. "For God's sake," he exclaimed, to the accompaniment of cheers from many of his fellow members, "let us if possible keep out of it!"[16]

To change Russell's attitude was one of the principal tasks of three Southern commissioners, who had been sent to Europe with the ultimate objective of obtaining recognition of Confederate independence. On May 4, forewarned both by Lyons and by the British consul in Charleston that they were coming and would probably take "high ground" toward England based on her alleged dependence on "King Cotton," Russell gave them a private and unofficial audience. He commenced the interview by telling the envoys that although it would give him pleasure to hear what they had to communicate, under present circumstances he should himself have little to say. He then listened patiently to a lengthy discourse by William L. Yancey on the causes and legality of secession, the extent of Southern resources, and the disposition of the Confederate government to cultivate peace and amity with all the nations of the world. According to the Southerners, the primary cause of their region's secession from the American Union had not been slavery at all, but rather the high tariff policy of the Republican party, backed by majority opinion in the Northern States. The commissioners concluded by expressing their hope that Great Britain would find it in her interest to "recognize the independence of the Confederate States of America at an early date." The foreign minister thanked them for the information they had furnished and said that the subject of recognition would be placed before the cabinet. In the meantime, however, he could not properly express an opinion upon the matter, nor could he hold any official communication with them. Not at all disheartened by this

39

interview, the Confederate commissioners reported to their secretary of state that although neither England nor France appeared likely at present to recognize the independence of the Southern states, "England in reality is not adverse to a disintegration of the United States, and both of these powers will act favorably toward us upon the first decided success which we may obtain."[17]

Perhaps the Southern envoys would have been less sanguine had they known that Lyons had earlier written, regarding the "King Cotton" thesis, that he feared "the very exaggerated and very false ideas they have in the South about cotton will lead to very foolish conduct. It is true that cotton is almost a necessity to us, but it is still more necessary for them to sell it than it is for us to buy it." Should the South actually withhold its great staple commodity from export to England, it seemed evident to the British minister "that other cotton would be got elsewhere or a substitute found." This was a view commonly held in Great Britain.[18]

On the same day on which he talked to the Southern commissioners, Russell received the crown law officers' opinion "that we must consider the Civil War in America as regular war—justum bellum—& apply to it all the rules respecting blockade, letters of marque &c which belong to neutrals during a war." The cabinet had adopted this suggestion without hesitation. On the evening of May 6, Russell told the House of Commons that the ministry had decided "that the Southern Confederacy of America, according to . . . just principles, must be treated as a belligerent." The right of the Confederate States to send out privateers, it followed, had to be recognized by Great Britain if she wished to be truly neutral in the American conflict. Earlier that same day, Russell had sent instructions to Lord Cowley, his ambassador at Paris, directing him to request France to join in recognizing Southern belligerent rights. He also suggested that the two powers join in asking both belligerents to treat neutral goods and ships (except contraband) as exempt from capture on the high seas, under the provisions of articles two and three of the Declaration of Paris of 1856, to which the United States government had never acceded. This, the British foreign minister hoped, would tend to minimize interruptions of British commerce with both the North and the South.[19]

Time passed while dispatches flew back and forth between London and Paris and the legal authorities of the two governments drafted their respective proclamations of neutrality. Meanwhile, William E. Forster, a parliamentary Liberal who on antislavery principles was strongly opposed to English recognition of Southern independence, nevertheless rose in the House of Commons to press the British government for a public announcement of a neutralist policy toward America. So clear and urgent did the necessity then seem for an official proclamation of neutrality, even one including a grant of belligerent rights to the Southern Confederacy, that Forster, later one of the Union's leading champions in Parliament, favored no delay in the matter. In this he agreed with the duke of Argyll, also a sympathizer with the Northern cause, who wrote a few days later that "the rights and interests of humanity demand that the rules and principles of some admitted law should be immediately applied to all such contests, and the rules affecting and defining the rights and duties of belligerents are the only rules which prevent war from becoming massacre and murder. I don't think the neutral governments of the world have any choice in this matter." On May 13, therefore, the Queen's Proclamation of Neutrality was issued. It recognized Southern belligerency and warned British subjects not to take any part in the American war. Published in the official London *Gazette* the following day, it presented the new American minister, who arrived in the British capital that same day, with a perplexing *fait accompli.*[20]

On the train from Liverpool to London, Charles Adams read in newspapers published during his two-week trip across the Atlantic Ocean not only that Russell had declared (without waiting to consult the new American envoy) that the Southern insurgents would be granted belligerent rights, but also that he had asserted: "further questions arise out of that question, with respect to which we are still in doubt." Did this suggest an apparent disposition of the British government to contemplate early diplomatic recognition of the Confederate government? Russell had indicated earlier that England might interfere in the American war if "British interests" were attacked. Was not the flow of Southern cotton that would be shut off by the blockade a British interest? Adams thought that there had been "not a little precipitation in at once raising the disaffected States up to the level of a belligerent power, before it had developed a single one of the real elements which constitute military efficiency outside of its geographical limits." As yet there was not "a single privateer afloat" under the rebel flag.[21]

Anxious to bring Seward's policies and views to the early attention of Russell, and especially to warn him that British recognition of Confederate independence would be viewed in Washington as a hostile act, Adams sought an interview with the foreign minister immediately upon his arrival in London. Delayed four days by the death of the duke of Bedford, Russell's elder brother, the interview finally took place on May 18.[22]

In his first conversation with Russell, the new American minister did not mince words. He wanted to impress upon Her Majesty's government, he declared, the necessity for grave consideration before adopting any course likely even in the most indirect way to encourage the insurgents in America. For the people of the United States now considered the termination of their "difficulty" but a matter of time, and any course adopted by Great Britain that might alter that calculation "would inevitably raise the most unpleasant feelings among them"—feelings that "would scarcely be effaced by time." For this reason Adams had felt great regret when upon his arrival in England he had learned of the decision to issue the queen's proclamation, raising the rebellious portion of the United States at once to the level of a belligerent state, "and still more the language used in regard to it by Her Majesty's Ministers in both Houses of Parliament, before and since." To characterize the rebellious states as entitled to belligerent status and the war there as *justum bellum*, whatever the motives for so doing, was "to encourage the friends of the disaffected" in Great Britain, as the tone of the press and of private opinion strongly indicated.[23]

To these remarks, Russell replied that he thought more emphasis had been placed on these events in America than they deserved. It had become necessary to set forth an official position defining the relation of the British people to the impending conflict in America. To that end the legal officers of the government had been consulted and they had concluded that a war in fact existed, that as yet all indications were of a contest of arms "more or less even." Other less formidable demonstrations had been "recognized" in the past. "Under such circumstances," Russell said, according to Adams,

> it seemed scarcely possible to avoid speaking of this in the technical sense as *justum bellum*, that is, a war of two sides, without in any way implying an opinion of its justice, as well as to withhold an endeavor, so far as possible, to bring the management of it within the rules of modern civilized warfare. This was all that was contemplated by the Queen's proclamation. It was designed to show the purport of existing laws and to explain to British subjects their liabilities in case they should engage in the war.[24]

To all of which, wrote Adams, "I answered . . . that the action taken seemed, at least to my mind, a little more rapid than was absolutely called for by the occasion." Lincoln's administration had had scarcely two months to renovate and purify a demoralized government and formulate its own policy. Yet it had accomplished the transition successfully and was

> just emerging from its difficulties, and beginning to develop the power of the country to cope with this rebellion, when the British government took the initiative, and . . . pronounced the insurgents to be a belligerent state before they had even shown their capacity to maintain any kind of warfare whatever, except within one of their own harbors, and under every possible advantage. It considered them a marine power before they had ever exhibited a single privateer on the ocean. . . . It did seem to me therefore as if a little more time might have been taken to form a more complete estimate of the relative force of the contending parties, and of the probabilities of any long drawn issue. And I did not doubt that the view taken by me would be that substantially taken by both the government and the people of the United States. They would inevitably infer the existence of an intention [on the part of Great Britain] more or less marked to extend the struggle.

Should the British ministry contemplate taking any additional step tending to invest the rebel government "in the eyes of the world with the notion of form and substance," Adams warned, he "was bound to acknowledge in all frankness that in that contingency I had nothing further to do in Great Britain."[25]

Again the British foreign minister denied that his government intended to pursue any course other than strict neutrality in dealing with the American difficulty. Should recognition of Confederate independence ever be contemplated, he should be "ready to listen to every argument that might be presented against it on the part of the United States." But if he was expected to pledge absolutely that the government of Great Britain "would not at any future time, no matter what the circumstances might be, recognize an existing State in America," that was more than he could promise. So he could only suggest, as the best course to follow, that he send Lyons directions "to give such a reply to the President as, in his own opinion, might be satisfactory." After hesitating a moment, Adams assented to this solution. For it might be best, after all, he thought, to allow Lincoln and Seward "to decide upon the sufficiency of the reply" to the American demand for explanations of the British position in regard to the Southern rebellion. For Adams to push further in London than he already had might elicit a reply from Russell so stiff and unsatisfactory to the American secretary of state that Anglo-American relations would be damaged instead of improved by Adams's initial discussion with the British foreign minister. The New Englander did not want thus to begin his tenure in London.[26]

When Adams's official report of his first conversation with Russell was received in Washington, the American secretary of state was pleased to learn that Russell wished him to "put the most favorable construction possible" upon anything that had been said earlier by the British foreign minister to Adams's predecessor. This, Seward wrote his London envoy, removed "the whole difficulty" about what had been said to Dallas. Adams was ordered to tell Russell that the president took "sincere satisfaction" in receiving the British denial that any intent of giving aid or sympathy to the Southern insurgents should have been inferred from his remarks to Dallas. For "this government," Seward asserted, "has no disposition to lift questions of even national pride or sensibility up to the level of diplomatic controversy, because it earnestly and ardently desires to maintain peace, harmony, and cordial friendship with Great Britain."[27]

Nevertheless, Seward thought it "remarkable" that after having promised Dallas that Adams would be given an opportunity to be heard "before any decisive action should be adopted," Russell should then have proceeded to proclaim to the world, simultaneously with the new American minister's arrival, that England recognized the Confederate conspirators "as a *belligerent* national *power*." Such a "grave" step, seeming to indicate a possible renewal of an "ancient alienation . . . under circumstances which portend great social evils, if not disaster, to both countries," required, in Seward's opinion, cautious treatment. He decided, before sending his London representative further directions about how to treat the British neutrality proclamation, to seek further information on the subject from Lyons.[28]

He asked Baron Gerolt, the Prussian minister, to take Lyons what the latter described as "a sort of friendly overture." The British minister had been hiding "under cover, like a prudent man, while the storm was raging, but . . . had been carefully watching the signs of the weather." At Seward's suggestion, Gerolt told the British minister that the secretary of state had "the best disposition now towards England; that . . . he hoped [Lyons reported] I should be ready to enter upon friendly explanations with him." Suspecting that "the real object of Mr. Seward in sending to me" was, however, to trick the British and French envoys in Washington into dealing with him separately in regard to the delicate question of Confederate belligerent rights, Lyons was determined to "counteract these schemes" by establishing "beyond contradiction that France occupies precisely the same position as England" in officially recognizing those rights. He intended to accompany Mercier to Seward's office, where the two ministers would "make the concert between England and France on the American question as manifest as possible."[29]

First, however, Lyons decided to pave the way for such an interview by sending Mercier to sound Seward out about it ahead of time. The Frenchman began his conversation with the secretary of state by offering the usual homilies about his government's friendly feelings for the United States. After listening patiently to these declarations, Seward replied that he shared these feelings of amity, but that he had also observed that "the first marks of sincere sympathy that he had received from abroad had come to him from the sovereigns of Russia, Austria and Prussia; that England obviously had ill intentions in regard to America; that she had proved this by her haste in recognizing the belligerent rights of the rebels; and that he had been shocked that France, whose interests were so different, had shown a disposition to allow herself to be led astray in the same direction." After defending his government's decision to recognize Confederate belligerent rights on the ground of practical necessity, Mercier found himself eased out the State Department door before he realized that he had failed to obtain the desired joint appointment for Lyons and himself with the secretary of state. When he tried again, a few days later, Seward told him that he would never officially admit that the United States was involved in a regular war. "To us," he asserted, "the rebels are only rebels, and we shall never consent to consider them otherwise. If you wish to recognize their belligerent character, either by addressing an official declaration to us, or by your actions, we shall protest and we shall oppose you." In the meantime, he said, he preferred not to be asked to receive any official communications from Mercier and Lyons simultaneously.[30]

Despite this warning that Seward objected to seeing them together, the two European envoys, looking determined, appeared at the State Department on June 15. Seward was well aware that they intended to notify him officially that the French and British governments had decided to recognize Confederate belligerent rights. Having persuaded them to allow him a preliminary examination of the papers they had brought with them, he declined to receive them officially. For a reference in the British dispatch to "the position of Great Britain as a neutral between the two belligerents" was unacceptable, as was similar language in the dispatch presented by Mercier; indeed, according to Lyons, the secretary of state said that he would not receive *any* "communication founded on the assumption that the Southern rebels were to be regarded as belligerents." Only if "he should be forced to do so" by some official public statement would Seward "take official cognizance" of the neutrality proclamations of England and France. The United States government was willing to concede all those two governments wanted with respect to neutral maritime rights. It regarded recognized principles of international maritime law "to be quite as applicable to measures of coercion adopted against rebels as to the operations of a regular war." Therefore, "there was no need that any question should be raised by those two powers with the United States, as to whether the Southern rebels were or were not invested with belligerent rights."[31]

Although Lyons complained to Russell that Seward's refusal officially to receive the communications brought to him by the British and French ministers "savoured of arrogance," he thought it wise not "to be punctilious in such matters" and to push the secretary of state "to the wall," which would "almost certainly have brought on a crisis." Moreover, although Seward had firmly declined to discuss the question of Confederate belligerent rights with either Lyons or Mercier, he had said that he would acquaint his ministers in London and Paris with his position on the matter, so that they might in turn explain it to Russell and Thouvenel, if asked to do so.[32]

It was obvious to Lyons that Seward was stalling for time in the hope of a decisive Northern victory on the battlefield, or a rift in the Anglo-French alliance, either of which might reduce the pressure abroad for intervention to make permanent the dissolution of the American Union. Lyons saw no sign, however, that the North might soon win an important military engagement. The trend of the war, he wrote Russell, was as impossible to predict as the future

47

conduct of the American secretary of state. At any moment Seward might explode with "a declaration of war. Any symptom of disunion between England and France, any necessity on the part of the [Northern] Cabinet, or of some of its members to arouse popular passion, or pander to it, might bring on a war." The best way to prevent such an occurrence was "to keep up strict concert with France, and to make that concert manifest to the public here."[33]

Seward's "motive for provoking a war with England," Lyons thought, would be his "personal ambition . . . as candidate to succeed Mr. Lincoln." The American secretary of state sought to play on the "irritability and ignorance in the multitude," especially with "the important Irish vote, by hostility to England." He entertained visions of "beginning the war with eclat, by an invasion of Canada, before any preparations could be made for the defence of that province." And although he had been thwarted by presidential editing of his bellicose instructions to Adams one month earlier, and then checked again in mid-June by the refusals of Lyons and Mercier to press an official announcement of Confederate belligerent rights upon him, he was still "the same man, with the same motives and the same recklessness"—and a new "critical question," that of the legality of the blockade, was pending. Although Mercier seemed to think it "impossible" that Seward would risk conflict with France and Great Britain united by insisting on the maintenance of an illegal form of blockade, Lyons thought that the French minister hardly gave "due weight to the indications of such an intention, which are only too plain."[34]

While Lyons was warning Russell that Seward appeared oblivious to the "absolute madness of quarreling with England and France" together, the secretary of state was sending Adams his reasons for declining to take official notice of the British and French dispatches regarding neutral maritime rights, so that his representative in London might, if he found "it necessary or expedient, communicate them to the government of Great Britain." Seward professed to be "anxious to avoid all causes of misunderstanding with Great Britain; to draw closer, instead of breaking, the existing bonds of amity and friendship." But the United States government could hardly agree to accept any announcement of the British government, especially one issued "without previously conferring with us upon the question," which derogated from "the unbroken sovereignty of the federal Union." Believing that the British had "acted inadvertently," influenced by exaggerated fears of damage to their commerce, Seward hoped, nevertheless, that good relations between the two countries would remain fundamentally undisturbed by the incident. For this to happen, however, the British government would have to let the government of the United States "manage and settle this domestic controversy in our own way."[35]

Seward's hopes were soon lifted by encouraging reports from England. After three weeks in London, Adams reported that his early pessimistic impressions of the state of British opinion toward America had been greatly modified. He now believed "that good feelings predominated and that there was no considerable disposition to encourage the disaffected." With the possible exception of the chancellor of the exchequer, William E. Gladstone,[36] whose family fortune was based partly on West Indian slavery, the leading members of the queen's cabinet all seemed friendly toward the United States. It appeared that the issuance of the British Proclamation of Neutrality might have been unjustly construed in America "to mean more than they intended by it." For the Palmerston ministry, by afterwards announcing that belligerent warships and privateers would not be permitted to bring prizes into the ports of Great Britain and her dependencies, had dealt Southern hopes a bitter blow.[37]

Adams had previously concluded that without some regulation such as this one,

> the preceding practice in this country would authorize the retention of such captures until condemned as prizes in some Admiralty Court set up by the insurgents at home, and the sale of them afterwards. The effect of this in giving them courage can scarcely be estimated. It would at once enlist in their behalf most of the daring and the desperate adventurers of every nation, whose sole object is plunder,

and would initiate a struggle between a community of planters who have nothing to lose on the ocean, and a commercial nation which whitens every sea with the sails of a peaceful navigation.

Hence Adams heard of the British government's new regulation "with great satisfaction." Although it did not remove "the main difficulty of putting the legitimate and the spurious authority in the same category," it did exhibit an unmistakable desire on the part of the British government "to avoid in any way a collision with the United States, or any direct encouragement of the insurgents."[38]

What appeared to be the friendly disposition of the British government toward the United States was further exemplified on the evening of June 7, when William H. Gregory's thrice-postponed motion for the recognition of the Confederacy, re-scheduled for consideration on that date, was withdrawn at the last moment in the face of the government's announced intention to oppose it strongly in debate. The "sense of the Commons," Adams estimated, would make likely an indefinite postponement of motions of this sort. Although Southern envoys Pierre Rost and William Yancey remained optimistic in the face of this setback, writing back to Richmond that England only awaited a Southern victory "to justify a recognition" before being forced, "when the cotton crop is ready for market, . . . to conclusions favorable to the South," the true magnitude of the Confederate defeat was better reflected in an enormous scowl on the face of Ambrose Dudley Mann, the principal Confederate envoy in England, as he left the House of Commons alone on the night of June 7, in bitter disappointment.[39]

Adams's jubilation was only momentary. His uncertainty about the good health of Anglo-American relations was soon renewed, when he opened his dispatch bag on June 10 and ran his eyes over Seward's instruction of May 21. In this missive which, one remembers, had felt the editorial scribble of the president's own pen, the secretary of state had ordered Adams to have nothing further to do officially with the British government if Russell should persist in talking with the Southern envoys. Should England grant diplomatic recognition to the insurgent government, Seward added, she would be treated as an enemy of the United States. For recognition would be tantamount to intervention in behalf of the Southern rebels, in response to which the United States would have no other choice than to resist. [40]

After reading this instruction from his superior, Adams wrote dejectedly in his diary that the government at home seemed "almost ready to declare war with all the powers of Europe. . . . I scarcely know how to understand Mr. Seward. The rest of the government may be demented for all that I know, but he surely is calm and wise." Risking a conflict with Great Britain at the present time, however, seemed to Adams "like throwing the game into the hands of the enemy." His son Henry reacted even more strongly to Seward's words, characterizing his instruction as

> so arrogant in tone and so extraordinary and unparalleled in its demands that it leaves no doubt in my mind that our Government wishes to face a war with all Europe. That is the inevitable result of any attempt to carry out the spirit or the letter of these directions, and such a war is regarded in the despatch itself as the probable result. I have said already that I thought such a policy shallow madness, whether it comes from Seward or from any one else. . . .
>
> I cannot tell you how I am shocked and horrified by supposing Seward, a man I've admired and respected beyond most men, guilty of what seems to me so wicked and criminal a course as this.
>
> I do not think I exaggerate the danger. I believe that our Government means to have a war with England; I believe that England knows it and is preparing for it; and I believe it will come within two months. [41]

That the Adamses should have been so much disturbed by Seward's instruction, and should have misinterpreted it as a gesture designed to provoke a conflict with Great Britain, instead of an attempt to prevent one, seems surprising now. Other American diplomats found the paper quite suitable to the situation. The anglophile John L. Motley, for example, thought it "unobjectionable in every way—dignified, reasonable, and not menacing, although very decided." But perhaps the context in which the Adamses first encountered it affected their appraisals of its meaning. For the same mail that brought it to the American minister's writing table also contained newspaper accounts of great hostility toward England throughout the Northern States, based upon reports that the British government contemplated placing the Southern rebels upon an equal footing with the United States by proclaiming neutrality between them. In an article that appeared to have an official flavor, the *New York Times* reported: "Depend upon it, if the official dispatches shall justify the impressions given by the papers, the [*sic*] will be no hesitation on the part of this Government in at once assuming a position hostile to that declared by the British Government. . . . the people will promptly accept the issue made by Great Britain, and fight it out to the bitter end."[42]

On the same day on which he received Seward's instruction and the contentious press commentary which seemed to give it point, Adams also read in the London *Times* an announcement that "in consequence of events which have convulsed the American Republic, . . . it has been determined to reinforce the garrison of Canada with a brigade of British infantry." He did not know, of course, that the move had been taken as a result of warnings from Lyons that Seward might be planning an attack on British North America. But he feared that this move would enhance the already great resentment at home and would probably lead to further remonstrances by Seward, or worse.[43]

Foreseeing that his duty was now "to prevent the mutual irritation from coming to a downright quarrel," Adams applied to Russell for an interview in which to deliver Seward's disturbing communication. On June 12, after a short preliminary conversation about secondary topics, the American minister "approached the most delicate portion of my task." Declaring that Americans had almost unanimously construed the queen's proclamation "as designed to aid the insurgents by raising them to the rank of a belligerent state," he informed Russell that the Lincoln administration had adopted a "very decided tone" on the subject. He was not yet personally convinced, Adams said, that such a motive existed. But any protraction of the known relations between the "pseudo-commissioners" of the South and the British foreign minister "could scarcely fail to be viewed by us as hostile in spirit and to require some corresponding action accordingly."[44]

Russell replied that it was an old European custom to receive such persons as the Southern deputation unofficially, but that this did not imply recognition. He added that although he had seen these gentlemen twice already, "he had no expectation of seeing them any more." Adams took this to be a satisfactory reply; at least, he wrote his chief, "I shall venture so to regard it and shall continue my relations here until I discover some action apparently in conflict with it or receive specific orders from the Department indicating an opposite course."[45]

Adams went on to tell Russell that although much prejudice against Great Britain "not now easy to be eradicated" had resulted from the hasty issuance of the queen's proclamation, he did not propose to aggravate the evil by discussing it in a spirit of animosity. He desired as much as possible to help avoid additional irritations that might worsen relations between the two countries still further. In this connection he felt obliged to mention a subject upon which he had as yet received no instructions—what had been reported in the press as a considerable movement of British troops to Canada. Such a step would naturally excite attention in the United States, and Adams was "therefore desirous to learn whether they were ordered with any reference to possible difficulties with us."[46]

Russell answered that Canada had lacked a full complement of military manpower for some time, and that the restoration of a portion of her usual armed force was only "a proper measure of precaution in the present disordered condition of things in the United States." Frankly, Russell added, he did not know whether the Americans "might do something." But there was no intention of any aggressive movements against the United States.[47]

After about forty-five minutes had passed, Adams terminated the discussion, satisfied that he had carried out his instructions, while at the same time he had avoided giving offense to the British government. He thought that a serious conflict between the two countries could now be prevented only "if no more impulse be given." But the recent transmission of British troops to Canada would probably be interpreted in the United States as evidence of an intention to launch an attack at an opportune time. "And then the rebound will come here again," he thought. Adams had never anticipated that his ministerial duties would be so difficult. "But," he resolved, "I will not permit a quarrel here if I can help it."[48]

IV

Misunderstandings Proliferate

How much harm [the false statements concerning Seward's alleged warmongering] may be doing cannot yet be appreciated. But if by means of them we get plunged into a war solely from misunderstanding of our reciprocal intentions, we might come to conceive an idea of it.

C. F. ADAMS TO HIS SON,
21 June 1861.

ONE OF THE SELF-APPOINTED DUTIES of the American secretary of state was to subject himself to a continual round of lavish receptions and dinner parties. The president and his wife were notorious for their social inadequacies, and many of the high-ranking military officers and politicians in Washington had become accustomed in previous years to a feverish social whirl conducted mostly by Southerners now absent from the capital city. Especially did the foreign diplomats have to be accommodated in this respect. So the Washington and New York newspapers for the period are full of accounts of "brilliant" parties at the Seward home on Lafayette Square, at which the secretary's daughter-in-law served as hostess, in the absence of the invalided Mrs. Seward, who remained at home in Auburn, New York.[1]

Seward's efforts at conviviality were unappreciated, however, by the British minister. Lyons interpreted Seward's outspoken love of country as arrogance and his bantering sense of humor as recklessness. A humorless foreigner who was perennially ill at ease in the jovial atmosphere that usually surrounded Seward, and who was affronted that the wishes of his government did not always meet with the deference he expected from an inferior people, Lyons was apt to misconstrue determined patriotism as mere contentiousness.

In his letters to London, the British envoy poured out tales of woe and impending war.[2]

The British prime minister found "these communications . . . very unpleasant." After a dinner at his house on June 1 he drew the American minister aside to say that, in his opinion, Seward had been needlessly "ungracious and unpleasant" to Lyons. Adams, who construed the secretary of state's alleged discourtesy "as some of his awkward brusquerie which he means to be playful, but which Lyons does not understand or appreciate," told Palmerston that he "wondered at this, for I believed that Mr. Seward was not disposed to be offensive, and his temper was mild and conciliatory." Soon he wrote Seward privately that Lyons was evidently "annoyed by some language or manner of yours which he construed as intentionally offensive." Palmerston had hinted that his minister "felt a little sore about it, and that his views had more or less effect on this side." Perhaps it would be better, Adams implied, to avoid "these little irritations."[3]

Never had he intentionally offended the British minister, Seward wrote back, but at the same time he had "not intended to leave Lord Lyons at liberty to believe that the conduct of his Government was . . . satisfactory." If British statesmen really desired good relations with the United States, they ought to "look deeper than the mere manner of conducting diplomatic intercourse." Americans were "shocked, offended, and disgusted" by the British stance of "neutrality," by the British government's "arrangements with the French Government to deny the sovereignty of the United States, and its countenance of the insurrection." Every government in Europe, except Great Britain, had expressed sympathy for the United States in its hour of trial. Seward wished to think well of England, but he did not intend to be "demoralized" by her. Of late, however, Seward declared, he and Lyons were "generally getting along quite well."[4]

Lyons was less sure of this. Although he had recently written Russell that there was "no ground whatever" for newspaper stories that any "misunderstanding" had taken place between Seward and himself, and he had asserted that, on the contrary, "no dispute, altercation, or even animated discussion has taken place between us, either orally or in writing,"[5] he proceeded to add new "evidence" to buttress his previous condemnations of Seward as reckless and unfriendly to England. He reported his discovery that Seward had prepared an instruction to Adams that was practically a direct declaration of war, and that only the intervention of the president and some of the "more reasonable" members of the cabinet had prevented the secretary of state from sending it unaltered. He had already written Russell that "no greater service could be rendered to the cause of peace" than to make Charles Sumner, chairman of the Senate Foreign Relations Committee, aware of the peril in which Seward's chauvinism placed the United States. The Massachusetts senator was known to exchange letters regularly with many persons in England, including the duke and duchess of Argyll. "If," Lyons wrote, "Mr. Sumner's correspondence from England convinced him that there was a real danger in Mr. Seward's proceedings, he might do a great deal to put a stop to them." Lyons's suggestion was no sooner received in London than Argyll, probably the member of the British cabinet most friendly to the cause of the United States,[6] was informed of its contents. Immediately, he sent Sumner a note earnestly entreating the senator to "use your influence and official authority to induce your government, and especially Mr. Seward, to act in a more liberal and a less reckless spirit than he is supposed here to indicate towards foreign governments and especially towards ourselves." Particularly was Argyll troubled lest Seward touch Englishmen in a sensitive spot involving British honor, in which case "the irritation would be extreme and could not be controlled." The duke was unaware that Sumner himself, for his own political reasons, had played an important role in creating the myth of a warmongering Seward; thus the Massachusetts senator was peculiarly unfitted to dispel the story, even had he wished to do so.[7]

Shortly after warning the secretary of state that Lyons had sent unfavorable comments about him to England, Charles Francis Adams learned from his closest friend at home that Sumner had been for some time in the habit of making derogatory remarks about

Seward. According to Richard Henry Dana, Jr., the Massachusetts senator could not "talk five minutes without bringing in Mr. Seward, and always in bitter tones of denunciation." Dana understood that Sumner's large correspondence with influential Englishmen and his conversations with foreign diplomats in Washington were "in the same style," but his diatribes were "in no sense confidential, for it is the same all over town." His one mission in life seemed to be to undermine, to discredit, and eventually to destroy, Seward, "and into that mission," Dana wrote, "he puts all his usual intellectual and moral energy."[8]

"I am sorry to hear the accounts of my friend Sumner," Adams wrote his son in Boston, "even though they do not much surprise me." It was hardly in the "public interest" that such prolonged and unjust attacks be made on the secretary of state by such an influential fellow countryman. "He is sowing the seeds of discord," Adams complained, "where we ought to have a more perfect union. He is disseminating distrust in our Government when it depends upon confidence." Adams had been surprised to discover how prevalent the dislike of Seward was in England, even among Americans. He had already traced enough of the rumors and impressions to Sumner to discern the channels through which they came. He suspected that the effect of Sumner's calumnious campaign had been "considerable, and that we shall feel . . . it in our future relations with this country for a good while to come." As far as he could, he had done his best to counteract all such "mischief."[9]

Adams was so worried about the impact which Sumner's slanders seemed to be having on his English correspondents and on Lyons that he sent Seward a confidential warning to be on his guard against the "effect produced on yourself and your influence" by the "hostile manner in which one of the Senators of my State is in the constant habit of speaking about you everywhere in private." This seemed to be the explanation for "what I cannot fail to observe here, a prevailing tone of distrust of your policy and motives." All over London people expressed an apprehension that leading men in the United States government hoped to cement the reunion of North and South "upon the basis of hostile measures against Great Britain." Adams suggested that it might "be desirable" for Seward to entice Lyons "a little out of that association [with Sumner] and nearer to yourself."[10]

Seward returned a reassuring reply regarding Sumner. "Do not give yourself uneasiness," he wrote Adams, "about what he can do here or near you." The enmity of the Massachusetts senator toward Seward dated from the latter's refusal to heed his "energetic remonstrances" against Adams's own appointment to the London mission, which Sumner had desired for himself. As for the rumors of his quarrelsomeness and his alleged craving for the conquest of Canada, the secretary of state assured his London representative that he had "no designs hostile to Great Britain, so long as she does not officially or unofficially recognize the insurgents or render them aid or sympathy." While the British government remained friendly to the United States, the more effectively it protected Canada "the better we shall be satisfied." But if that government should purposely "do us any injury, which we have not the least idea now that she proposes to do, we should not be deterred from vindicating our rights and our unbroken sovereignty against all the armies and navies that she could send here." The United States government would never acquiesce in the proposition that its sovereignty over the Southern States was lost or diminished by the rebellion there. "At the same time, if Her Majesty's government shall continue to practice absolute forbearance from any interference in our domestic affairs, we shall not be captious enough to inquire what name it gives that forbearance, or in what character it presents itself before the British nation in doing so." Hence to remain unyielding on the main point of unbroken American sovereignty did not necessarily signify hostility to Great Britain. But such a policy did demand of Seward himself, at least for the moment, a rigid and overt patriotism, one of the truest tests of which might well be its unpleasant effect on foreigners. The secretary of state, therefore,

> could not hope to reconcile the energetic and vigorous resistence to English injustice which my duty to my own country has exacted, with the preservation of partial sentiments towards myself in Great Britain.

You could do no greater harm, than by inducing an opinion that I am less decided in my intercourse with the British minister than I am reputed to be, or less determined to maintain the pride and dignity of our government.

The British, Seward believed, had been well underway on the road to a recognition of "the independence of the Southern Confederacy," when his remonstrances against such a course had changed it. For Englishmen then to complain was a natural and expected reaction. The important thing to remember was that "the safety, honor and welfare" of the United States should always take precedence in the words and deeds of her leaders over the natural desire to please the statesmen and people of powerful foreign nations.[11]

The impressions of Seward's hostility held by most of the English oligarchy did not rest solely upon affirmations of his belligerence by Lyons and Sumner. Some of his diplomatic agents in Europe had issued pronouncements that tended to reinforce the widely held impression that either he failed to understand the simplest rudiments of diplomatic courtesy, or he planned to provoke England beyond bearable limits. During May, several of Adams's diplomatic colleagues, who arrived in Europe bursting with patriotic devotion, made public statements in behalf of the Unionist cause that infuriated English leaders of all factions and classes. For example, Cassius M. Clay of Kentucky, newly appointed American minister at St. Petersburg, wrote a letter to the London *Times* in which he asked, rhetorically, whether England could afford to offend her erstwhile colony in its hour of distress by failing to support the Union cause. To fall short in this respect, he wrote, would be to antagonize England's best customer, her best foreign source of foodstuffs and raw materials, and a nation that in another half-century would contain one hundred million people. Was England's future so secure "as to venture, now in our need, to plant the seeds of revenge?" England was the Union's natural ally, Clay concluded. "Will she ignore our aspirations? If she is just, she ought not. If she is honourable and magnanimous, she cannot. *If she is wise, she will not*."[12]

"Mr. CLAY," the *Times* replied editorially, "must really allow us to give our own version of the honour and interest of England," which in respect to the American contest was to remain neutral, "and to leave those who take to the sword to fall by the sword." Clay and his countrymen ought to concentrate on the present, the *Times* warned, where they would "find enough to occupy their attention without troubling themselves with long visions of humiliation and retribution which no man now alive will ever see accomplished."[13]

Not content with the damage done by his letter, Clay crossed the channel to Paris and delivered an address to a meeting of Americans in that city, in which he proclaimed that if England sided with the South, France would join the North in humiliating the power that had confined Napoleon I on St. Helena, after destroying both his glorious empire and, earlier, that of Louis XIV. "I am accused of threatening England," Clay trumpeted. "I am not in the habit of casting about me to see how I may make truth most palatable. Let those who stand in the way of truth look out."[14]

Following Clay's remarkable exhibition of diplomacy-by-bluster, Anson Burlingame, Lincoln's new ministerial appointee at Vienna, loudly expressed his own resentment at the language of part of England's press and some of her statesmen, saying: "We will put down rebellion on our own soil, and shall reserve a quick hand and a dauntless heart for whoever, for whatever cause, shall be found in complicity with the most causeless revolt that ever lifted its audacious hand against a noble government and a generous civilization." All over England men discussed this "latest example of American arrogance and brutality." Clay and Burlingame were "noisy jackasses," Henry Adams wrote, probably reflecting his father's opinion. They had done more harm in England "than their weak heads were worth a thousand times over." Moreover, another letter published in the *Times* was even worse. Written by Theodore S. Fay, late United States minister in Switzerland, it was full of Biblical allusions and likened the Civil War to a struggle between Satan and God. As a later letter-writer put it, rather mildly, the sympathy with the South of a large portion of the British population could not be "diverted either by Mr. Clay's ridiculous threats or the sanctimonious adjurations of Mr. Fay."[15]

Even those in England most disposed to favor the Union cause were deeply offended by the forensic efforts of Clay, Fay, and Burlingame. Expressions of distaste ran the gamut from the mild editorial comment of the *Illustrated London News* that the American propaganda was "ill-judged," to a suggestion in *Punch* that "cassius had been moistening his clay" when he vented his "queer opinions," to Richard Cobden's expression of "mortification and disgust" at the "shallow antics" of "individuals, *accredited by your Government*," at Paris. Adams bluntly informed Clay that he had done his country great harm. Not only had he violated a State Department regulation prohibiting its accredited officials abroad from writing to the newspapers, but in so doing he had given "our enemies an opportunity to strike the key-note of determined hostility on the part of our government to that of England which has been most dexterously used ever since." While Adams had been attempting to assure the British ministry of the friendly disposition of his government, "other representatives of the government equally entitled to credit were appealing to France by drawing distinctions unfriendly to England." The result had been "to fix upon Mr. Seward the suspicion of bad faith and of secret hostility to England which no efforts of mine have had any success in eradicating."[16]

As time passed, further word came to Adams in London of additional attacks on the American secretary of state by Charles Sumner. The Massachusetts senator continued loudly and fiercely to accuse Seward of planning "to force the country into a foreign war." He wrote John Bright, a leading radical M.P., that he had been obliged several times "to oppose the secretary of state, who has been disposed to a course of much harshness" toward England. And to the Argylls he wrote of "sinister" influences on President Lincoln to turn him against England, which he was himself "constantly" striving to check. By the end of summer his cannonades had not only helped to turn England against Seward, but had badly damaged the secretary of state at home as well. One of Adams's sons wrote that Seward's "fall has been tremendous. Few men are now more violently attacked on all sides." And former secretary of state Edward Everett expressed a hope that Adams was trying to counteract Seward's "belligerent spirit, which Mr. Sumner leads me to think either has been or is very active against England."[17]

Quickly Adams replied to Everett that Seward was "no more belligerent than any high-toned American ought to be." Sumner had done great injury to his country by telling his English correspondents that Seward was their enemy. The secretary of state had merely been firm in asserting American rights. Nothing more had ever been required of Adams by his instructions. Worried by the crescendo of animosity against Seward in England, Adams was moved to send him another warning that he was still "sedulously held up here as in spirit very hostile to this country," an impression furthered by "leading persons in America." Nevertheless, Adams asserted, he retained complete confidence both in Seward's ability and in his disposition "to set at nought all these devices of our enemies, whether at home or abroad."[18]

Adams continued at every opportunity to disseminate among leading British statesmen his conviction that Seward had no ill-will toward their country and no intent to raise questions with them, except regarding those matters "to which it was his duty to object." He had been responsible for the appointment of Adams, who was known to desire friendly relations. So if there was at times in Seward's dispatches "an unconciliatory tone," it was probably less owing to the secretary of state's natural disposition than to "the excessive amount of care and anxiety to which he had been subjected." On the whole, Adams believed, the many communications from Seward received in London would "do him honor whenever they come to light." As for Senator Sumner, if he thought he could obtain some political advantage over the secretary of state "by taking the side of Great Britain against his own country, he is only showing one more example of his want of acquaintance with the world."[19]

Less harmful to the Union cause than Sumner's fulminations against Seward and the "patriotic" publicity of pseudodiplomats like Clay, was a long letter to the London *Times* by John L. Motley, then at the height of his literary reputation in England as the author of the *Rise of the Dutch Republic* and the *United Netherlands*. Motley, according to Clay, had persuaded the latter to write his short "popular" diatribe, while Lincoln's later minister at Vienna tried his own hand at a more elaborate constitutional argument addressed to English intellectuals. Protesting the disposition in England to accept the collapse of the American Union as an accomplished fact, Motley asserted that the United States government would be "false to the people if it does not do its best to preserve them from the horrors of anarchy, even at the cost of blood." However, in resting the Northern case entirely on arguable constitutional grounds, and in denying that Lincoln intended to interfere with slavery where it was already established, Motley provided ammunition for those in Great Britain who denied the existence of any great ethical principles behind the Union war effort. If, Europeans reasoned, the great moral issue over which the war was being fought was not the freedom of the slave, then it could only be the right of the Southern people to political independence.[20]

The apprehensions about Seward's intentions which the combination of Motley's misguided reasonableness, Clay's ranting, Sumner's malicious whispers, and Lyons's peevish complaints tended to implant in the minds of British leaders were reinforced, during May, by two peculiar episodes involving Canada, which the British minister in Washington construed in terms derogatory both to Seward's motives toward England and to his personal character. The first was the case of the ship *Peerless*. Lyons wrote Russell during May that Seward had sent for him on the first day of that month and had informed him "that he had reason to believe that a Union steamer, the *Peerless*, had been sold to the de-facto Southern government, and was on her way out of Lake Ontario to be used as a privateer." Seward added that the ship, which was alleged to fly the British flag and to possess British registry, appeared temporarily to be docked at Toronto. He asked Lyons, therefore, whether he thought the governor general of Canada might be induced to detain the vessel before it reached the high seas and did damage both to the Northern merchant fleet and to Anglo-American relations.[21] The British minister objected, however, "that if her papers were in order, and there was no direct proof of her being actually engaged in any unlawful enterprise, the Governor-General might not have legal power to interfere with her."[22]

Faced with Lyons's reluctance to consider taking any action to stop the alleged privateer from sailing, unless her true character could be established in advance, the secretary of state produced a draft of a telegraphic order to the commanding officers of American warships at sea "to seize the 'Peerless' under any flag and with any papers," if they had probable information that she had been sold to the Southern insurgents. After reading the order to Lyons, he said: "I suppose you will hardly assent to this."[23]

The British minister at once replied that, far from assenting, he solemnly protested "against any attempt to seize a vessel under the British flag, and with any regular British papers." Although Seward assured him that if the seizure took place, the United States government would take full responsibility for justice being done in the case, Lyons argued that "even if the Peerless should in fact be sold to the seceded States, she could never cause the United States anything like the inconvenience which would follow a deliberate violation of neutral rights." The step proposed, he implied, was impolitic and dangerous.[24]

Saying "that he would give due weight to the protest, and that nothing would be done without the sanction of the president, whom he was about to see at a Cabinet council," Seward ended the interview. Later, after meeting with the president and the cabinet, and after receiving "a solemn protest" in writing from the British legation, the secretary of state notified Lyons that

> notwithstanding your lordship's protest, [I have] given conditional directions for the seizure of the Peerless. . . . I need hardly add that this proceeding is taken with no feeling of hostility against the government of Great Britain. The President feels satisfied that Her Majesty's government will not think the seizure unnecessary, or unwarrantable, or injurious, if the information upon which it proceeds shall prove to be correct; and, on the other hand, if it shall prove to be incorrect full satisfaction will be promptly given to the government of Her Majesty and the parties aggrieved. The British government will be satisfied that such proceedings are sometimes

indispensable when a flag is abused to cover aggressions upon a friendly nation.[25]

Determined to maintain his "firm stand" in the face of what he termed another instance of "the arrogant spirit and disregard of the rights and feelings of Foreign Nations, with which the American government seemed to be disposed to conduct the Civil War," Lyons fired another note back at Seward, saying that he was compelled to "maintain and repeat the protest which I made to you, both by word of mouth and by written note, before the orders were issued." Almost one week later the British minister was still fuming about the incident. Calling it "a painful illustration of the character of the man we have to deal with," he suggested to his superiors that it showed Seward's "strong inclination to try to what extent he may make political capital by high-handed conduct and violent language towards us." Backed by "the ignorant mob of the North," the American secretary of state was likely to initiate "similar proceedings at any moment. The next step," Lyons warned, "may be to seize a suspected privateer in Canadian waters, or to commit some other violation of Canadian territory." Warning Russell that "our best chance of preventing further difficulties is to be firm in the beginning," Lyons left "entirely open" for his chief's consideration "the means to be adopted to prevent a recurrence of similar acts of violence or threats of violence."[26]

When he received Lyons's report of the incident, the British foreign minister reacted calmly to what he called "very serious despatches." He thought "Lord Lyons was right to protest, but . . . I cannot blame the U.S. authorities for stopping by any means in their power the arming, purchase, or issue of exports to carry on hostilities against them." If, however, the Americans should actually seize a legitimate British ship, they would "do so at their peril."[27]

In Washington, Lyons continued to take a jaundiced view of the question. He asserted that when Seward had proposed that he try to get Canadian Governor General Sir Edmund Head to stop the *Peerless*, the secretary of state had reason to know that Governor

John Andrew of Massachusetts had already requested the Canadian governor general to do the same thing and had been turned down. Lyons agreed with Head that the order to seize the vessel had been issued for no better reason than "that a certain vessel had probably been sold to somebody, because she was going to Quebec, and that such vessel if improperly used would be dangerous." Meanwhile, Seward had sent a special agent, George Ashmun,[28] surreptitiously into Canada as a Union propagandist and also "to watch and prevent just such transactions as the sale or fitting out of the *Peerless* for a pirate would have been."

News of the Ashmun mission had leaked to the *New York Herald*, apparently through Senator Sumner, and Lyons inquired at once at the State Department about it on the ground that all official communications with Canadian authorities ought to be made through him and not directly. When asked about the venture, Seward gave Lyons the impression that he wanted to conceal it; he refused to provide "any information on the subject," the British minister complained, "even after Mr. Ashmun's mission had become so public as to be mentioned in the newspapers." Remarking that in his opinion the proceeding was "not inconsistent with Mr. Seward's individual character," the Englishman expressed perplexity about "what he can have hoped to effect by it in the present instance."[29]

Not long afterwards, however, Lyons decided that the *Peerless* and Ashmun incidents comprised part of a scheme for provoking war with England, in order to annex "Canada, as a compensation for any loss which might be occasioned by the disaffection of the South." Whether war was actually sought, or whether Seward "had no ground for his extraordinary proceeding . . . except his desire to seize an opportunity of making a Bravado against England for Party purposes," the secretary of state's "recklessness" in offering such provocations rendered "it only a matter of prudence to put Canada at once into a complete state of Defence."[30]

Commenting upon these speculations, Russell said that whatever the object of the United States government in sending secret agents into Canada, Her Majesty's government felt compelled to complain that no notice had been given to the British minister of an intention to dispatch them. A "frank explanation" should have been offered to Lyons, when he inquired "respecting the mission with which these agents were charged." He was ordered not to "conceal from Mr. Seward the unfavourable impression which this transaction has made on Her Majesty's government."[31]

Lyons took pleasure in transmitting these remarks, apparently verbatim, to Seward when next they conversed on the subject. Seward, however, protested that the mission had been an innocent one not designed to cause irritation. Its purpose had merely been to ascertain public feeling in Canada regarding the fitting out of Southern privateers on the St. Lawrence River. As soon as the British minister had objected to the venture, Seward added, he had recalled Ashmun.[32] Lyons, however, insisted on "telling him that H. M. Government considered that they had a good right to complain of his having been sent at all without proper communication being previously made to them and to me."[33]

In London, Russell told Adams, who reported his words to Seward, that he was not pleased

> at the mission of Mr. Ashmun, without any notice given to them of his purposes; and he likewise said something about a threat uttered by yourself to Lord Lyons to seize a British vessel on Lake Ontario without ceremony. To this I replied, that inasmuch as I had understood Mr. Ashmun's mission had been made known to the governor of Canada, it did not seem to me that it could be of much concealed significance; and that as to the other matter, if there was any reality in the threat, it surely was an odd way of proceeding to furnish at once the warning in time to provide against its execution.[34]

In his diary that night, Adams characterized the British anxiety over the Ashmun mission and over the *Peerless* incident as attributable to Lyons's lack of appreciation of "Seward's horseplay." He wrote Seward as much, suggesting that the British troops recently sent to Canada might well have been embarked as a consequence of Lyons's apparent tendency to "mistake pleasantry for earnest," and to "communicate unfavorable impressions when he might do otherwise."[35]

Seward's response to these warnings, however, indicated that his bout with Lyons had been more than mere "horseplay." While asserting that he had "every desire for a good understanding with the British government," and professing "no concern" that British land and naval reinforcements had been sent to America, the secretary of state explained that he had acted decisively in the Ashmun and *Peerless* cases to ensure "that the peace of the two countries should not be disturbed by the unlawful action of covetous and ill-disposed persons" in Canada, who were scheming to send out privateers against the maritime commerce of the United States. It was important to indicate to such persons from the beginning that the United States government would act decisively to protect its own interests and national integrity.[36]

When he had requested Lyons to ask the governor general of Canada "to look into the facts" of the *Peerless* case, Seward continued, and to prevent the vessel from sailing if it was found to be a rebel privateer, the British minister had replied "that he had no authority to do so." However, after Seward had said that he would direct American naval forces to detain the vessel if it still appeared to be a privateer, and Lyons had duly protested, the governor general of Canada had (so Seward declared) been persuaded somehow after all to interfere, "and the Peerless was prevented from sailing until the danger of her being converted into a pirate was prevented." Had it become necessary for United States forces to seize that vessel, Seward added, "we should at once have avowed the act and tendered any satisfaction to the British government if it should appear that the character of the vessel had been misunderstood." As for Ashmun, his visit to Canada was not meant to be objectionable. Indeed, his presence there, by providing a reliable source of information about just such vessels as the *Peerless*, might help to avert serious maritime collisions growing out of false or incomplete information. Ashmun was personally acquainted with Governor General Head, and his mission was no secret to Head.

Nevertheless, when Lyons complained of the step, Seward said, "I instantly recalled Mr. Ashmun."[37]

Had the *Peerless* been allowed to sail unhindered out of the St. Lawrence under a British flag to become a rebel privateer, other such corsairs would probably have followed her in increasing numbers, until serious danger of war with Canada, and thus with Great Britain, might have resulted. In the long run it had been best to risk the momentary tension that might have followed a single seizure based on a case of mistaken identity, which could have been eased at once by an apology and the payment of damages. Lyons, however, took Seward's refusal to heed his warning not to bother the *Peerless* as a personal affront. Even after he became satisfied that Seward's gesture in regard to the ship had been based on a genuine suspicion of her hostile character, Lyons wrote Russell that the affair had been "a sad indication of the carelessness and precipitation with which a matter which ought to be so grave, as a violation of the Rights of the British Flag, may be treated by him." Consequently, Lyons suggested, Anglo-American amity remained in a precarious state.[38]

Contributing to this uneasy situation was an officiousness that continued throughout the year 1861 to emanate, occasionally, from leading statesmen in England. As early as December, 1860, Palmerston had considered offering recognition to the nascent Southern Confederacy on the condition that it make "some engagement" against renewal of the slave trade. He had welcomed a suggestion by Edward Everett that England, France, and Russia should together declare a willingness to mediate in the American civil conflict. And to a similar proposal by the governor of Maryland that the British minister himself should act as a mediator, Palmerston had responded that he still thought mediation a possibility "to be fully weighed & considered." But Great Britain must move cautiously in that direction. For the danger was that, "in the excited state of men's minds in America, the offer of anyone to interpose to arrest their action, and disappoint them of their expected triumph, might be resented by both sides; and that jealousy of European, especially of English, interference in their internal affairs might make them still more prone to reject our offer as impertinent." When the time came, the premier declared, the best proposition to lay before "our North American cousins" would be "that the North and South should separate amicably; . . . and that each confederation should be free to make for its own internal affairs and concerns such laws as it might think fit."[39]

Russell, too, began edging toward a proposition of mediation in mid-May, when he instructed Lyons, "in case you should be asked to employ your good offices, either singly or in conjunction with the representatives of other powers, to give your assistance in promoting the work of reconciliation." After receiving Russell's dispatch, Lyons appears to have tendered some kind of mediation offer to Seward. According to the American secretary of state, Lyons expressed in behalf of his government "their willingness to undertake the kindly duty of mediation, should we desire it." Seward sent his answer to Adams:

> The President expects you to say on this point to the British government, that we appreciate this generous and friendly demonstration; but that we cannot solicit or accept mediation from any, even the most friendly quarter. [No] . . . dispute arising among us should ever be referred to foreign arbitration. . . . the British government . . . will do wisely by leaving us to manage and settle this domestic controversy in our own way.[40]

Seward's warning prevented any direct attempt at mediation by Great Britain for several months afterwards. It discredited the opinion of Baron Gerolt, the Prussian minister in Washington, who encouraged the idea of an effort at mediation by the Great Powers of Europe on the ground that Seward would probably welcome it. It justified Lyons's comment on his plan that its "object was no doubt excellent, but that . . . there was in my mind one objection which was fatal to it. I was certain that neither party would accept the mediation." It added weight to Palmerston's remark that it was only "human nature that the wiry edge must be taken off this craving appetite for conflict in arms before any real and widespread desire for peace by mutual concession can be looked for." But the itch in London to settle the American quarrel in favor of the Southern insurrectionists was too strong to be entirely suppressed. It merely took a clandestine form—that of an attempt secretly to open a diplomatic negotiation with the government of Jefferson Davis, a step that in itself implied recognition of the sovereignty and independence of that government. [41]

The Declaration of Paris Negotiation[1]

1. Privateering is and remains abolished. 2. The neutral flag covers enemy's goods, with the exception of contraband of war. 3. Neutral goods, with the exception of contraband of war, are not liable to capture under enemy's flag. 4. Blockades, in order to be binding, must be . . . maintained by a force sufficient really to prevent access to the coast of the enemy.

THE DECLARATION OF PARIS, 1856.

WHEN NEWS that the American Civil War had broken out reached England, the British foreign secretary realized that encounters between British mercantile seafarers and American belligerent warships might lead to serious trans-Atlantic disputes. In order beforehand to avert, as much as possible, such confrontations, Russell instructed his representative at Washington to seek an American commitment not to interfere with British maritime commerce, except by regular blockade of enemy ports, or except in cases when a prize court could clearly establish the conveyance of contraband of war. Lyons was told, first, to remind Secretary Seward that the United States government had never acceded to the Declaration of Paris of 1856, which had been contracted by the Great Powers of Europe, following the Crimean War, in order to resolve some of the most persistently difficult questions of international maritime law. Secondly, Lyons was ordered to request American acquiescence in the last three articles of the Declaration of Paris, which provided that noncontraband enemy goods on neutral ships, and noncontraband neutral goods on enemy ships, would both be exempt from capture in wartime, and also that blockades, in order to be respected by neutral governments, had to be "maintained by a force sufficient really to prevent access to the coast of the enemy." Finally, the British representative in Washing-

73

ton was commanded to "take such means as you shall judge most expedient to transmit to Her Majesty's Consul at Charleston or New Orleans" a copy of the dispatch calling for the adherence of the United States government to the aforementioned three provisions of international law, "to be communicated at Montgomery to the President of the so-styled Confederate States." Implicit in this instruction was the wish that the Southerners would agree as recognized belligerents to observe the rules of war laid down in the last three articles of the Declaration of Paris.[2]

The one remaining article of the Declaration of Paris bound participants to renounce the practice of privateering, whereby belligerent governments supplemented their naval strength by issuing "letters of marque" licensing privately owned vessels to seize and plunder the merchant ships of an enemy nation. Russell wrote that the French foreign minister was reluctant to propose that the United States government accede to this first article because the Confederate president had already begun issuing letters of marque to Southern privateers, and as long as Abraham Lincoln's administration classified the Confederates as "rebels" and claimed full jurisdiction over the Southern States there was a danger that any agreement to ban privateers reached at Washington would be interpreted by the United States government as applying to the South as well as to the North. From this perspective France and Great Britain would be bound to enforce a prohibition of privateering against the Southerners and to treat their vessels sailing under letters of marque as pirates. French and British neutrality between the belligerents could not be maintained under such circumstances. Hence, although Lyons would "not err in encouraging the Government to which you are accredited to . . . recognize the Declaration of Paris in regard to privateering," he was also to

> understand that her Majesty's government cannot accept the renunciation of privateering on the part of the government of the United States if coupled with the condition that they should enforce its renunciation on the Confederate States, either by denying their right to issue letters of marque, or by interfering with the belligerent operations of vessels holding from them such letters of marque, so

long as they carry on hostilities according to the recognized principles and under the admitted liabilities of the law of nations.[3]

The British foreign minister drew up his proposals for American adherence to the Declaration of Paris in ignorance of the fact that Seward had already instructed his envoys in Europe to initiate negotiations with the same object in view. As soon as the Civil War began at Fort Sumter, Seward anticipated that European governments "would naturally feel a deep anxiety about the safety of their commerce, threatened distinctly with privateering by the insurgents," as well as by the possibility "that we too should take up that form of maritime warfare in the present domestic controversy." Apprehending, then, "that the danger of . . . depredation upon commerce equally by the government itself and by its enemies" would stimulate the great maritime powers of Europe to proclaim their neutrality in relation to the developing conflict in America, Seward hastened to offer them assurances that

> we did not desire to depredate on friendly commerce ourselves, and we thought it our duty to prevent such depredations by the insurgents by executing our own laws, which make privateering by disloyal citizens piracy, and provide for its punishment as such. We thought it wise, just, and prudent to give, unasked, guarantees to . . . friendly nations for the security of their commerce from exposure to such depredations on either side. . . . The accession to the Declaration of Paris would be the form in which these guarantees could be given. . . . In this way we expected to remove every cause that any foreign power could have for the recognition of the insurgents as a belligerent power.

Any declaration of neutrality by a foreign government granting belligerent rights to the Southern rebels would constitute a serious step toward full diplomatic recognition of the South as an independent nation. From the American point of view the conflict was only a domestic rebellion, in which neither party, not being technically at war, could be classed as a belligerent under international law; hence neither party could legally issue letters of marque as a "belligerent right," although the United States government might adopt such measures as a right of internal police power. Therefore,

Seward was willing to give up the right of privateering, which the United States government, intending to build a great navy, would no longer need to exercise, in order, by adhering to the Declaration of Paris, to obligate European powers to shut their ports to Confederate privateers as piratical vessels with no legal right to use the high seas. Jefferson Davis's proclamation, which encouraged the commissioning of Confederate privateers, had inspired a virtual panic in Northern shipping circles. Tales of buccaneering expeditions fitting out in the South had caused Yankee shipowners, insurance underwriters, importers, and exporters to apply frantically to their representatives in Washington for added protection for their property. If the great sea powers of Europe could be induced by Seward not to interfere with the efforts of the United States Navy to rid the world's waterways of Southern privateers, the panic might soon be brought under control; otherwise, American statesmen were beginning to realize, the United States merchant marine might eventually be driven from the seas.[4]

Seward also envisioned a long-term advantage of subscribing to the Declaration of Paris. As a probable neutral in future wars, the United States might expect to grow rich off the profits derived from trading with belligerents on both sides, provided that by adhering to the Declaration of Paris it could then both protect its neutral trade and minimize the danger that had been ever-present during the era of the French Revolution and that of the Napoleonic Wars of being drawn into a foreign fray.[5]

These considerations resulted in an instruction circulated by Seward to most of his ministers in Europe, in which the secretary of state directed each of these gentlemen to ascertain whether the government to which he was accredited would negotiate a treaty with the United States for its accession to the Declaration of Paris. Seward observed that a treaty, rather than the mere exchange of diplomatic notes by which other nations had acceded to the Declaration of Paris, was necessary to enable the United States Senate to fulfill its constitutional prerogatives of "advise and consent." It would be "eminently desirable," the secretary of state continued, that the so-called Marcy amendment, proposing a fifth article exempting noncontraband belligerent private property from seizure aboard belligerent ships, should be incorporated into the Declaration of Paris. For the United States government had not abandoned the idea that maritime wars ought to be limited to battles between government warships, leaving all commerce, except in munitions, relatively unhindered. But, in view of the outbreak of rebellion in the South and the further possibility of war occurring in Europe at any moment over such imbroglios as the Italian and Polish questions, the United States government was no longer disposed to sacrifice the immediate advantages of being included among the parties to the Declaration of Paris merely because of a temporary inability to gain further immunities for private property in future wars.[6]

When Adams had his first interview with Russell on May 18, the foreign minister had already learned unofficially that the United States government had instructed its envoy to propose its formal accession to the Declaration of Paris. Lyons had written that Seward had spoken to others, but not to him, "of the United States being now willing to adhere to the Declaration of Paris abolishing privateering." But the British minister in Washington was "afraid of touching" the matter and did not believe American adherence, if actually given, would survive "the present crisis." In fact he thought that "the time at which the offer would be made renders the thing rather amusing. It would no doubt be very convenient if the Navies of Europe would put down the Privateers, and thus leave the whole Navy of the United States free to blockade the Ports against European merchant vessels."[7]

When Adams told Russell that his government had given him full powers to negotiate an Anglo-American agreement on neutral rights, and added that he had brought with him a draft convention incorporating the American position on the subject, Russell replied that Great Britain and France had already instructed their ministers at Washington upon the subject, and that Lyons had been given authority "to assent to any modification . . . which the government of the United States might prefer" on the question of privateering; hence he anticipated "no difficulty whatever" in reaching agreement on the question there. This being the case, he said, it would be advisable to leave the question in Lyons's hands. Adams answered that he would refrain from complicating the negotiation by proceeding any further in London, unless he should receive further instructions on the subject from his government.[8]

In a second interview with Russell on June 12, however, Adams discovered that although Lyons had been authorized to accept American accession to the last three articles of the Declaration of Paris, he had apparently been instructed to omit any reference to the privateering article. At this point, Adams probably should have pressed Seward's proposal for inclusion of the United States among the signatories to the entire Paris declaration. But Russell, failing to comprehend the need for a written agreement, upon which the Senate in Washington could exercise its constitutional role of "advise and consent," failed to inform Adams explicitly that his representative in America had no authority to enter into a formal treaty on the subject of neutral rights. Thus uninformed, Adams continued to assume that the negotiation which Seward had instructed him to undertake was already begun in Washington, and therefore he did not pursue the subject with the British foreign minister.[9]

Dispatches were received in Washington on June 2 directing Lyons and Mercier to propose that the United States government adhere to the last three articles of the Declaration of Paris and to transmit the same proposal to the Confederate government. The two envoys agreed that "unless communicated with much tact and caution," any overture to the authorities at Montgomery might be "resented here and regarded as a recognition of the Southern Confederacy." In fact, Lyons thought, "a sudden declaration of war by the U. S. against Great Britain" might well result if he initiated any contact with the Confederates whatever.[10]

After much anxious consultation about "what would be the most conciliatory form in which we could execute the instructions we had received respecting . . . maritime rights," Lyons and Mercier went together to see Seward. Although the secretary of state was "calm, friendly and good humoured," as Lyons later admitted, Seward refused to listen to "a communication founded on the

assumption that the Southern rebels were to be regarded as belligerents." Rather did he prefer, he said, to treat the question of
neutral maritime rights separately in London and Paris, where he
had already sent detailed proposals, instead of in Washington.
Moreover, he added, although he would not issue a formal complaint on the subject, he did not think it was friendly procedure for
two European powers to consult and act closely together upon a
course to be pursued toward his own country. As for the queen's
proclamation investing the insurrectionists with belligerent rights,
that had been "addressed only to Her Majesty's subjects," and
Seward hoped that he would not be forced to recognize it officially.
With these words he ended the joint interview, showing Mercier
into another room for further talk with him alone, and inviting
Lyons to dinner in order that he, too, might be at liberty to discuss
the question additionally, but also informally and alone.[11]

Although Lyons resented Seward's refusal officially to receive
"the communication which we were instructed to make to him," he
assumed, as a practical matter, that it would not be prudent to press
the secretary of state further on the question. After all, Seward had
stipulated that the United States government would adhere to the
last three articles of the Declaration of Paris. And when Lyons had
informed him that the British cabinet, "without in the slightest
degree recognizing the Southern government diplomatically,"
nevertheless insisted on its right to "hold intercourse with it more or
less formally, so long as the personal safety and the interests" of
British subjects living in the South were "dependent upon that
government," the secretary of state had suggested that the Lincoln
administration "might even shut its eyes" to unofficial European
intercourse "with the Rebel government of the South," provided no
"regular announcement" was made which might be interpreted as a
declaration of diplomatic recognition.[12]

This hint by the secretary of state appeared at least momentarily
to offer Lyons and Mercier an opportunity safely to transmit the
proposals of their governments to Montgomery. Fearing that "the
Southern Government will no doubt do all in their power to give
importance and publicity to the communication" about neutral

rights, and that Seward would then "probably withdraw the Exequatur of the Consuls who make it," they moved cautiously, nevertheless, to instruct their consuls at Charleston to seek "securities concerning the proper treatment of neutrals."[13]

Perhaps this overture would have escaped question in Washington had not Lyons included in his letter to Consul Robert Bunch the statement: "I am authorized by Lord John Russell to confide the negotiation on this matter to you." To apply the word "negotiation" to any relationship with the Southern insurgents was a serious mistake, for no government would "negotiate" with another regime unless it either recognized it diplomatically or was making preparations to do so. Moreover, a diplomatic negotiation was not generally considered to be within the permitted sphere of activity of a consul, whose exequatur allowed him only commercial and not political functions. Hence, even though Lyons warned Bunch to "act with great caution, in order to avoid raising the question of the recognition of the new confederation by Great Britain," and not to place himself in direct communication with the Southern government, but to work "verbally" through Governor Francis Pickens of South Carolina, the way was paved for misunderstanding of the venture in the Northern States. For sooner or later the news was bound to leak out that Bunch had been asked to induce "the government at Richmond to recognize, by an official act, the rights secured to neutrals by the second and third articles of the Declaration of Paris, and to admit its own responsibility for the acts of privateers sailing under its letters of marque." Whether the advantages of obtaining such a commitment from the Southerners would out-weigh the risks of great irritation in the North, once the people there learned that a "negotiation" had been attempted, remained to be seen.[14]

Meanwhile, the American minister in Paris, William L. Dayton, violated his instructions to offer his government's unqualified adherence to the Declaration of Paris. Instead, Dayton told the French foreign minister that he was authorized to sign a convention incorporating the four articles of the declaration, *with the addition of a fifth article containing the Marcy amendment*, designed to protect belligerent-owned private property from seizure aboard belligerent ships. Edouard Thouvenel quite properly replied that before he could act on the American request for a convention, he would have to consult the other signees of the original agreement.[15]

When the British foreign minister was informed about Dayton's proposal to the French government, he immediately suspected that, as Lyons had warned might happen, the "violent men" in the United States government were trying to manipulate "some shade of difference in the conduct of England and France, in order to use violent language, or even to take violent measures against England without necessarily involving themselves in a quarrel with France also." Moreover, the delay in getting the negotiation underway which followed Dayton's insubordinate act gave Russell time to receive additional warnings from Lyons in Washington that there was "no doubt" that the American adherence to the Declaration of Paris was being offered "in the expectation that it will bind the government[s] accepting it to treat the privateers of the Southern Confederacy as Pirates." Thus would the crafty Seward draw foreign governments into the Civil War on the side of the North.[16]

The fact that his envoy at Washington had contradicted himself—suggesting both that Seward was trying to separate England from France in order to arrange a quarrel with the former power, and that Seward was also trying to trick England and France together into using their warships to help the United States government suppress the Southern privateers—seems not to have occurred to Russell. Although he agreed during a conference with Adams on July 13 to put the question of an Anglo-American convention incorporating the Declaration of Paris, "pure and simple," before the British cabinet, he used the ensuing interval both to work out arrangements with foreign diplomats for identical conventions to be signed simultaneously at Paris and at London, and to reach an understanding with the French regarding an announcement that "this convention cannot in any way alter the Proclamation and other Instruments by which Great Britain and France have declared their intentions to treat the two Parties engaged in the Civil

War in America as belligerents." Such an announcement, Russell said, would prevent a misunderstanding about the obligations of European governments regarding Southern privateers.[17]

At Washington, meanwhile, Seward paid a visit to the British legation in an attempt, he told Lyons, "to disentangle a complication" produced by Dayton at Paris. What his representative in France did not seem to understand, Seward asserted, was that the purpose of his proposal for American accession to the Declaration of Paris was to provide England and France with as much security for their maritime trade as possible during the current emergency. British shipping would be saved from the uncertainties of a paper blockade by article one; British civilian goods on Confederate vessels and British vessels carrying noncontraband Confederate cargoes would be protected by the second and third articles; and the United States government "would do all in its power," under article four, "to protect the commerce of friends from the attacks of the so-called privateers of the rebels." It would *not* insist that its accession to the Declaration of Paris imposed an obligation on other parties to that agreement to aid in suppressing Southern privateering. It only asked that the British government, in contracting to accept the adhesion of the United States to the Declaration of Paris, refrain from implying a recognition of Confederate belligerent rights, which would follow from any statement "that it did not intend, by accepting the accession of the United States, to contract any engagement affecting the states in revolt."[18]

Notwithstanding this explanation, Lyons promptly wrote the British foreign minister that he continued "to think it very important, with a view to preventing serious disputes in future, that Great Britain and France should not accept the accession of this government to the Declaration of Paris without stating to it, formally and distinctly, beforehand, the exact effect which their so doing is intended by them to have with regard to the seceded States."[19]

Russell agreed. He wrote Palmerston that he would let Adams know before the two men met to sign the convention that its provisions would not in any way alter the British neutral position toward the war in America. In reply, the prime minister suggested that the statement to Adams be "given in writing," in order to have a "record of the precise words." Russell, therefore, wrote Adams that he was prepared to sign an Anglo-American convention embodying the four articles of the Declaration of Paris. However, "to prevent any misconception as to the nature of the engagement to be taken by Her Majesty," he proposed to accompany the convention with a written declaration in the following form:

> In affixing his signature to the convention of this day between her Majesty the Queen of Great Britain and Ireland and the United States of America, the Earl Russell declares, by order of her Majesty, that her Majesty does not intend thereby to undertake any engagement which shall have any bearing, direct or indirect, on the internal differences now prevailing in the United States.[20]

Adams wrote Russell that he could not permit himself to complete the negotiation "when clogged with such a declaration." For the British had suddenly interjected "a proceeding somewhat novel and anomalous"—one which prevented the parties to the convention from signing it "upon terms of perfect reciprocity . . . without equivocation or reservation of any kind." Should the United States government accept the qualification brought forward by Russell, asserted Adams, it would justify the implication that it sought to participate in the Declaration of Paris agreement for the sole purpose of "securing some small temporary object in the unhappy struggle . . . at home." The United States government was motivated only by its historic "high purpose" of support for neutral rights. Rather than allow any other inference, Adams said, he must decline to proceed in the negotiation until he received further instructions to do so from home.[21]

By September both sides understood the Declaration of Paris negotiation to be ended. Russell was happy to abandon it. It had begun to look "as if a trap had been prepared" by Seward to trick the European powers into assisting the United States in suppressing Southern privateering and thereby to involve them in the war on the side of the North. Seward, whose real motive throughout the negotiation was to reduce, not increase, the possibility of foreign involvement in the American Civil War by committing his country as much as possible to the protection of neutral maritime commerce, was forced to reject the British and French qualifying declarations. For they would have put the United States government in the position of recognizing that a state of war, rather than merely one of rebellion, existed within its borders. Once the government had admitted this, the way would have been open for European diplomatic recognition of Confederate independence. Then, finally, might have come outright foreign interference in the conflict, to ensure the perpetuation of that independence.[22]

All the parties to the negotiation tended to blame its failure upon connivance and bad faith on the other side. The suspicions that Russell and Lyons had of Seward's motives, and that Seward and Adams had developed of British intentions, had now been magnified as a result of successive misunderstandings that none of the statesmen involved in the affair could believe had been accidental.[23] Thus existed a dangerous conjunction of attitudes at the very time that serious new differences arose between the two countries, in the autumn of 1861.

The Blockade as a Dangerous Issue

We are of opinion that no belligerent power has a right by mere prohibitory enactment, to require neutral nations to abstain from all commercial dealings with another belligerent power. . . . We are therefore of opinion that any [such] paper enactment by Congress . . . may be treated as nugatory by the Law of Nations & any attempt to enforce it by the seizure & confiscation of a neutral ship may be justly regarded as an act of hostility.

BRITISH CROWN LAW OFFICERS,
July, 1861.

FROM THE OUTBREAK OF FIGHTING in North America the British were greatly disturbed by signs that the United States government contemplated closing Southern ports to their trade. Lincoln's secretary of the navy, Gideon Welles, an old political antagonist of Seward's, had opposed the adoption of a maritime blockade as a war measure in conformity with international law, favoring instead a presidential proclamation simply declaring the Southern ports domestic areas closed to foreign trade. Seward, however, had argued that to try to close the ports in the hands of the insurrectionists without adhering to the traditional procedures of international maritime law might involve the United States in dangerous complications with European powers in quest of cotton, while the same powers, having bound themselves by the Declaration of Paris of 1856 to respect a regular blockade, would be less likely to interfere in behalf of the rebels if a blockade were publicly proclaimed. President Lincoln adopted Seward's advice against what Welles later alleged were the contrary opinions of a majority of the members of the cabinet, but the secretary of the navy, bitterly Anglophobe as well as anti-Seward, labeled early blockade instructions "confidential," so that the secretary of state could not carry out his promise to send Lyons full information about which ports were going to be blockaded and when.[1]

Before the end of May, the British minister began to complain that no foreign envoy had "succeeded in obtaining a relaxation of the rigour of the Blockade, either in favour of any Neutral Flag, or in individual cases of hardship." Yet he was soon anticipating the necessity of making an official protest to the United States government for having had its naval commanders announce a blockade of the entire Confederate coast, when in fact, he asserted, "up to the present moment nothing like an effective Blockade of the greater part of the Southern coast exists." Then, less than one week later, he once again objected to what he termed the excessively "harsh" restraints imposed on British trade by the blockading squadron.[2]

In answer to such reports that the blockade was inefficient, intermittently interspersed with lamentations that it was *too* efficient, Russell wrote that it was "desirable not to open a contentious correspondence on the separate cases in which the legality of the blockade may be disputed." Instead, Russell said, Lyons should recognize "the extreme importance of obtaining all the particulars possible respecting the Blockade," so that the British government might be able easily to substantiate "the claims which may possibly at a future time be brought against the government of the United States in connection with the Blockade."[3]

The foreign minister's intentions, then, were to acquiesce in the Northern blockade, as long as it was carried on in conformity with accepted rules of international law, and to postpone remonstrances about its inefficiency and about inequities arising under it.[4] He took quite a contrary view, however, of Gideon Welles's project of closing the Southern ports by mere proclamation, without employing a regular blockading force. He was greatly disturbed when Lyons wrote him that influential members of Congress favored such a bill, despite repeated declarations by the British representative in Washington that the maritime powers of Europe would recognize no such paper blockade. With some members of the cabinet, including Seward, in Lyons's opinion actually seeking a pretext for war with England, the *casus belli* most likely to be employed appeared "to be that of closing the Southern Ports by an Act of Congress, instead of by an Effective Blockade," and it was probable, according to the British minister, that Congress, due to convene on July 4, would quickly pass such an act.[5]

These reports were circulated by Russell to other members of the British cabinet and resulted in considerable disquietude. Having recognized the belligerent rights of the Confederacy, the British government could not consistently accept the idea that the United States government retained its sovereignty over Southern ports. Palmerston began to visualize "serious difficulties" should the proposed act pass the American Congress; while Russell, deploring the very thought of such a "wild measure," determined to give "fair warning" to the American minister at London.[6]

On July 4 the British foreign minister sent Lyons a written opinion of the crown law officers, in which those gentlemen asserted

> that any attempt on the part of the northern U.S. to close by an act of Congress all the Ports of the Southern (Confederate) States against British commerce, would be inconsistent with the pacific and commercial relations at present subsisting between the U.S. of America & this country.
>
> Further we are of opinion that . . . any paper enactment by Congress, to the effect anticipated by Lord Lyons, may be treated as nugatory by the Law of Nations & any attempt to enforce it by the seizure & confiscation of a neutral ship may be justly regarded as an act of hostility.[7]

After telling Adams that the crown law officers "had declared that with regard to ports in the hands of insurgents, the right of closing the ports, except by the recognized mode of blockade, did not exist," Russell wrote Lyons to inform Seward that the British government "would consider a Decree closing the Ports of the South actually in the possession of the insurgents or Confederate States as null & void, and they would deem it their duty to resist its execution by force if necessary." Although on second thought the foreign minister substituted for the last thirteen words of this declaration the less vigorous phrase—"could not submit to mea-

87

sures taken on the high seas in pursuance of such Decree"—the determination of the British government not to acquiesce in the proposed port-closing project was clear, and the dangers inherent in American defiance of Russell's admonition were equally obvious. [8]

Russell wrote Lyons: "It is of course desirable not to get into a quarrel sooner than we can help, nor at all if we can help it." In dealing with complaints growing out of an attempted enforcement of the act, Lyons was instructed "in every case of difficulty . . . to refer home, and not to act without previous instructions fitted to the case." Russell would, in turn, seek opinions from the crown law officers before taking a position on such cases. For he cherished a hope that "if we can tide the summer over without serious hostilities," perhaps the coming of "autumn may see an opening of negotiations between the two combatants." [9]

While Russell was preparing these latest instructions to Lyons, the United States Congress had convened and had begun action on a war message from President Lincoln, accompanied by special reports from the Navy, War, and Treasury departments. The Treasury Department report, which dealt with methods of financing military operations, carried a recommendation that Congress enact a law closing the Southern ports, and that it empower the president to collect customs duties on shipboard, if necessary, without a formal blockade. The penalties for violation of the act were to include forfeiture of both ship and cargo. Rushed through both houses of Congress within one week of being proposed, the port-closing act became law with the president's signature before a second week had elapsed. Lyons reported that the haste with which the measure had been passed was an alarming symptom of the reckless temper of both Congress and the country at the moment. The legal counsel to the British legation had responded to Lyons's request for an advisory opinion by saying that once the port-closing act went into effect, the President would no longer have legal power to continue the kind of blockade required by international law. The British minister thought, nevertheless, that if Seward and Lincoln really wanted to continue the blockade in force, instead of substituting a policy of arbitrary closing of ports, "they will find the means of overcoming any legal impediment to doing so."[10]

After being cautioned by both Lyons and Mercier that very serious consequences might follow any attempt to enforce the provisions of the port-closing act, Seward apparently paid a visit to the White House. For a senator from the president's own state of Illinois found Lincoln "very melancholy" because of portending "difficulties with foreign powers." The president informed his visitor that Europeans

> were determined to have the cotton crop as soon as it matured—that our coast was so extensive that we could not make the blockade of all the Ports effectual—and that England was now assuming the ground that a nation had no right, whilst a portion of its citizens were in revolt to close its ports or any of them against foreign Nations—that we had passed a law at this session of Congress, authorizing him, in his discretion, to close our ports, but if he asserted the right of closing such as we could not blockade, he had no doubt it would result in foreign War, and that under the circumstances we had better increase the navy as fast as we could and blockade such as our force would enable us to, and say nothing about the rest.[11]

Besides influencing the president to "say nothing" about carrying out the port-closing act, in the face of strong pressure from most of his cabinet members and from such powerful senators as Charles Sumner to put it into operation at once, Seward wrote Adams that the passage of the port-closing law did "not necessarily indicate a legislative conviction that the ports ought to be closed, but only shows the purpose of Congress that the closing of the ports, if it is now or shall become necessary, shall not fail for want of power explicitly conferred by law." Although the President was determined to use this new power to close the Southern ports "at the hazard of whatever consequences, whenever it shall appear that the safety of the nation requires it," Adams might assure the British that no change of policy was presently contemplated, "injuriously affecting foreign commerce . . . against nations which practically respect the sovereignty of the United States."[12]

Seward summoned Lyons to read him this instruction to Adams, and he also added oral assurances of peaceful intent. Relieved, the British minister wrote home that the question was at least temporarily settled: the secretary of state, who had suddenly entered into a "prudent and pacific mood," was single-handedly preventing the president's cabinet from putting the port-closing act into operation. Lyons hoped that Seward might be "opening his eyes to the real danger of a quarrel with England." But, if so, it was only because of past demonstrations of British firmness in sending troops to Canada, and in reinforcing the West Indian fleet. Lyons hoped that "the impression we have made will be strengthened by evident readiness on our part to make an attack upon any portion of our Dominions disastrous at the outset to the assailants—and by a manifest firmness in exacting due respect to us."[13]

Prior to receiving these reassuring remarks from Lyons, the British foreign minister had become so alarmed by the earlier reports from his envoy in Washington that he brought the question of the port-closing act before the British cabinet. The collective judgment of that body, as Russell interpreted it, was that England would have to risk war, rather than submit to any American "pretentions in violation of the law of nations." Well into the summer of 1861, Russell worried whether the Americans would ignore his warnings that the British government "could not submit" to any actual application of the new law. Instead, he learned from Lyons that Seward had been able "to fortify himself in the cabinet with our positive declarations" in order to prevent any attempt by Lincoln's Navy Department to put the port-closing act into operation. By September, the British foreign minister discontinued his agitation of the explosive issue—partly because the American secretary of state appeared to have it at least temporarily under control, and partly because it had been eclipsed by a new, no less dangerous, controversy in the form of the so-called "Bunch affair." The dangers inherent in the existence of the American port-closing act did not evaporate, however. They still lurked behind the scenes, ready at any time suddenly to reappear, perhaps afterwards to drive the two nations into a trans-Atlantic war.[14]

The Pressure from London Increases

You will see they are sending troops to Canada. I cannot make out what this is for. It has been customary for the English Government to move ships and troops whenever and wherever any disturbance is going on ("to be ready for any emergency," and generally to meddle in it). This is the tradition . . . , and Lord Palmerston and Lord Russell are saturated with it. . . . [Also] I don't place much faith in their minister at Washington. I . . . did not form a high opinion of his capacity. . . . Some persons here have not been without anxiety as to the manner in which he regards what is passing [in America].

JOHN BRIGHT TO CHARLES SUMNER,
September 6, 1861.[1]

BY MID AUGUST OF 1861, Secretary of State Seward had begun to believe it safe to moderate his vigorously worded warnings to Great Britain against interference in the American Civil War. For Adams had written that they had achieved the desired effect. "In lieu of the former rashness," the American envoy in London had reported, had "come a proportionate timidity. . . . I am now earnestly assured on all sides that the sympathy with the government of the United States is general; that the indignation in America is not founded in reason; that the British desire only to be perfectly neutral, giving no aid nor comfort to the insurgents. I believe that this sentiment is now growing to be universal." Thus assured that his warnings had jolted British leaders into a reasonable attitude toward the American rebellion, Seward concluded that it was time to adopt a more soothing stance toward the British representative in Washington. On July 20—*the day before* the Battle of Bull Run— he told Lyons, confidentially, in the latter's words, "that he himself was at heart always inclined to peaceful and moderate counsels; but that he could not afford to 'lessen his means of usefulness' by going against the current of public feeling. . . . If, for instance, he had used strong language in his earlier communications to Foreign Powers, it was from the necessity of making them clearly understand the state of public feeling here and the results it might produce." For any direct European aid to the South would have raised an irresistible outcry in the North for war. To avert this calamity had been Seward's sole motivation, and he "was very anxious to maintain this position," while in the future employing language as pacific as his intentions.[2]

Lyons rejected this overture. Commenting smugly that "I was not altogether unprepared for the change in Mr. Seward's tone," he added that the secretary's new subdued attitude was traceable, not to British backtracking as a result of the secretary's policy of "insolence towards Foreign Powers," but rather to Seward's own realization that his "bluster has produced no effect—that it has not changed the determination of Her Majesty's government, nor created dissension between England and France. Firmness appears to have a much more quieting effect than any amount of conciliation or concession." In the future, therefore, Lyons recommended that his government continue its policy of rigid defense of the "rights of British subjects and British interests."[3]

Thus did Lyons turn his back on an opportunity to relax the tension between the United States and Great Britain. For the Northern defeat at Bull Run on July 21 only reinforced Seward's determination to deal with European governments in a pacific spirit, as long as they refrained from extending aid or encouragement to the Southern rebels. Realizing that after that debacle few Europeans would credit the United States government with much military strength, Seward wrote Adams that, although he fully expected a "vigorous reconstruction" of the Northern war effort with greatly increased enthusiasm as a consequence of the defeat in Virginia, he also believed it "not likely that anything will now be done here, hastily or inconsiderately, affecting our foreign relations." Some of Seward's post-Bull Run instructions implied that the United States government would temporarily ease its pressure for withdrawal of the British neutrality proclamation. Also, in the belief that the Bull Run defeat would "for a time operate to excite apprehensions and encourage the enemies of the Union in Europe," Seward decided to postpone any further discussions with Lyons of the president's right to close the Southern ports without the imposition of a formal blockade. Adams had already anticipated this shift to a cautious defensive position when on July 13 he told Russell that he did not propose to enter into any further discussion about the merits of these questions without specific instructions to do so from his government. The differences of opinion about the question of Southern belligerency had been thoroughly expounded by representatives of both governments, and any reiterated definition of them could only create trouble. So long as the president proposed to persevere in the blockade, a course against which Russell had signified his intention not to raise any objection, Adams did not "deem it expedient to stir the matter until the necessity for it shall become positive."[4]

The defeat at Bull Run, Adams wrote Seward, had created a need for American restraint in dealing with the British government. Having a distinct tendency to be impressed mainly by "the idea of power and success," Europeans viewed the scenes of Bull Run painted by the press of both England and America with disgust. The British in particular had "little mercy for weakness physical or moral." By "vaporing" now, the United States government's leaders would only make themselves ridiculous.[5]

In his response to Adams's cautionary message, the secretary of state professed himself "entirely satisfied with the exercise of your own discretion as to the time and form you may choose for making the explanations to the British government on those subjects with which you are charged." He was fully aware, he said, of "the exultations of enemies of our country and its institutions over the disaster of the 21st of July." But the ultimate victory of the government over the rebels was no less sure than it had been before the Bull Run defeat; and this should not "be misunderstood" in Europe.[6]

In Lyons's dispatches, however, Seward's determination and his confidence in the eventual triumph of the North were translated by the British envoy into mere bravado, and the British envoy at Washington suggested, and the prime minister agreed, that although the result of the Battle of Bull Run might lower the hopes of the Northern leaders "as against the South," it might also proportionally turn their thoughts "to compensation" in Canada. In the Foreign Office, too, both Russell, who could not "believe the descendants of the men of 1776 & indeed of 1815 to be totally wanting in courage," and his permanent undersecretary were afraid that Seward might now create an incident in order "to send Lyons his passports; and [to] endeavour by so doing to retrieve the character of the administration which seems to have suffered much since the defeat of Bull's Run." An attack on Canada, Palmerston suggested, might well follow. [7]

Near the end of August dispatches arrived in London from Lyons warning the cabinet of possible seizures of British merchant shipping without notice, should the Lincoln administration decide abruptly to put the port-closing act into operation. Received at approximately the same time was a lengthy diplomatic note from Adams suspending the Declaration of Paris negotiation, a move which impelled Russell and Palmerston to agree that "relations with the Washington govt are in a ticklish condition." Neither Lincoln nor Seward could be trusted. The Americans were "a swaggering bullying set of men" wrote Palmerston. Their belief that the British were defenseless in Canada "might lead them to venture out of their depth in communications with us . . . ; and they might be led to go beyond the limits at which they could go back, or at which we could allow them to take their stand." The earlier dispatch of troops to Canada, the prime minister asserted, had exercised

a wholesome effect upon the tone & temper of Lincoln and Seward; but that effect was due not merely to the actual amount sent but also to the expectation that more would follow. The only security for continued Peace with men who have no sense of Honour, and who are swayed by the Passions of irresponsible masses, and by a reckless

94

desire to hold their positions by all and by any means, consists in being strong by sea on their coasts and respectable in our military force in our Provinces.

. . . I am strongly of opinion that we ought to increase our Regular Force in Canada and that by doing so, we should keep the United States government in check, give spirit and confidence to our own people in the Provinces and take the best chance for the continuance of Peace.[8]

Even Sir George Cornewall Lewis, secretary for war, at first subscribed to the view that the "reckless and unscrupulous" Yankees might be tempted to launch a foray against Canada by the "appearance of unguardedness" in London. Hence, even though he thought that the Northerners currently had "their hands too full to attempt an attack on Canada," he favored sending additional troops there at once.[9]

But the leak of the project to the press, which the colonial secretary attributed to "some clerk in the War Office," brought it to the attention of other members of the cabinet, who proceeded strongly to oppose it. On September 3, Lewis wrote Palmerston that, after all, the leaders of the Washington government were "not insane, and with the 'belligerent' in the South to deal with I can hardly think that they will wish to make an enemy of the principal maritime power in the world." He now leaned to the opinion that the mere knowledge that troops could be promptly sent to Canada by the *Great Eastern*, if it developed that they were needed there, would be enough to deter the Americans. A few days later, having received "dissent from the proposal for sending more troops to Canada" from Sir George Grey, the home secretary, Lewis wrote that he now entertained "great doubts as to the policy of the measure" and that the diversity of opinion that had arisen about it made it "necessary to call a Cabinet to discuss the question."[10]

By this time the influential duke of Argyll, who held the office of lord privy seal, and William Ewart Gladstone, chancellor of the exchequer, had joined Lewis, Grey, the duke of Newcastle, and the duke of Somerset, first lord of the admiralty, in opposing "the folly of sending troops to Canada." Argyll wrote: "I can't see any possible use—and I do not wonder at the interpretation put upon it by Americans."[11]

As cabinet opinion thus swung strongly against sending more reinforcements to North America, a sudden demand by Seward for the removal of a British consul serving in the seceded states reached London. This demand appeared to be the long-anticipated aggressive gesture which Lyons had repeatedly indicated might signal Seward's institution of an Anglo-American war. At once Palmerston resumed his advocacy of the immediate dispatch of more troops and warships to North America, while Russell, without hesitation, prepared to bring the full strength of British diplomacy to bear in favor of the accused consul.

The Bunch Affair Begins

The only authority in this country to which any dip-
lomatic communication whatever can be made is the
government of the United States itself.

W. H. Seward to C. F. Adams,
October 23, 1861.[1]

From the time news reached England of the American secession crisis at the beginning of 1861, the possibility that British consular activities in the Confederacy might increase Anglo-American tensions had never been absent from Foreign Office calculations. As early as the end of January, Lyons had warned that when vacancies occurred in consular offices located in seceding states, the appointment of replacements "might give rise to serious inconveniences." It was almost certain, he wrote, that the seceding governments "would refuse to recognize a Consul who should have obtained an Exequatur from the Federal Government. On the other hand the Federal Government would probably be seriously offended if their Exequatur were not applied for in the case of a newly appointed consul."[2] One way of dealing with this dilemma, Lyons eventually decided, was for him to make "temporary" appointments to fill consular vacancies and hope that neither the United States government nor any Southern state government would demand that an exequatur be issued in such cases.[3] He also insisted that if British consuls already holding exequaturs from the United States government were asked to recognize Confederate independence and take out new exequaturs in the South, they "should refer home for Instructions" before taking any action on the subject.[4]

During the first week of July, news arrived in London from Washington giving notice that in the future all passports issued by foreign diplomats or consuls within the United States must be countersigned by the secretary of state to be valid. Lyons had not objected to this step; indeed, he wrote the Foreign Office, "I thought it desirable, with a view to avoiding the risk of British Subjects making use of my Passport to assist them in acting as Partisans on one side or the other in the present struggle." But several days after receiving official notice from Seward of the new passport regulations, Lyons learned that they had resulted at least partly from an alleged indiscretion of Her Majesty's consul at Charleston. In a private note to the British minister, the American secretary of state had enclosed a police report complaining that Consul Robert Bunch had made use of his office "for facilitating the transmission of treasonable correspondence." The report asserted that a man who had been a dispatch courier for Bunch was engaged in purchasing arms for the Southern government in New York. And although Lyons had gone at once to the State Department to deny the report, to the extent of saying that if any improper correspondence had been transmitted, he was certain it had been carried without Bunch's knowledge, the suspicion had been nevertheless implanted in Seward's mind that Bunch might be involved in unneutral activity.[5]

This suspicion was reinforced when one Purcell M. Quillan, a British subject from Charleston, was arrested in the North, accused of being a rebel spy, and charged with traveling in the United States for the purpose of buying arms for the insurgents. Bunch had supplied Quillan with a British passport and a letter of recommendation.[6]

Soon a second consul, this one at New Orleans, attracted the secretary of state's interest. This gentleman, William Mure, was accused of forming a partnership with his brothers in Canada to engage in blockade-running ventures. There was also evidence that he had sent, under the protection of his consular seal, thousands of letters designed to aid Confederate commercial and diplomatic projects. Although Seward did no more than threaten to revoke Mure's exequatur, the secretary of state became convinced by August that at least some British consuls in the South made use of their offices to help transmit "treasonable" correspondence. He had also become unpleasantly familiar with the name "Mure."[7]

Such was the situation when Seward received a telegram from the New York City superintendent of police announcing that a resident of Charleston named Robert Mure had been arrested as he was about to sail, under suspicious circumstances, for Europe. After a hurried investigation, which turned up testimony that Robert Mure was a cousin of the British consul at New Orleans,[8] the secretary of state summoned Lyons to an interview. He told the British minister that Mure, who claimed the right to British protection, had been arrested on suspicion of "carrying despatches from the rebel government to the Southern commissioners in Europe." He also informed Lyons of his intention to "send by the first opportunity a special messenger" to London to deliver a confiscated dispatch bag, bearing the seal of the consulate at Charleston, to the British Foreign Office, and he said that he would direct Adams to explain to Russell "the circumstances under which the messenger had been arrested and the bag taken from him." The secretary of state objected, he said, to Bunch's having issued Mure a passport, which he had no legal power to do, and he pointed out that even if it had been issued by the proper authority, Mure's passport would still have lacked validity "because the regulation requiring it to be countersigned by the Secretary of State had not been complied with." About two hundred private letters addressed to persons in Europe had been found in Mure's possession and were being examined to see if they contained treasonable material.[9]

Lyons's report of the incident of Mure's arrest did not provide any warning that Seward would seek Bunch's removal from his post. The secretary of state apparently did not indicate this intention when he spoke to the British minister. He did say, though, "that it would be very easy" for a British consul to send dispatches from the Confederate leaders to their overseas envoys by enclosing them in a sealed diplomatic pouch addressed to the British foreign minister, "and let the messenger open the bag when he arrived in England—and separate what was really for [Russell] from the treasonable correspondence." Therefore, Seward desired the bag taken from Mure to be handed to Russell "exactly as it was sent off." Lyons "resented the idea that Mr. Bunch or any of our Consuls could play such foolish or improper tricks," but inasmuch as Russell, upon examining the contents of the intercepted dispatch bag, would be in a better position to evaluate the case than he would, Lyons kept his indignation to himself. "I made no endeavour to get him to give me the bag," Lyons wrote. "I did not wish to afford the smallest motive towards these people including me in their small suspicions."[10]

For the American minister in London, the Bunch affair began on September 2, when a special messenger arrived from Washington bearing a mysterious package—the confiscated dispatch bag, seals unbroken—wrapped in brown paper. Accompanying the package were two instructions. One required Adams to deliver the bag to Russell, apologize for the delay in its transmission, and request that its contents be examined, so that if any portion should prove to be treasonable to the United States, Consul Bunch should "be promptly made to feel the severe displeasure of the government which employs him." In the other instruction, which Adams received on the same day, Seward castigated Consul Bunch "as a conspirator" against the United States. He quoted from an intercepted letter, which represented Bunch as saying that his British superiors, by ordering him to open a "negotiation" with the Confederate government, had taken the first step toward recognizing the insurgent regime. Finally, Seward directed Adams to request that the British government remove Bunch from office and replace him with someone "who will not pervert his functions to hostilities against the United States."[11]

Adams made the representations required of him in two notes delivered along with the errant bag to the Foreign Office on September 3. A long delay followed, while Russell tried to determine how best to reply. Having apparently had a premonition of trouble, the British foreign minister had earlier rushed off a dispatch to Washington directing Lyons "not to make any announcement to the authorities of the South" of the proposals made to the United States government for its adherence to the Declaration of Paris. He had begun to fear that "any intercourse with the South may create fresh irritation without any adequate result." Only if official steps had already been taken, Russell wrote, should his Washington representative "proceed in them to the end."[12]

Unfortunately, Russell's countermanding order had reached Lyons too late to stop the envoy from committing himself and his government to a "negotiation" with the Richmond authorities. And Seward, true to Russell's apprehensions, had seemed to snatch at the incident as a pretext for attempting "to pick a quarrel." Russell was determined to meet any fresh American belligerence head-on. Though reluctant to believe the Americans "foolhardy enough to quarrel with England and France," he was still sorry that fellow members of the cabinet had so stubbornly "opposed my wish to send a squadron to N. America" in order to support the troop reinforcement earlier sent to Canada. He was sure such a gesture "would have inspired respect, & we might have been spared this trouble."[13]

The composition of an answer to Adams elicited the personal supervision of the prime minister. Palmerston wrote that Lincoln and Seward might

> follow up the refusal of their demand by sending Lyons away; if this should be so, would it not be best to direct him to go in the first instance to Canada and there to wait for further orders? This would look like giving the Washingtonians an opportunity to settle matters in a friendly way . . . .
>
> . . . As to our Admiral I conclude that he should be told that in the event of a breaking off of diplomatic relations between the Northerns and us, he should wait for further instructions and not commit hostilities unless the rupture was followed by a declaration of war or by acts of hostility on the part of the Northerns. . . . I almost doubt Lincoln and Seward being foolish enough to draw the sword against us, but they have shown themselves so wild, that any act of intemperance may be expected from them. At all events we must immediately send more troops to Canada and more ships to Adml Milne. . . . Theoretical political economists may discuss at their leisure the question as to the value of Colonies to the mother country, but no man with half an eye in his head, or half a idea in his brain, could fail to perceive what a lowering of the position of England in the world would follow the conquest of our N. American Provinces by the

N. Americans, especially after the Bull's Run races. We must defend Canada: and to defend it, we must have troops there.[14]

Russell replied: "I quite agree with you about sending troops to Canada." Since Seward's demand for Bunch's recall, relations with the United States had become "the great question of all, . . . and that grows darker and darker every day." Like Palmerston, the foreign minister thought it possible that Lyons might be handed his passports, if "Seward and Co." should try "to revive their waning popularity by a quarrel with Great Britain."[15]

In answering the American demand for Bunch's recall, Russell maintained that no rebel correspondence had been found in the consul's dispatch bag and that there was consequently no reason to remove him from his post. "In pursuance of an agreement between the British and French governments," the British foreign minister added, "Mr. Bunch was instructed to communicate to the persons exercising authority in the so-called Confederate States" the desire that they would observe the last three articles of the Declaration of Paris. Bunch, therefore, had "acted in obedience to the instructions of his government, who accept the responsibility of his proceedings so far as they are known to the foreign department, and who cannot remove him from his office for having obeyed his instructions."[16]

He could not, Russell declared, accept any responsibility for a statement by "some person not named, that the first step to the recognition of the Southern States by Great Britain has been taken." Although the British government intended to continue treating the Southerners as belligerents, Russell wrote, "Her Majesty's government . . . are not prepared to recognize the so-called Confederate States as a separate and independent State."[17]

In transmitting these statements to Seward, the American minister at London observed that Bunch's "granting a safe-conduct to an emissary of secession, charged with treasonable papers, is no objection to his neutral character in the eyes of his employers." Beyond this, the implication that the British had not been dealing with the United States in good faith, evident in the revelation that Her Majesty's government had secretly entered into negotiations with the Southern insurgents, could not be ignored. Seward might proceed to revoke Bunch's exequatur with no great difficulty, despite Russell's refusal to sanction the removal, but one of Adams's sons put his finger on the real issue when he wrote: "They feel that they have been *found out*, and this for an Englishman is anything but pleasant." The incident could hardly fail to increase tension, as British brazenness in maintaining righteous innocence clashed with enhanced American suspicion that additional English trickery might yet remain unrevealed. "The affair will hardly end here," Henry Adams predicted.[18]

The Bunch Affair Reaches Crisis Proportions

*Mr. Adams's logic is as keen as Lord Russell's sarcasm.
The astute Englishman, with all his specious reasoning
and condescending irony, was never able to divert Mr.
Adams's attention from the fact that a consular agent
had engaged in diplomatic negotiations.*

MILLEDGE L. BONHAM,
British Consuls in the Confederacy, 43.

LORD PALMERSTON'S DETERMINATION to demonstrate with shipments of troops and munitions that England possessed both the will
and the means to withstand any attack against Canada met strong
opposition in the British cabinet. Argyll, for example, did not think
there could be any great danger to Canada as a result of the Bunch
affair. He could "hardly believe that the Yankees will be mad
enough to embroil themselves with us at such a moment," even
though they might be greatly influenced by "the audacity & passion
of such a man as Seward—the very impersonation of all that is most
violent & arrogant in the American character." Gladstone and
Lewis, too, both agreed that there was no immediate need to send
more troops to Canada, merely, as the chancellor of the exchequer
put it, to draw a line in the dust for the benefit of the "bully" in the
state department. For, he added, "there remains the question who
is the bully, and possibly whether we have not, with the world in
general, a good deal of that character." Meanwhile, both Newcastle
and Somerset raised the specter of a heavy incidence of desertion in
any forces that might go to Canada as a result of the Bunch incident.
Finally, Russell and Palmerston, the latter admitting that the desertion argument had "shaken my previous opinion," decided once
more to postpone action. Saying that to send "one large frigate . . .
might perhaps be enough" for the present, the Premier added: "The
next fortnight or 3 weeks will probably throw light on the subject."
And Russell, expressing a hope that "Seward at least will probably

be satisfied" with the British disclaimer that Bunch's approach to the Confederate authorities was 'a first step to recognition,' added: "As to [naval] reinforcements to the American station, we should know in three weeks what the American government will do. If they do not quarrel about Bunch we may rest on our oars for the winter; if they do . . . the cabinet must meet. But I do not expect it."[1]

Closely following the advice of the premier, Russell wrote Lyons that if Seward employed the complaint against Bunch as a pretext for breaking off relations with Great Britain, the envoy at Washington should content himself with expressing "in the most dignified and guarded terms that the course taken by the Washington Government must be the result of a misconception on their part, and that you shall retire to Canada, in the persuasion that the misunderstanding will soon cease, and the former friendly relations be restored."[2]

After three weeks had indeed passed without any further news from Lyons about the Bunch case, Her Majesty's ministers began to relax a little and to wonder whether Seward really contemplated making it a serious grievance. Momentarily, Russell found his Washington envoy's dispatches less gloomy than usual. But, unfortunately (and, it appears, almost inevitably), Seward and Lyons were both forced by circumstances which neither could control to continue their confrontation over the activities of Consul Bunch. As they gingerly traded arguments over the issues brought into the open by the Bunch controversy, they both strained to prevent any major irritation from developing out of their discussions. One thing was clear: if the British consular corps was to remain active in the South, as the Northern blockade tightened all along the Confederate coast, and as Northern armies gradually choked off the infiltration through the border states of insurgent spies and messengers, some new method of communication between the British consuls in the cotton states and their superiors in Washington and London had to be arranged. And any direct contact between London and the British consuls in the Confederacy, unchanneled through Washington, presented the dangerous possibility of growing into direct contact between representatives of the British government and the officials of the Jefferson Davis administration. This Seward could not permit.

On the suggestion of Bunch at Charleston, Lyons took the first step toward change by directing that two British warships serve, temporarily, as packets to carry dispatches from New York to Charleston and back again. He proposed, however, to avail himself "very sparingly" of this means of communication, and to make use of a similar program set up by the French government for the purpose of keeping open communications with its consuls in the South.[3]

He was careful to consult Seward on every detail of this project. During October he kept diplomatic notes on the subject of contact with the Southern consuls flowing constantly into the State Department. Complaining to Russell about "the extreme punctiliousness of the U. S. government on the subject of any communications between Her M's. Diplomatic or Consular servants in this Country and the de facto authorities in the Southern States," he condemned such an "unreasonable pretension," which he said was "so injurious to British interests that Her Majesty's government will no doubt deem it necessary to deliberate very seriously as to the proper mode of dealing with it." But in his own relations with Seward, he added, he was "anxious to avoid as far as possible giving any pretext to this government to take violent or offensive measures" against England; therefore, he intended to abstain from agitating the difficult and dangerous question of reopening communications with the South until he should receive instructions from London to do so.[4]

Russell wrote Lyons that the cabinet was not prepared to insist that British consuls in the Confederacy were entitled to have their correspondence transmitted North by ordinary public conveyances; hence he agreed with Lyons that the latter should arrange for an expansion of the system of communicating with those officials by means of English ships of war. One disadvantage of this system was that it tended to encourage the periodic consular outcry for frequent visits from British ships of war as a means of awing Americans into respecting the rights of British subjects. As Lyons put it, "This is the solution for every difficulty in the Consular mind, as my experience in the Mediterranean taught me long ago; though what the ships were to do, except fire a salute in honour of the Consul, I could never discover." Both he and Admiral Alexander Milne strongly objected to showing the British flag in Southern ports, "unless with a specific object and definite instructions," and they both warned against the danger of exposing "a detached ship to capture by sending her to look after our countrymen," which might in turn precipitate an extremely serious international crisis. Moreover, the temptation to desert, Lyons admitted, was very strong among British seamen allowed to go ashore in North American ports, and was "very generally yielded to." Finally, the wartime practice "of putting out lights and removing beacons and buoys" made it "easier to get a ship into one of these harbours or rivers than to get her out again." Except in cases of unusual danger, Lyons insisted, he could not permit British ships to linger long in American coastal waters. The use of warships as diplomatic couriers represented an exception to that rule, but the fewer the instances in which the British flag flew in Confederate ports, in Lyons's opinion, the better.[5]

Seward could hardly object to the maintenance of communications between British officials in London and Washington, on the one hand, and British consuls in the Confederacy, on the other hand. But he repeatedly warned Lyons against extending these communications officially to include the Southern authorities. On October 12, for example, the secretary of state told the British minister confidentially "that his desire was to find some mode of escaping the necessity of treating the communication of Her Majesty's government with the government of the Confederate States concerning Maritime Rights as an unfriendly act." Although he was persuaded that the leading men in the Palmerston ministry were not really unfriendly to the United States, the "unfortunate affair of Mr. Bunch" had, nevertheless, revealed that not only had the British government made an official communication to the Southern rebel regime, but it had also in the process formally announced to the United States government its recognition of

Confederate belligerent rights. The secretary of state seemed to Lyons "to be taxing his ingenuity to find the means of avoiding on the one hand a quarrel with us," and on the other hand of averting the unpopularity among his countrymen that would follow the discovery of his "having pusillanimously retreated from the high position he originally took up." He would assume, Seward said, that the decision in London to approach the rebel authorities had been made in early May, "before his more recent declarations of the policy of the United States"; moreover, he would not act further on the Bunch question until he had received through Adams further explanations from the British ministry. For he was "above all things anxious to gain time"—especially for the North to take possession of a deep-South port and open it for the renewed exportation of cotton, which, he hoped, "would very materially change the views of the European Powers."[6]

In response to these comments by Seward, the British minister expressed a desire to "go far to relieve Mr. Seward from embarrassment in treating the [Bunch] question," but he "took care to make it plain" that the United States government "had no ground of complaint against Mr. Bunch personally." Both England and France had distinctly and "openly declared their recognition of the South as a belligerent." In the future "it would be impossible to carry on the diplomatic business between those powers and the United States on the false hypothesis that the United States government had not cognizance of this." Seward apparently made no direct reply to this declaration; instead "he begged," according to Lyons, that if the British minister should receive from London any further communications to deliver to the United States government on the subject of Southern belligerent rights, he "would speak to him privately and confidentially before making any official communication." Lyons reported that he "of course readily entered into all his proposals that we should keep up a confidential intercourse with a view to make our official communications as conducive as possible to the maintenance of good will between the two countries."[7]

Hoping that Seward's new "moderate" mood signified his disposition to reconsider withdrawing Bunch's exequatur "as a sop to public opinion" in the United States, Lyons was sorely disappointed two weeks later to learn from the newspapers that the consul was to be sacked after all, in vindication of Seward's position that for a foreign official "to hold any communication at all" with the government of the Southern insurgents "was an offense against the United States." Lyons fully expected the secretary of state to follow this gesture with "other half-violent acts of the same kind." Should he then gain popularity, the British minister wrote, "he will probably play out the play, and send me my passports, on the plea of some Consul's having communicated with the Southern government under instructions from me." Lyons had "hitherto by taking the greatest pains to avoid annoying this government" contrived to keep himself from becoming personally involved in a "scrape" with Seward. But this unstable situation could not last much longer. Lyons despaired "of getting on at all" with the Lincoln administration "unless Great Britain and France come to some distinct understanding with it, on the nature and extent of the communication which they mean to hold with the de facto government of the Confederate States." The governments of England and France ought to stipulate their joint determination to communicate with the Confederate authorities in all "cases of necessity." Only by making such an announcement, Lyons declared, could the two European powers avoid keeping "perpetually in hot water" with the Lincoln administration. Otherwise he was afraid that Seward and his cabinet colleagues would be led "to insolent if not hostile treatment of us," and he himself could under such conditions "have little or no hope of keeping the peace."[8]

Early in November, in a conversation with Seward, the British minister took the first step toward reestablishing the official communication with the Confederate government that had been forestalled by Seward's revocation of Bunch's exequatur. He reported telling the secretary of state that

> I could not but think that the extreme punctiliousness which he displayed with regard to communications between the British and French governments and the *de facto* government in the South was

neither politic nor reasonable: the effect of it must be to keep open a constant source of irritation. It was impossible that such communication should not take place. . . . Was it wise to push England and France to the wall? What could be the advantage of rendering it difficult to conduct this necessary intercourse in the quiet and unobtrusive manner which had been adopted?[9]

In reply, Seward, forbearing from pointing out that what Lyons had called the "quiet and unobtrusive" methods of the British in dealing with the South had been adopted only after continuous strong remonstrances from himself, said mildly that he probably "should not take notice" of any British communication to the Southern authorities such as a request for the restoration of confiscated property; indeed, Lyons reported him as saying, "he should perhaps not have taken up the affair of Mr. Consul Bunch, if he had known at the beginning how far it would lead him; but having 'made the point,' he could not stop short of what he had done in the affair."[10]

The key to the Bunch question, however, was not to be found in whether British subjects might be forwarding improper correspondence out of the Southern States; such activities, although irksome, were not crucial, and were easily settled in conversations between Lyons and himself.[11] From the American point of view, the peculiar significance of the Bunch affair lay in the publicity it had created for the idea, true or false, that the British government had instructed its representative at Charleston to conduct a *diplomatic* negotiation with the rebel authorities at Richmond, which did imply, no matter how much Lyons and Russell might deny it, a preliminary step toward full-fledged British diplomatic recognition of the national independence of the Confederate States of America. Bunch, who had violated the "national rights" of the United States by reporting "that the proceeding in which he was engaged was in the nature of a treaty with the insurgents, and the first step towards a recognition by Great Britain of their sovereignty," would have to go. Seward had no alternative other than to revoke his exequatur.[12]

When he received Lyons's report that Bunch's exequatur had been revoked, Russell wrote Palmerston that Bunch's dismissal was what might have been expected from that "singular mixture of the bully and coward" who held the office of American secretary of state. Having heard that Adams had apparently not yet received Seward's instructions to announce Bunch's expulsion from office, Russell added that he supposed the announcement was delayed in order that Seward might "be able to say it before Congress without my answer. I hardly know how to deal with such a man."[13]

Russell's remarks about the Bunch affair caused the British prime minister so much concern that he was moved to speak personally to Adams about the matter. For Bunch's exequatur to have been revoked, Palmerston told the American envoy, was much to be regretted. What difference did it make to the United States government whether Bunch was in Charleston or not, as long as the city was not in the possession of the Union forces? The effect of demanding Bunch's removal was "simply irritating," which in the restless state of British public opinion in relation to the United States was "unfortunate."[14]

Adams himself worried that the demand for Bunch's removal from office seemed "sufficiently aggressive to render my duty a highly responsible one" in transmitting it to Russell. "Much as I regret the mistakes that have been committed by the Government here," he added, "so long as I consider them only such, I shall endeavor to keep the peace with them. Any other policy seems to me to be fatal."[15]

On November 21, Adams worked the entire day composing an official diplomatic note containing the official American request for Bunch's recall. He remolded the arguments of Seward's instruction, "so that while losing none of its force, it might be stripped of some of its avid character." He pointed out that Bunch had violated a law of the United States forbidding any person residing therein "from counselling or advising, aiding or assisting in any political correspondence with the government of any foreign state whatever, with an intent to influence the measures of any foreign government, or of any officer or agent thereof, in relation to any disputes or controversies with the United States, or to defeat the measures of their government." Moreover, the consul had been authorized by his exequatur to perform only consular duties; yet he had addressed a communication to domestic enemies of the United States that, even if it could have been justified otherwise, had "transcended the just limits" of his authority, which did not permit him to assume duties legitimately exercised only by a diplomatic agent. Finally, Bunch's "personal conduct," well before his attempt to conduct a diplomatic negotiation with the Richmond rebels, had "been that, not of a friend" of the United States, "nor even of a neutral, but of a partisan of faction and disunion." Adams had been instructed, therefore, to announce that the consul's exequatur would be revoked, "because his services are no longer agreeable to the government of the United States." The "privileges thus taken from him," however, would "be cheerfully allowed to any successor whom her Majesty may be pleased to appoint, against whom no grave personal objections are known to exist."[16]

Five days later, Russell furnished Adams with a spirited rejoinder. He began by labeling as "unsupported by any proof whatever" and "entirely unfounded" both the statement that Bunch had taken the first step toward British recognition of the Confederate government and the charge that the consul was a Southern partisan. He then proceeded to ridicule the proposition that any applications by the British government for redress of grievances in the Southern states "ought to be made through the President of the United States." It was an "undoubted principle of international law," Russell declared, that "in cases of apprehended losses or injury to their subjects, states may lawfully enter into communications with *de facto* governments to provide for the temporary security of the persons and property of their subjects." The commission executed by Bunch to get Southern acquiescence to certain articles of the Treaty of Paris had been carried out in strict conformity with this established principle. If it became necessary in the future, in order to protect British subjects, for the British government to contact Confederate authorities, the foreign minister wrote trenchantly, "such communications will continue to be made, but such communications will not imply any acknowledgement of the confederates as an independent state." In conclusion, Russell took some of the sting out of his note by expressing his opinion that "the conduct of Mr. Adams, while upholding the authority and interests of his own government, has been such as to acquire the esteem and respect of the government of her Majesty and of the British nation."[17]

In spite of these kind words, the fighting spirit of Adams's lineage was stirred by the body of Russell's note; and he soon fired back a devastating rejoinder. A vastly more serious dispute that was threatening to plunge his country into war with England at almost any moment had suddenly erupted, and Adams was anxious to quiet the British foreign minister on the subject of Consul Bunch, so as to reduce the springs of controversy to a minimum level. Russell's position, he wrote, appeared to be that the authorities of the United States, by whose recognition Bunch held his position as consul, were "expected to acknowledge his right whilst acting in this capacity, at the same time to treat with any of their citizens who defy their authority." Adams recognized Russell's concern for the protection of British interests in the regions of rebellion, he said, but he also felt it necessary to remark that whatever the course which the British government considered proper for regulating its relations with the Southern insurgents, he hoped it would not include requiring of the United States government "that it should recognize the agents through whom they may be carried on." The main reason for Bunch's deposition was that while enjoying as a British consul "the advantages of a solemn recognition of the United States," he had engaged himself in official proceedings both in violation of the law and far outside his consular authority, for any negotiations carried on to extend the number of adherents to the Declaration of Paris constituted exclusively "a pure diplomatic act" far outside the scope of a consul's authority.[18]

On reading Adams's note of November 29, Palmerston became furious at what he termed the "absurd as well as untenable" arguments contained therein. "Nothing is more common," he wrote, "than the employment of persons not having diplomatic credentials to conduct diplomatic negotiations. All that the government which is addressed has a right to ask is, whether the messenger is really &

fully authorized to make his communication." South American governments had often in the past attempted to evade British demands for redress from injury "by saying the demand was diplomatic & that a consul should confine himself to strictly commercial and consular functions." The answer, Palmerston declared, had usually been that the consul was charged with the care of British interests, "& that if the offending government did not chuse [*sic*] to receive representations from our consul, it would be compelled to receive them from a British admiral, whose manner of dealing with such matters might be less agreeable to the government in question."[19]

In the official British reply, however, Russell avoided bluster and confined himself to quibbling over small details of the Bunch case. He rested his main argument upon the United States Constitution and laws, "of which," Adams said, "he knows nothing." Taking up his pen for the last time to reiterate his government's determination to send Bunch packing, Adams asserted: "I doubt whether he gets much by his notion." Forcefully repeating several of his previous arguments justifying the necessity of Bunch's removal, Adams ended by informing the British foreign minister that because the consul had conducted "these extraordinary negotiations" with rebels against the authority of the United States, the Union government could not risk "an implication of a doubt of its own rightful authority" by failing to withdraw Bunch's exequatur, which in any case had already been done.[20]

Russell could do no more than to accept the *fait accompli* by stating that he did "not perceive that any advantage would be obtained by the continuance of this correspondence." Later, he even sent peremptory instructions to Charleston prohibiting his new consular representative there from forwarding letters from private individuals in all cases whatever. It was, indeed, total capitulation by the foreign secretary. Early in 1862 he wrote Lyons that "Her Majesty's government do not dispute the right of the government of the United States to withdraw the exequatur of Mr. Consul Bunch," and he agreed with his representative at Washington that although it would be desirable for Bunch to remain in Charleston, so that his experience and "local influence" could continue to be utilized for the benefit of British interests, all official consular acts should be done thenceforth over the signature of his vice consul.[21]

Having attempted covertly to establish contact with the Confederate authorities in Richmond, the British government had been discovered and belabored heavily by Seward and Adams, and had afterward been forced to retire from the field minus one valuable consul and with lost prestige. Despite the professed determination of the British to maintain their alleged right to deal directly with the Southerners, in order to protect British interests in the slave states, the Bunch affair seems to have ended any real disposition to put this theoretical claim into extensive practice. From this time on the British government transacted only the most necessary business with the Confederate government, and that was done gingerly, at arm's length.[22]

When, near the end of the year, Russell, insisting that "it is a recognized principle of International Law that a State may communicate with de facto authorities in any case where the persons or the property of its subjects is endangered by the acts of the de facto authorities," asked that France cooperate in a joint approach to the Confederate authorities on the subject of seizures of British and French property in the South, he was careful to instruct Lyons not to say anything to Seward about these or any other future contacts with the slaveholders. And Lyons was quick to agree that all communications, official and unofficial alike, between British subjects in the South and England should be "sent to their destination without passing through this legation." For he feared that it would "be impossible for me to avoid constant altercation with the United States government, and indeed very serious embarrassment, if I am placed in a situation in which that government can hold me individually responsible for communications with the de facto government or local authorities in the South."[23]

To keep the British government from opening up regular official communications with the Southerners, the Americans paid a high price. Seward's reputation in England for boorish bellicosity was reinforced by his uncompromising stand on the withdrawal of

Bunch's exequatur and by his evident determination to run the most serious risks to prevent all official British diplomatic contact with the Southern insurrectionists. The leading members of the British cabinet were becoming impatient with the secretary of state's "insolence." They were growing tired of the inconveniences suffered by Englishmen as a consequence of the American Civil War. And they were seriously considering, by October of 1861, whether they ought to take some step designed to reduce or to eliminate these annoyances and, at the same time, to chastise Seward. Yet—in the face of the American secretary of state's apparent irascibility during past encounters—they hesitated, nervous and irritable because of their inability to shake Seward's will to resist foreign meddling in the struggle for the survival of the American Union. Perhaps unconsciously, they awaited a favorable moment for a test of strength.

Seward Jails British Subjects

These North Americans . . . are following fast the example of the Spanish Americans and of the Continental despots. They commit all sorts of violence without regard to law, take up men & women and imprison them on mere suspicion, and rule the land by spies and police and martial law.

PALMERSTON TO RUSSELL,
September 26, 1861.[1]

BRITISH PIQUE with the American secretary of state was intensified late in the summer of 1861 by still another controversy, one which threatened to injure Anglo-American relations as much as the Bunch case. It grew out of what Lyons called the "monstrous" practice of locking up civilians, including British subjects, in military jails without due process of law. The British minister reported that both the high officials of the United States government and "the Mob" that had installed them in office appeared to favor "placing their own lives and liberties, . . . without any reserve, into the hands of the officers of the army." The American people were "recklessly applauding the suspension, without law, of all their liberties." Any person, including British subjects, who had "an enemy to inform against him," Lyons wrote, "is in danger." For the United States government "sends any one it pleases to a Fortress —and orders the Commandant to decline to make any return to a Writ of Habeas Corpus."[2]

The imprisonment, without *habeas corpus*, of self-proclaimed British citizens like Robert Mure and Purcell Quillan caused Russell to seek an opinion from the crown law officers about the legality of such confinements. In response, Her Majesty's legal advisers held that in each case, according to the information supplied by Lyons, "there was so much illegality, coupled with so much harsh treatment, as fairly to entitle Her Majesty's government to call upon the government of the United States for a full explanation if it should be deemed expedient to do so." However, with Quillan having in the meantime been set free by Seward, and with the case of Robert Mure entangled in the serious matter of Consul Bunch's alleged misconduct, Russell decided for the moment to instruct Lyons not to agitate the imprisonment issue with Seward, unless a similar case should afterwards occur.[3]

Two additional imprisonment cases were soon brought to the attention of the British minister. William Patrick and John C. Rahming, both British subjects, had been separately seized, apparently "without any warrant of law," and confined in the federal prison at Fort Lafayette. Despite strong efforts by "influential supporters of the administration" to procure Patrick's release, Lyons saw little hope that even a personal representation on his part would accomplish that purpose. He was "alarmed and distressed by the system of arbitrary arrest" which he believed to be "entirely illegal." The leading men in Lincoln's administration, "Mr. Seward not least," seemed to Lyons "to enter with great gusto upon a system of espionage, persecution and arbitrary arrests." The secretary of state appeared to take "personal pleasure in spying and arresting" and was prone to "torment" the British minister by mentioning "reports" he had received about "improper language and what not" of British consuls and British subjects. Lyons had not yet had "serious conversation with Mr. Seward on the subject," but although he intended at the first opportunity to convince the secretary of state "of the imprudence of giving us so strong a cause for dissatisfaction," he had "little hope of doing any good."[4]

Russell's reaction came back at once. The exercise by the American secretary of state, "upon the reports of spies and informers," of the "despotic and arbitrary" power of imprisoning British subjects and retaining them or releasing them "by his sole will and pleasure," was in the British foreign minister's opinion "inconsistent with the Constitution of the United States, . . . at variance with the Treaties of Amity subsisting between the two nations, and must tend to prevent the resort of British subjects to the United States for purposes of trade and industry." Congress had sanctioned no such "departure from the due course of law." Lyons was ordered, therefore, "to remonstrate against such wanton proceedings and to say that in the opinion of Her Majesty's government, the authority of Congress is necessary in order to justify the arbitrary arrest and imprisonment of British subjects."[5]

Before Lyons received his chief's comments regarding the arrests of Patrick and Rahming, however, Seward had once again responded to a plea from the British minister by issuing orders to have them both released from prison. The secretary of state, wrote Lyons, had behaved in a "very calm and on the whole reasonable and friendly" manner about it. He had invited the British minister to have dinner at his house, "nobody else except his own Family being present," according to Lyons. On that occasion he had expressed anxiety "to avoid arresting British subjects except by regular legal process." Although he added that he could not abandon the *principle* that the United States government had the right, on a charge of treason, "to arrest foreigners as well as citizens, and confine them indefinitely without cause assigned," he did intend, *in practice*, he declared, to attend promptly to any representations which Lyons might make to him in behalf of any individual prisoner. With Seward so "well disposed," the British minister wrote, he was reluctant "to enter the lists" with him "on the question of principle"—whether the United States government had the constitutional right to imprison foreigners without *habeas corpus*—in the absence of orders from London "determining exactly how far I ought to go."[6]

During most of the month of September, Lyons worried that his superiors in London would think him "too tame about the arrests of British Subjects and such matters." He had been concerned, he explained to Russell, that the

> natural temptation to a man placed as I am is to write what the public regard as spirited Notes. My own view however at the present moment is that so far as I can get redress in individual cases, it is better for me to be as quiet as I can here—and not to embarrass you by getting into a dispute. I therefore avoid raising questions of principle, and keep clean of strong language, so as to leave all the cases for your

consideration unhampered by declarations made by me to this government.[7]

Russell, however, was not satisfied with Seward's failure to adopt the British position on the abstract question of arbitrary arrest. Ignoring his minister's conclusion "that it is vain to resort to the courts of law for redress," because all "the officers of the army decline to make any return to Writs of Habeas Corpus," he nevertheless wrote Lyons

> that advantage might arise from testing the legality of such proceedings by instituting in one of the Federal Courts an action for false imprisonment against those who may have been instrumental in making the arrests.
>
> If Your Lordship were to intimate to Mr. Seward that such a course would be pursued in the event of British subjects being arbitrarily arrested, the Federal government might not like to have the question brought under public discussion by a trial at law.
>
> . . . unless you foresee some great inconvenience in the course proposed, Your Lordship will make the intimation to Mr. Seward, and if subsequently a case of palpably illegal arrest of a British subject should occur, Your Lordship will take proper steps for bringing the matter before a Court of Law.[8]

The unrealistic nature of the foreign minister's suggestion was tactfully indicated in Lyons's response to it, in which he pointed out that any lawsuit against the power of arrest claimed by the executive branch of the United States government would probably fail to result in a favorable decision. Acting upon orders from Russell, Lyons had already written Seward that although his government was willing "to make every allowance for the hard necessities of a time of internal trouble," the American secretary of state had gone too far in exercising, "upon the reports of spies and informers, the power of depriving British subjects of their liberty, of retaining them in prison, or liberating them, by his own will and pleasure." The British crown law officers, Lyons declared, had ruled that in the absence of explicit congressional sanction, "The arbitrary arrests of British subjects are illegal." The British minister, therefore, had been instructed to remonstrate against this illegal use of "despotic" power and to demand that it cease.[9]

Instead of yielding to this strongly worded protest, Seward had promptly issued a challenge to further discussion by publishing it in the newspapers, along with his official reply. In the latter document he had suggested that while he did "not question the learning of the legal advisers of the British Crown or the justice of the deference which her Majesty's government pays to them," he also hoped that Russell and Lyons would not expect President Lincoln to be guided by "explanations of the Constitution of the United States" provided by British lawyers whose advice conflicted with the opinions of "the highest authorities of our own country."[10]

Greatly irritated that Seward had enlisted "popular passions" in support of his policies by causing a disagreement with a foreign power to be revealed and discussed in American newspapers, Lyons nevertheless acknowledged that the Federal courts would probably sustain the secretary of state against any legal challenge. And Seward "would probably consider it fortunate" to have the imprisonment question brought to court by a British subject, rather than by a prominent American citizen. Indeed, Lyons said, he would not be surprised if the secretary of state made some conspicuous arrests of more British subjects in order to precipitate this event. Therefore, it seemed best to defer initiating any suit for false imprisonment, either until positive orders came from London to do so, or until "an especially flagrant case" which might offer a reasonable chance of success appeared.[11]

When Lyons's report of these proceedings reached London, accompanied by American newspapers in which his exchange of notes with Seward had been published, Russell appeared unable to do more than remark: "I have only to observe in reply that Her Majesty's government did not before understand that the President was invested by the Constitution with powers so despotic and so arbitrary." Russell was disconcerted to discover that, in discussing the published diplomatic notes, London newspapers tended to support Seward, not Lyons. The *Times*, for example, ridiculed the

British envoy for the lack of "dignity and propriety" in his "slovenly" note to Seward, while the Tory mouthpiece, the *Herald*, lectured Russell for having ordered his Washington representative to deliver a communication "offensive in its purport, discourteous in its language, and very probably wrong in its law" to the United States government—thus having brought upon Great Britain "national rebuff without the right to resent it."[12]

Nevertheless, once the newspaper notoriety had blown over, Russell renewed the assault against Seward's imprisonment policy. Sending Lyons a recapitulation of what the British government understood to be the facts in the Patrick case, he declared: "Among the necessities of civil war this wanton and capricious arrest of Mr. Patrick cannot be reckoned, and the remonstrance of Her Majesty's government must remain on record." He added: "You may give a copy of this despatch to Mr. Seward."[13]

Noticing, however, that the foreign minister had said "You may" instead of "You will" in connection with the delivery of his remarks to Seward, the once-burned Lyons replied that under the circumstances he thought that it would not be "prudent" to avail himself of "this permission," and that he would await further orders from London before acting.[14]

Russell was quick to send these orders. Although armed conflict with the United States seemed almost inevitable to most Englishmen at the time, because of the *Trent* crisis, the British foreign minister lost not a day in commanding Lyons to deliver his remonstrance to Seward with no further vacillation. Fortunately, the secretary of state was content to let Russell's protest lie unanswered "on the record," in the belief that history recorded "no instance in which any government or people has practiced moderation in civil war equal to that which, thus far, has distinguished this government and the American people."[15]

While Lyons was still delaying as long as possible before sending Russell's remonstrance to Seward, more British subjects were arrested and their cases were handled much as before. At least five cases of arrests, some involving apparent mistreatment of British subjects, were brought to Lyons's attention during September by

Her Majesty's consul at Baltimore. Within a few weeks, however, Seward had been persuaded to let these men go, and by the end of October the British minister was able proudly to report: "I have hitherto succeeded in procuring the release of every British subject arrested in this way, whose case has been brought to my knowledge." When such released captives sought indemnities for their losses as a consequence of having been imprisoned, however, Lyons refused to diminish his usefulness in regard to such important matters as personal freedom by raising additional questions pertaining to a "few dollars." Instead he referred these cases to London for advice. Russell's reaction was one of grumpy resignation. "The President of the United States," he wrote,

> maintains that he has the right to arrest without cause or reason assigned any British subjects residing in the United States; and it would serve no purpose to ask the President to give indemnity in a case in which he maintains that he has acted lawfully. . . .
>
> Her Majesty's government are unwilling to enter into an irritating and useless controversy with the United States, and can only hope that the present exceptional state of things will not be of long continuance.[16]

Before settling into this position of reluctant acquiescence, however, Russell first had a final fling at righteous indignation. When he learned from Lyons during October that nine British subjects captured aboard vessels attempting to run the blockade had been confined in irons in Fort Lafayette, he decided that Seward's release of these men, immediately upon application from the British legation, was insufficient to obscure "the barbarous treatment" to which they had been "thus wantonly exposed." He therefore instructed Lyons "to bring the matter again to the notice of the United States government, and you will express the hope of Her Majesty's government that due compensation will be awarded to the sufferers." Her Majesty's envoy obeyed orders; his note[17] bringing the matter to Seward's attention, however, elicited a defense of the treatment of the nine men, as well as a refusal to grant any compensation. The fact that the secretary of state referred to the nine men as "prisoners of war" intrigued the British minister; to him this was further evidence of how hypocritical was the United States government's position that the conflict with the South was nothing more than a local insurrection. Indeed, the phrase "civil war" frequently appeared in Seward's communications to the British government.[18] But while quibbles about terminology might palliate British egos, they did not alter the fact that Seward forced the British foreign minister, ultimately, to abandon his demands for compensation. "Although these men appear to have been treated with most unjustifiable severity during their confinement," Russell eventually wrote his envoy at Washington, "yet . . . I do not think it necessary to instruct your Lordship to take any further steps in the matter." The British seamen, Russell admitted, had served voluntarily under Confederate colors, and the United States had every legal right to treat them as prisoners. Her Majesty's advocate general had ruled that since Seward had promptly set them free upon receiving Lyons's application for their release, "no demand for compensation can properly be made by Her Majesty's government in their behalf." Perhaps it was unfortunate that Russell had not waited for this opinion before rushing off his initial demand.[19]

During November the British legation in Washington was deluged with arrest cases. Lights burned far into the night as clerks labored to keep up with the correspondence that ensued. Lyons's requests for leniency toward imprisoned British subjects were almost invariably honored, and ultimately the persons involved, including some very shady characters, were released from custody.[20]

Despite Seward's cooperative attitude in regard to most of these cases, however, some of them dragged on for months while evidence was being gathered, as Federal agents sought to accumulate incriminating data, and as the British consuls and representatives of the imprisoned parties rounded up what proof they could of innocence or extenuating circumstances. In the meantime unpleasant publicity often found its way to England, where it was widely believed that the United States government was engaged in a calculated, methodical policy of wholesale arrests and cruel treatment of British subjects within its jurisdiction. For their part,

American officials who were intimately informed about these cases tended to be persuaded by what they revealed about the activities of a significant number of British subjects, that support for the Southern rebel cause was strong among Englishmen residing in both the Northern and the Southern states, and that this could well be considered an indication of underlying unfriendliness toward the United States in Great Britain.

XI

England Edges Toward Intervention

*The great point now is the blockade. . . . I cannot
conceal from myself the fact that as a whole the English
are pleased with our misfortunes. There never was any
real good-will towards us—and the appearance of it of
late years was only an effect of their fears of our
prosperity and our growing strength.*

C. F. Adams to J. M. Forbes,
August 30, 1861.[1]

AS SOON AS IT BECAME APPARENT in England that the American
Civil War would probably produce a serious scarcity of cotton
there, the British prime minister considered what steps might be
taken to alleviate the prospective cotton shortage. Was there not
cotton grown in India, Australia, the "Feejee" Islands, Syria,
Egypt, and on both the eastern and western coasts of Africa, "not to
mention China, and probably Japan?" Should not the board of
trade take "active measures . . . to draw from these places" enough
cotton to make up some of the anticipated losses in the American
crop, and "to make a better supply spring up for future years" in
areas outside the American slave states?[2]

It was important, Palmerston asserted, for the British cabinet to
take the lead in meeting the emergency. For the English manufacturers would

> do nothing unless directed and pushed on. They are some of the most
> helpless and shortsighted of men. They are like the people who held
> out their dishes & prayed that it might rain plum-puddings.
>
> They think it enough to open their millgates and that cotton will
> come of its own accord; they say that they have for years been *looking*
> to India as a source of supply; but their *looks* seem to have had only the
> first effect of the eyes of the rattlesnake, viz., to paralyse the object
> looked at, and as yet it has shown no signs of falling into their jaws.

The question of future cotton supply, the premier wrote the president of the board of trade, "deserves early attention."[3]

In replying to Palmerston's query, however, Thomas Milner Gibson asserted that the British government could not legally "take any direct part in procuring an additional supply of cotton beyond that which the manufacturers and merchants can get for themselves." If England was "to be prevented altogether from getting cotton this autumn from the Southern States of course it must produce a most serious pressure which no measures of Government could prevent."[4]

As Northern warships swarmed in ever-increasing numbers along the coastline of the Southern Confederacy during the summer months of 1861, Englishmen began to realize that little of the autumn cotton crop would be likely to filter through the blockade, even if the Confederate authorities should abandon their announced policy of embargoing that commodity as a means of pressuring European governments to intervene in the war in behalf of the slave states. In July, Richard Cobden, M. P., who had reached political eminence as a spokesman for the interests of Lancashire textile workers, warned: "If the American Civil War goes on, and all the ports of the South remain blockaded after the new cotton crop is ready, . . . then all parties will be very sick of blockades." And on the following day his friend and fellow Radical M. P., John Bright, himself a leading textile manufacturer, observed that English "mills are just now reducing their working time, [some] to four days, and some of them to three days in the week. . . . Working half time we can go on till April or May perhaps, but this will cause suffering and discontent, and it is possible pressure may be put upon the Government to take some step supposed likely to bring about a change."[5]

The American minister in London had similar thoughts. He had foreseen as early as July 5 that "the substance of what sympathy there is here with the rebellion" was bound up in the widely held belief that the stock of cotton on hand in British warehouses would not last beyond the end of the year. The cotton manufacturers had already begun to contemplate putting their workers on short time. But even with curtailed production, Adams gathered from the newspapers and economic journals, most authorities calculated that the stocks of cotton on hand could not last beyond March, 1862. "One of two things must follow," the American minister foresaw. "Either there will be great misery and destitution in the manufacturing cities, leading perhaps to serious political consequences, or there will be a direct interference on the part of the two great powers" of England and France with the Union blockade of the Southern cotton ports.[6]

Confederate policy-makers were as conscious as Adams of the strong desire among the Lancashire magnates and their Liverpool shipping associates for cotton. In his initial instructions to three commissioners sent by the Southern government to Europe, Confederate Secretary of State Robert Toombs asserted that

> the gross amount of the annual yield of the manufactures of Great Britain from the cotton of the Confederate States reaches $600,000,000. The British ministry will comprehend fully the condition to which the British realm would be reduced if the supply of our staple should suddenly fail or even be considerably diminished . . . an occurrence, I will add, that is inevitable if this country should be involved in protracted hostilities with the North.

After the Battle of Bull Run, the Southern commissioners called Russell's attention to the fact that the 1861 cotton crop would soon be picked. To be obtained by British buyers, it had to be sought in Southern ports on whose wharves it would be delivered "by our planters and merchants, as usual, . . . when there shall be a prospect of the blockade being raised and not before." The blockade was not effective, the commissioners declared, for it had been repeatedly broken by vessels slipping in and out of ports all the way from Wilmington to New Orleans. It was for the European nations whose trade had already been harmed by this illegal "paper blockade" to determine how long such a situation should endure.[7]

The threats of the Confederate agents did not, however, elicit a favorable response from Russell. Ever since Seward had belabored him so roughly in June because of his unofficial reception of the

Southern envoys, the British foreign minister had given them no further encouragement. Now he merely reiterated the British intention to preserve "a strict neutrality between the contending parties in America," and he stated that his government did not intend to acknowledge Confederate independence until the contest should take a decisive turn toward some definite issue.[8]

By early October, however, the Southern commissioners were "reliably informed" that, notwithstanding Russell's previously firm tone, the British cabinet was "anxiously considering the question of recognition." In view of the growing destitution and resultant discontent in the cotton-manufacturing districts of England and France, the Southern envoys reported, "we have brighter and better assured hopes of achieving [diplomatic recognition] than we have had at any time before since our arrival in Europe." If foreign ships should continue to reach Confederate ports with relative ease, they reasoned, and the fact thereof widely publicized, perhaps under growing pressure from Lancashire the British government would intervene to raise, forcibly if need be, the manifestly inefficient (and hence illegal) blockade. Recognition could be expected to follow as a matter of course.[9]

The Southern commissioners were right in thinking that members of the British cabinet had become deeply disturbed about the prospective shortage of cotton. If the American Civil War should continue until Parliament met early in 1862, Russell wrote Palmerston, the dearth of cotton would "be an ugly question." Still he wondered why the Southerners did "not see that our recognition *because* they keep cotton from us would be ignominious beyond measure & that no English Parliament could do so base a thing."[10]

Palmerston agreed that "This cotton question will most certainly assume a serious character by the beginning of next year." If the American conflict had not subsided by that time, he wrote, "I suspect that we shall be obliged either singly or conjointly with France to tell the Northerners that we cannot allow some millions of our people to perish to please the Northern States, and that the blockade of the South must be so far relaxed as to allow cotton loaded ships to come out." In the meantime, he added, it was "of the utmost importance" to establish a regular supply of cotton from Africa or India, "because as long as we are dependent on America alone for supply we are not politically in a condition to deal with the United States with free and independent action."[11]

Russell and Palmerston were disconcerted by information given the Foreign Office by William S. Lindsay, M.P., one of the largest shipowners in England with many commercial ties to the American South. His letters from the Confederacy showed that the announced determination of the slaveholders to resist the Northern effort to reunite the country, even to the point of keeping cotton in storage on the plantations, was no mere bluff. Moreover, as Russell pointed out gloomily, not only did the American Southerners "wish to force us into recognition"; the French, too, were increasingly more insistent in the same direction. Palmerston, however, believed that it was possible that the Northern navy might not be able to maintain the blockade during the winter months to come, "and that thus the cotton ships will be free to come out. If this should be so it is scarcely likely that the Southerners would refuse to realize the value of their cotton by selling it at good prices to England & France. They cannot be so flush of money as to forego such means for defraying the expenses of their wars." Russell, too, could "not see how 3,000 miles of coast and 1,500 miles of land frontier are to be guarded against that excellent disciple of Adam Smith, the smuggler." Even Cobden, though bitterly disagreeing with Palmerston and Russell on a host of political questions, agreed nevertheless that American "cotton will find its way somehow to the capital & labour awaiting it. How it is to reach us, I am unable to say. But to keep it locked up is too great an outrage on the laws of commerce, which are the laws of nature, to be successful."[12]

Charles Francis Adams continued to be well aware that the blockade was an economic headache for England and France, one with special political implications. "No doubt exists in my mind," he wrote a friend in Boston, "that the two powers would like to have some excuse for violating it. But Great Britain has so tied itself by the law heretofore enunciated by its Judges in times when blockades suited the national policy that it is not easy to break out of the bonds now that it would be convenient."[13] The effects of the blockade, however, "most sensibly felt already" in Great Britain, would intensify "the temptation to raise questions upon it" during the last four months of the year.[14]

Adams feared that when the leading figures in the Palmerston government finished "ruralizing" early in October and re-assembled in London for the first cabinet meeting since their summer vacations began, they might seriously discuss intervention in America. For the "prevailing rumors and the tone of all the leading newspapers" appeared to him "to point in a direction which will put an end to my stay here at once." The situation appeared "extremely critical."[15]

There was a distinct "impression in commercial circles," Adams warned Seward, "that a recognition is in agitation. Large quantities of stocks of the Northern States have been sold out in consequence." Moreover, the aristocratic press was "unfavorable, if not hostile," to the United States; and the commercial classes were "strongly in favor of bringing the war to a termination as speedily as possible. This feeling," Adams reported, "has its representatives in the Cabinet as elsewhere." He had little faith in "the good will of the leading men" of Great Britain, especially in that of Palmerston, one of whose private secretaries was a "friend of the insurgents," and kept the premier in close touch with their activities. He had been reliably informed, Adams wrote, that the Southerners were "buoyed up by a reliance upon positive interference by the New Year. Would this have been so had the authorities here been perfectly explicit?"[16]

"There is no doubt in my mind," Adams added "that the general conviction here is that the [American] disruption is final; and that among the higher classes at least, the wish is father to the thought." Such sentiments, the American minister declared, were well represented in an article published in the July issue of the *Quarterly Review* by Lord Robert Cecil, who initiated a series of pro-Southern articles in that extremely conservative journal by pronouncing the United States permanently fragmented.[17]

Cecil's parliamentary colleague, Sir Edward Bulwer-Lytton, a popular novelist and playwright who had served as colonial secretary under Derby several years before, had made an even stronger statement favoring separation between North and South, which he said would "be attended with happy results to the safety of Europe." For the United States, undivided, "would have hung over Europe like a gathering and destructive thundercloud. No single kingdom in Europe could have been strong enough to maintain itself against a nation that might consolidate the gigantic resources of a quarter of the globe. . . . But in proportion as America shall become subdivided into different States, . . . her ambition," he wrote, would "be less formidable to the rest of the world."[18]

Meanwhile, such journalistic echoes of English aristocratic thought as the editors of the London *Times* repeatedly assured their readers that it was best for the United States to be split into not less than two rival confederacies, so that, as the "Thunderer" proclaimed, "the strength of the American people will be self-consumed. . . . Instead of a great, united, irresistible nation, they will be two jealous States watching each other." Thus would the unnatural experiment of democratic government die a long-overdue death. *Punch*, appealing to the lighter side of British upper-class natures (perhaps best embodied in the queen's pixilated prime minister), proclaimed that "Never murder, was absurder," and it advised the combatants in America that since

> You will never
> More for ever,
> North and South, together pull;
> Each from other
> Rent, as BROTHER
> JONATHAN from old JOHN BULL . . . ,

the two sections should stop fighting and agree peaceably to go their own ways.

> YANKEE DOODLES,
> Oh, you noodles!
> Why prolong this idle strife,
> Costing treasure
> Beyond measure,
> Waste of money and of life?[19]

Behind the public manifestation of belief that the American Union was permanently divided lurked the body of private English opinion, virtually unanimous in sustaining the same idea. From British travelers in the Confederate States,[20] from Lyons in Washington, and from the British consuls in the South, the Foreign Office had received for months past the undivided and undiluted opinion that no reconstruction of the Union was possible, whether or not the North was militarily successful. As a result of their victory at Bull Run, Russell declared, the Confederates could "remain on the defensive for two years to come," if not longer, and the Northern people would not have the resources or the patience to fight that long. Even if they should do so, and ultimately bring the South back into the Union politically, the foreign minister believed, it would only "be with ample guarantees for the maintenance & limited extension of Slavery. Thus strengthened, the cause of Slavery would prevail all over the New World. For this reason I wish for separation." He added, however, that the conduct of the British government must continue to "be strictly neutral." In all of this he was seconded by Palmerston, who wrote: "It is in the highest degree likely that the North will not be able to subdue the South, . . . but the operations of the war have as yet been too indecisive to warrant an acknowledgement of the Southern Union."[21]

Even Englishmen whose friendly feelings toward the United States could not be questioned were convinced that the fight to restore the Union was hopeless. One of these, William Howard Russell, had an excellent reputation as a judicious and impartial foreign correspondent. He had traveled extensively on a "fact-finding" mission through the Confederate States in the spring of 1861; he had spoken with knowledgeable men on both sides from Lincoln and Seward, Davis and Benjamin, on down through the two governmental hierarchies; and he remained "faithful to my original belief that it's all up with U.S. . . . Even conquest, subjection & submission won't make it so, as it was."[22]

John Bright, one of the most vehemently pro-Northern Englishmen of all, had written Charles Sumner early in September: "I confess I am unable to see any prospect of reunion through a conquest of the South." Despite a message from Seward, to whom Sumner had shown Bright's letter, declaring that the rebellion was arrested and that it would soon perish when "its authorities here, no longer sustained by false hopes from abroad, will fall before the returning allegiance of their misguided people," Bright remained convinced late in November that the subjection of the South was "barely, if at all, possible, and that a restoration of the Union is not to be looked for."[23]

The American minister in London had been given ample opportunity by the autumn of 1861 to hear Bright's opinions, as well as those of many other frankly spoken Englishmen from their own lips. Once the North had been defeated on the battlefield at Bull Run, therefore, he could only report to Seward the said truth: that everywhere in England the "division of the Union is now regarded as a *fait accompli*."[24]

Having also heard from "almost everybody" that a permanent disintegration of the United States was "inevitable," John L. Motley, passing through England on his way to his ministerial post at Vienna, urged prominent English acquaintances "to resist the program that will be brought upon government to break our blockade." The outcome of such a measure, he asserted, "would be one of the longest & bloodiest tragedies that history has ever recorded." Avidly, he explicated this warning in conversations with members of the British cabinet, including Palmerston and Russell.[25]

Such arguments only momentarily dissuaded the mercurial Russell from toying with the idea of blockade-breaking, or at least threatening to do so. By October the foreign minister appeared to be losing patience. Reinforced by news of growing French restiveness on the cotton supply question, he sought to obtain the prime minister's approval of a typical Old World power play for cotton.[26]

What probably most stimulated Russell's activity in favor of intervention during October was a communication from Lyons. This letter reported that the French minister in Washington had strongly recommended to his government that England and France together seize a "favourable moment" to recognize Confederate independence and declare the blockade no longer binding on their ships seeking cotton. The time to act, Mercier declared, would be at the first hint that the North was becoming disheartened over its prospects of military success; such a bold move on the part of the two powers, acting in close harmony, he asserted, would deter the United States government from declaring war.[27]

Although Lyons deprecated Mercier's scheme, writing the Foreign Office that the moment "when the intervention of England and France in the quarrel would be . . . tolerated by the American peoples" was "far distant," Russell, for his part, thought that there was "much good sense in Mercier's observations." He had already hinted in a public speech that European interference in the American Civil War would soon become desirable. At a political banquet in Newcastle he had declared that the American combatants were

> contending together, not upon the question of slavery, . . . not contending with respect to Free trade and Protection, but contending as so many States of the Old World have contended, the one side for empire and the other for power. . . . I cannot help asking myself, as affairs progress in the conflict, to what good can it lead?

For if the Southern states re-entered the Union with the same status as they had at the outbreak of war, the festering question of slavery would soon render a resumption of the quarrel inevitable. And if the North conquered the South, the task would entail the destruction of the economies of both sides (including the South's cotton economy, the good health of which was so essential to Great Britain). Meanwhile the vaunted liberty of the Americans would also be crushed under the heavy weights of militarism and corruption, while the task of keeping the South afterwards in subjection would "very materially interfere with the freedom of nations" to carry on a peaceful international commerce. There was really only one way, Russell implied, to avert such unhappy results: independence must be granted to the Southern States—and the sooner the better. Although the British government did not propose immediately to exert its power or influence on the belligerents, the foreign minister concluded, no man could deny that the war in America had raised questions "deeply affecting us all."[28]

Three days later, while Russell's Newcastle address was still the talk of cockney pubs and fashionable London drawing rooms alike, the foreign minister wrote Palmerston that France and England ought to act together "on a grand scale" to propose mediation to the American belligerents, saying: " 'Make up your quarrels; we propose to give terms of pacification which we think fair and equitable. If you accept them, well and good. But if your adversary accepts them, . . . our mediation is at an end, & you must expect to see us your enemies.' " Russell thought France "would be quite ready" to join in issuing such an ultimatum. After all, Napoleon had offered mediation once already, in May, only to have his offer refused by Seward. "If such a policy were to be adopted," Russell wrote the premier, "the time for it would be the end of the year."[29]

Palmerston was not impressed by his colleague's proposal. Tactfully he poured cold water on the notion that some form of *activity* was called for. "As to North America," he cautioned,

> our best and true policy seems to be to go on as we have begun, and to keep quite clear of the conflict between North and South. It is true, as you say, that there have been cases in Europe in which allied Powers have said to fighting parties . . . , In the Queen's name I bid you to drop your swords. But those cases are rare and peculiar. The love of quarreling and fighting is inherent in man, and to prevent its indulgence is to impose restraints on natural liberty. A State may so shackle its own Subjects; but it is an infringement on national independence to restrain other nations.

The distress in Europe over a lack of cotton would have to become "far more serious than it is likely to be," the prime minister asserted, before it could justify such intervention. "The probability is," he continued, "that some cotton will find its way to us from America, and that we shall get a greater supply than usual from other quarters." Canada would be greatly endangered by any conflict with the Yankees, especially in the winter time when it would be impossible to reinforce the inadequate British garrison there. Therefore the best policy was "to lie on our oars, & to give no pretext to the Washingtonians to quarrel with us, while on the other hand we maintain our Rights and those of our fellow Countrymen."[30]

The sedative administered by the premier caused Russell to postpone his interventionist scheme and to rely instead principally on his former hope that English "sufferings may be mitigated by the ingenuity of trade." Although he continued to "wish for separation" of the Union, he wrote Lyons, he was determined that "our conduct must be strictly neutral & it will be." How long the capricious foreign minister would adhere to this resolution, however, was a question which Americans already had good reason to ask.[31]

European Intervention Averted

We ask nothing of you save moral support. Have confidence in the reestablishment of the Union, and let this be well enough known, so that the South is convinced of it, and for our part we shall find a way to supply your industry with cotton.

SEWARD TO MERCIER,
23 October 1861.[1]

FOR SEVERAL WEEKS the American minister in London had sensed that something unpleasant was in the wind.[2] After reading the version of Russell's Newcastle speech published in the London *Times* on October 16, Adams inferred that the foreign minister believed the British should intervene to end the civil war in America. Perhaps it was only "a mere fault of expression, not altogether unusual with his Lordship, but it certainly does seem as if he not only felt that the United States were wrong, but that we ought to be somehow made sensible that we were so."[3]

Fortunately, the London *Morning Post*, which the American envoy understood often reflected "the sentiments of the Prime Minister," published a leading article on October 19, asserting that no foreign power had "the smallest right to interfere" with the Northern blockade. Recognition of Confederate independence by England and France would not have the effect of releasing cotton from Southern ports for export to Europe; rather would it "render the blockade more stringent than ever." The editors of the London *Times*, too, had stated on October 21 that to interfere with the Federal blockade in any way would be to wage war against the United States—"an unjust war. . . , which, whatever its issue, would stain the reputation of this country and expose us to the just reproaches of the Americans in after times." The *Times* reminded its intervention-minded readers that it was hardly logical to complain that cotton was not sent because it was shut in by the blockade and then, in the next breath, to assert that the blockade should be broken because it was everywhere ineffectual. "If ships can get in, they can also get out," the editorial pointed out, "and, if the South desired to send us Cotton, it has not lacked the opportunity." But the fact was that the Confederate government had forbidden cotton exportation in order to force foreign nations to aid the South in attaining its independence. "It would ill become England," the "Thunderer" concluded, "to make herself the tool of such machinations."[4]

In the meantime other London newspapers had printed a letter from Edmund Hammond, permanent undersecretary for foreign affairs, warning a group of Liverpool merchants that "Her Majesty's government will not afford the slightest protection" to British ships attempting to run the blockade of Confederate ports. Implied was British official acceptance of the Northern blockade as "effective."[5]

Another hopeful sign mentioned by Adams was "a speech by the Duke of Argyll which may fairly be construed as representing the sentiment that has prevailed in the Government." The lord privy seal had told his tenantry at Inveraray that the British government would under no circumstances submit to any pressures to interfere in the American Civil War, or "to take some steps which may ultimately involve us in it." For he believed it the "absolute duty" of Englishmen to "remain absolutely neutral in that contest," which position included abstaining "even from offering advice, though it might be conceived in a kind and friendly spirit. No good whatever can arise from offering such advice."[6]

By the end of October it was clear that, as the Manchester *Examiner* editorialized: "Lord Palmerston and his colleagues . . . adhere to their policy of non-intervention in the American war." Members of the British cabinet were embracing "every opportunity of speaking on this point with laudable emphasis and precision." On the same day, October 30, the London *Morning Post* printed a statement by a prominent member of Parliament that it was "the true policy" of the British government "not to interfere in the strife" in America, although all Englishmen "wished to see it ended."

Adams thought this declaration "unequivocal enough" to send specially to Seward, along with his personal reassurance that there was "no immediate danger of any change of policy . . . on this side of the Atlantic."[7]

In the long run, Adams declared, the English were not apt to risk a conflict with the United States which would cut off the source of about one-fifth of their supply of grain. Traveling in Southern England during the wheat harvest season, the American minister noted with satisfaction that Great Britain depended upon the United States "for more things than cotton. She must have five million quarters[8] of wheat more than she can raise even in the best of years." By October it had become clear to him that the English, Scottish, and Irish wheat crops for 1861 were quantitatively very poor (though perhaps not as poor as during the previous year, when the United States had furnished 36 percent of the wheat, and more than double that proportion of the flour, imported into Great Britain from abroad). The continued demand for Northern grain, coupled with "the scarcity in France," would suffice, Adams thought, "to keep up a demand that may in a degree neutralize the consequence of the loss of the cotton supply." The newspapers were full of stories of a gold drain from both England and France to the United States, to pay for imported grain. "Bread is rising at a rate which pours thousands in our pockets daily," Adams wrote during October. As the money flowed westward across the Atlantic Ocean to pay for wheat to feed the British workingman, it was obvious that no responsible British statesman would openly propose initiating a conflict with the United States that would risk cutting off the Lancashire cotton worker's bread, merely in an attempt to save his job.[9]

Adams was also confident that to agitate any measure involving interference in the American Civil War among the members of the British cabinet would be to threaten "considerable danger to their internal harmony." For the Palmerston ministry, he wrote Seward, was "very insecure as to its hold on power," and therefore its members were "not anxious to stir up any cause of internal discord." Meanwhile, the Tory opposition was "not so confident of its strength as to be ready to put out a declaration of policy which might shake it to pieces." It seemed "plain enough to every eye that the current of opinion and feeling" in Parliament favored a policy of preserving the *status quo*. Ever since the end of May, when the Tories had attacked Gladstone's budget and had been repulsed by a desperate effort, the queen's ministers had "gradually retreated from every measure or movement calculated to preserve a line of distinction between them and their opponents, as well as from all appearance of sympathy with the radical wing of their supporters. As a consequence," Adams wrote, "they have nothing left to stand upon but their personal popularity, a very unsteady prop in the direction of so many and so difficult public questions as must be perpetually presenting themselves for the decision of a leading power like Great Britain."[10]

"Besides which," the American envoy in London wrote home, "the aspect of things all over Europe is so threatening as to inspire caution in every quarter." Italy was the most troubled area. Austria and France were still maneuvering for dominance there, with the pope, despite threats from Turin, holding tightly to the region around Rome. The Italian people seemed impatient to complete the process of unification, and Adams calculated that this impatience might "precipitate a war with Austria that will involve all Europe. I do not say that I wish it, for that would be too selfish and cruel, but I do hope that it may keep so close on the verge of it as to draw away the attention of the great powers from our side of the Atlantic."[11]

Serious political problems existed as well in Denmark[12] and Poland,[13] while Alexander II's emancipation of the Russian serfs early in 1861 indicated growing restiveness in the colossus of the East. Adams wrote home that the sudden death of a key figure—say Napoleon or Palmerston—"would set everything afloat, and make the direction of things in Europe almost impossible to foresee." Great Britain depended on other countries for huge quantities of raw materials for her industries, as well as for foodstuffs. Her advocacy of free trade principles was "therefore not the disinterested thing she would make other nations believe." Moreover, it was vital to England that she continue her "perpetual expansion of her markets abroad in order to counteract her dependence upon others for the first articles of necessity." Hence it was the requisite "labor of her government to keep down the universal tendency of Europe to internal and external commotion." Yet not a single nation in Europe was "easy or quiet." Each government was "arming and drilling all their effective male population." In England it almost appeared that "the enemy was at the door. Even the boys parade with guns and drums," Adams wrote. "The dockyards are filled with novel inventions to fortify ships and to increase the range of artillery fire. Surely," Adams speculated, "this means something." He could think of no other reason for all the warlike commotion than the British fear of the adventurous French emperor. For Napoleon "must please his people, and they gasp after the conquest of Great Britain." At the same time France also appeared ripe for domestic insurrection, remaining quiet only because of the terror inspired by six hundred thousand men under arms. Any sudden sign of weakness in Napoleon's government "would be the signal for a general uprising," which might quickly spread beyond the boundaries of France. On the other hand, an alteration in the government of England, Adams believed, would lead to "a retreat from France and an advance towards the old connection with Austria, the consequences of which would not be slow to appear at home as well as abroad." Never had "true wisdom" dictated to the British government a more cautious course in dealing with foreign nations.[14]

Trusting to the solid sense of self-interest that invariably ruled the decisions of Palmerston and his cabinet colleagues, Adams predicted in a dispatch written for Seward on October 11, "that we shall be suffered to pursue our course in America without molestation to the end and that whatever that end may be the [British] Government will accept it with a disposition to make the most of it for Great Britain either way, and without the waste of any superfluous sentiment about the matter." British statesmen, as Adams was soon to remind Edward Everett, were renowned for their lack of scruples in the pursuit of their own interests. Hence they inspired little good will toward themselves among the leaders of other nations. Yet they also had a reputation "for acting up to their word, which was not always the case with their more courteous neighbors." Officially, Adams wrote, "I think they act better than they talk. Whilst my good-will is steadily diminishing I grow more confident in the steadiness of their policy." The United States would be granted nothing more "than a fair and full opportunity to recover its authority." If it suffered any great disaster while pursuing that aim, British public opinion would probably favor "a recognition," a move which would be joined in by France, after which would come similar action by "the rest of Europe."[15]

Almost four thousand miles west of the grimy building from which Adams faithfully sent off his weekly reports of developments in England, the American secretary of state kept watch on the European situation. For a while the news from that quarter, especially that portion of it emanating from London, was encouraging, so that on September 24, Seward felt able to write his wife: "My fears of foreign intervention are subsiding. The prestige of secession is evidently wearing off in Europe." Late in October, however, Seward received his first reports of Russell's Newcastle speech. He read the British foreign minister's remarks in the context of news, received about the same time, that England, France, and Spain had formed an alliance for the purpose of sending an army to invade Mexico. Thus, although Adams wrote reassuringly, Seward began to worry. His trepidation was enhanced by alarming reports from other envoys in Europe, who did not share Adams's calm confidence in the current reluctance of European governments to get entangled in the American Civil War. Carl Schurz, for example, wrote from Madrid that rumors were floating around in the "European press that Spain was about to recognize the independence of the Southern Confederacy and to break up the blockade of our Southern Ports." And Dayton notified Seward of rumors printed in European newspapers "of an effort being made, upon the part of the British government, to induce the French government to aid in an interference in our affairs under a pretext of bringing about a peace. . . . The English, on the other hand, pretend that France is urging them to join in such interference and they are holding back."

Meanwhile, the French Emperor had made no secret of his pro-Southern sympathies. He told the British ambassador that he thought "the insolence and presumption . . . of the North merited a severe lesson, & . . . he hoped it might be given them."[16]

Even more disturbing to the secretary of state was a visit from Mercier on October 23. The French envoy brought a dispatch from Napoleon's foreign minister. In it Edouard Thouvenel complained of the serious disruptions of French commerce already attributable to the war in America and suggested that the prolongation of that conflict was likely to produce even greater economic injuries for France. For after having allowed many of her industries to become so dependent upon American cotton that they consumed four hundred thousand bales of it annually, France was now threatened with "complete deprivation" of that commodity; consequently, as cotton reserves rapidly approached exhaustion, the first symptoms of a serious economic depression were appearing.[17]

The season for buying cotton had arrived, Thouvenel declared, and if the French importers were unable to obtain it, the government at Paris would soon be deluged with demands from influential French citizens for some drastic action to procure economic relief. Should this situation arise, the French foreign minister implied, the flow of events might "leave no longer full freedom of thought or action to anybody." He therefore believed it requisite that the United States government consider relaxing its blockade to the extent necessary to allow Frenchmen seeking the "indispensable" Southern cotton to fetch it from the ports of the American insurgents. In considering this suggestion, he added, the president of the United States would of course recognize the necessity of avoiding "difficulties the imminence and importance of which need no demonstration."[18]

Seward was not oblivious to the menace implicit in Thouvenel's communication. But before replying to it he asked Mercier whether it had been prepared in concert with the British government, or whether, if not, the British might at least have been informed about its contents. Mercier replied that he "presumed" the dispatch had not been written in concert with the British government, nor did he think it had been communicated to them. (This last statement was untrue, for Mercier himself had read Lyons the dispatch in question, and he had even allowed the British minister to make a copy of it.)[19]

After receiving this false reassurance, Seward (according to Lyons's account of this particular interview, as related to him by Mercier) said that an official reply to Thouvenel's message would have to be considered carefully by the president; hence it would be several days before more than an offhand preliminary opinion of it could be given. In the meantime, Seward said, he thought he could assure Mercier that the people of the North would not quit their struggle until they had reunited the entire nation "under one government, be its character the same or changed." Therefore, if France wanted cotton, let her at once exert her moral influence on the side of the United States government. This would help end the war quickly and reestablish the old trade. Any attempt to get cotton by interfering in the fray on the side of the South would be resisted. Even if all Europe opposed them, the American people would, as France herself had done at the end of the eighteenth century, defend their country heroically; and although they might suffer, they would not be conquered. During such a conflict commercial ruin would visit Europe. So let France understand that if she desired cotton, the only practicable way to get it was "to promote by every means in her power the speedy suppression of the rebellion."[20]

The French minister[21] answered Seward by saying that, although his feelings, and likewise those of his government, were perfectly friendly to the United States, he had long regarded the reunion of the North and South as "absolutely impossible," and he had expressed this opinion to his government in dispatches. Having formed this conviction, he had recommended that, as the only way to remedy the evils that the Civil War had already brought to Europe, France and England should "try to use their influence to produce an amicable separation" of the Northern and Southern states into two countries. For the only alternative seemed to be for Frenchmen and Englishmen "to stand with folded arms, and quietly contemplate the sufferings of their own people at home, and the ruin of both divisions of this great, and once prosperous, country." Therefore, Mercier seemed to imply, Thouvenel's request that the blockade be opened enough to let France get cotton might, indeed, be a first step toward a policy of outright intervention to support the cause of Confederate independence.[22]

Lyons appeared surprised to learn from Mercier that the latter's frank revelation of his recommendations to his government did not provoke an exhibition of great irritation on the part of the American secretary of state. On the contrary, the French minister reported, Seward quietly conceded the possible "dangerous consequences of the prolongation of the war." Yet he also remained firm in his warning that the United States government would not voluntarily allow cotton to be exported through the blockade until the South submitted.[23]

Viewed against the background news from Europe that a great power coalition was forming to invade Mexico, possibly as a trial run for a venture north of the Rio Grande, and viewed also in the light of Russell's Newcastle address, the French threats about cotton appeared truly ominous. The secretary of state's health began to show the strain. In the oppressive damp heat of a lingering Washington summer, the piles of diplomatic notes and dispatches on his desk grew ever higher, and the clamoring of increasingly larger numbers of people for interviews grew steadily more burdensome. Plaintively, Seward wrote his wife that under the pressure of his growing diplomatic correspondence he could "scarcely find the time to see anybody or do anything else." The American war had begun "to produce intolerable suffering in Europe, and the European statesmen," he wrote, "begin to complain." As the conflict began to tug at their economic interests, they had ceased to mock the efforts of loyal Americans to hold the Union together, and had begun "to argue, and to reason with us, how to avert from them the suffering they heedlessly provoked for themselves." Europeans should have recognized that "the treason of slaveholders" was injurious to the American Union hardly more than to "the interests of mankind," and they should therefore have refrained from encouraging the rebellion. Nevertheless, as European pecuniary interests became engaged, the danger of intervention from across the Atlantic to aid the Southern insurgents had now become acute.[24]

Shortly before Seward's conversation about cotton with Mercier, newspapers in both Washington and New York had published a circular letter from Seward addressed to the governors of Northern states with coastlines on the Great Lakes or the Atlantic Ocean. Whereas rebel agents abroad, the secretary had written, sought to involve the United States in "controversies" with foreign nations, it was necessary "to take every precaution that is possible to avoid the evils of foreign war, to be superinduced upon those of civil commotion, which we are endeavoring to cure." An "obvious" precaution of this kind, Seward had continued, was to put "our ports and harbors on the seas and lakes" in an effective state of defense. The president had directed him to invite consideration of this question by governors and state legislators, under the supposition that Congress might well later authorize reimbursement from Federal funds of whatever expenditures a state government might make to fortify its coastline.[25]

Lyons had theorized to Russell that Seward's letter might be merely a gesture—intended as a "show of energy" to "gain time" in the face of a steady tide of movement toward European intervention in the American Civil War by conveying the impression that the United States government was still willing and able to act with vigor if provoked. It was much more likely, however, wrote Lyons, that the circular letter represented "a sudden and very unfortunate return . . . to an inconsiderate and unconciliatory policy towards the Powers of Europe." When this estimate arrived in London, it was, as usual, taken seriously at the Foreign Office and was reflected in an editorial in the London *Times*, whose editors promptly characterized the fortifications circular as another example of Seward's "usual resource of getting up a quarrel between England and the United States." "Does he think," they asked, "that England will go to look for cotton on the shores of Lake Ontario, and Lake Erie, and Lake Champlain?" Lyons's warning even helped to motivate the prime minister to take the unusual step of summoning Adams to hear a word of caution in regard to Seward's alleged belligerent intentions.[26]

The public announcement of a second step, taken by Seward to counteract the growing pressure from Europe for Southern cotton, soon followed. The secretary of state had already grasped at the idea of seizing a Southern port as a means of access to that commodity. As Attorney General Edward Bates had confided to his diary on September 30, the cabinet had agreed that the enterprise should "easily get out enough cotton to make a full supply for home consumption, and some for Europe." Early in October, Lyons had noticed in the newspapers that a great naval expedition was on its way to the Southern coast to obtain cotton. He thought the project rested "upon two suppositions, both improbable": First, that there existed in the South a pro-Union group that would help bring the cotton to the waterside, and, second, that Southern greed exceeded Southern patriotism and would countenance the evasion of official restrictions against exporting cotton. Consul Bunch had reported that pressure from vigilante groups in the South had prevented cotton from being loaded even upon British blockade-runners. Plantation owners, the consul had added, would burn their cotton rather than allow it to go to a port held by the Northern armed forces. Nevertheless, on November 2, Seward hinted to Mercier that the projected maritime expedition to the Carolina coast would procure the cotton that the French needed, and Mercier at once passed the statement on to Lyons. Upon hearing this, Russell commented: "I hope this expedition by sea will clear the atmosphere. If the cotton planters bring their cotton to a port held by the Northerners, I think it will be nearly up with the South." But if not, the foreign minister added, he could not conceive of any way for the North to reunite the Union by force of arms. Russell thought that perhaps the North might indeed succeed in capturing "such a port—but the Southern govt will probably take care that very little Southern cotton is found in it, or passes the pickets of the Confederate army." Russell's estimate in this respect was correct enough —the sky for miles around Port Royal smoked and glowed day after day, once the hated Yankees had arrived there early in November, as the local planters put their cotton to the torch—but the expedition did help, as Bates put it, to "satisfy foreign nations that we are in earnest, and willing and able to win success—and then, we will have little trouble about *Blockade*."[27]

While Seward awaited news of the impact on European leaders of these latest diversions, he could only hope that Lyons had found his earlier tough talk credible enough to dissuade his government from adopting Mercier's recommendations for European intervention. Seward's hopes were rewarded. For although Mercier kept urging the British minister to join him in "pressing the United States without offending them" to open up the blockade to European trade for one or two months, after which he thought the way would be paved to recognize the sovereignty of the Confederate government at the first opportune moment, Lyons was afraid such a course of action would result in war. He told the Frenchman that he "had no reason to suppose that Her Majesty's government considered that the time had come for entertaining at all the question of recognizing the South." And he vigorously disputed Mercier's assertion that such a recognition, by discouraging the Northern "war party" and giving strength to the already numerous peace advocates, would put an end to the Civil War, establish the Confederacy as a separate nation, and thereby fully restore European trade with both North and South. Likewise did he differ, lastly, with the Frenchman's further declaration that in his opinion England and France, acting together, might recognize the Southern Confederacy without any danger of provoking war with the United States. It would be impossible, Lyons declared, for the Lincoln administration to allow the announcement of such a recognition

at this moment without some strong mark of resentment. If they did not declare actual war, they could hardly avoid breaking off diplomatic relations at best; a half measure . . . which would nevertheless cause a good deal of inconvenience and ill feeling. I would not deny that a contingency was possible in which the recognition of the South might produce the advantages which M. Mercier expected, but I did not think that at the present juncture it would have much effect towards putting a stop to the Civil War.

Lyons had previously warned Mercier that it would be "impossible" for European powers to obtain cotton without breaking the Northern blockade, which would mean war with the United States. So the choice was between two evils: whether to do without cotton until the Civil War ended, or whether to enter upon a costly war in the hope of thereby obtaining cotton.[28]

Lyons's recommendations still had great influence with the British cabinet. His reports of his conversations with Mercier on the subject of recognition, which contained his personal contention that the governments of the two great Western European powers should carefully avoid taking any step that might ignite Seward's wrath and thus possibly provoke an incident that could lead to war, were carefully considered in London. In reply, Russell commented that he considered discussions of intervention, as suggested by Mercier, "premature," and he reassured Lyons that Great Britain would remain neutral for a while longer.[29]

Meanwhile, Seward carefully composed his answer to Thouvenel's demand for cotton. Speaking through Dayton, he pointed out, first, that while "the direct benefits of the proposed relaxation" of the Northern blockade "must result to others, the whole cost and all the hazards which would attend it, must necessarily fall upon the United States," by weakening the Federal coercive power and supplying further "means of resistance to the insurgents." The French "suggestion," he wrote, had placed no limits on the interruption of the blockade, either

> of time or of the quantity of cotton that foreign consumers shall procure in the insurgent ports; nor does it show how discrimination shall be made between commercial nations, or by what rule the proportion of cotton that each of them shall be permitted to take shall be adjusted. Nor does it indicate what shall be the nature or the form of the equivalent to be paid to the insurgent owners of the cotton; whether it shall be bullion, paper, articles of luxury or articles contraband of war.

Nor was it clear whether such a "concession of commercial privileges to the insurgents" would also be equivalent to a grant of political privileges as well. Meanwhile, although these disadvantages to the United States were all so obvious, Thouvenel had not offered one single inducement for the concession he had proposed. On the contrary, he had declared only that he hoped the United States government would act to anticipate and prevent "difficulties" which might follow action by the French government, "if no relief to the commercial distress of France" should come soon.[30]

The secretary of state then addressed himself directly to the threatening aspect of Thouvenel's dispatch. "Our respect for France," he wrote,

> forbids us from supposing that Mr. Thouvenel is to be understood as implying that she will adopt any injurious or hostile policy, whether in arms or without, if we should refuse to yield a concession which . . . is . . . solicited as a favor and not claimed as a right. . . .
>
> While we have never seen anything in the conduct of France to justify us in giving so uncharitable an interpretation to the argument of Mr. Thouvenel, we have seen so much of sagacity and generous aspirations on the part of his government as to assure us that when the history of the second revolution in the United States shall be written, it will appear that we were not so far misunderstood by the people who were our allies in the first as to be supposed incapable of maintaining against all opposition from abroad . . . the invaluable institutions of liberty and Union. . . . When European nations shall think of intervening to maintain [slavery] here for their own advantage and to the subversion of our own government, they will I am sure calculate not only the cost but the probabilities of success in an enterprise which the conscience of the civilized world would forever reprobate and condemn. We do not expect any such proceeding on the part of France.[31]

This warning delivered, Seward proceeded to put several specific questions to Thouvenel, saying that after they were answered the president would then inform him of his final decision on the subject. First, if the Federal blockade were relaxed, as Thouvenel proposed, would "France thereafter maintain an attitude of cold indifference to our exertions for the preservation of the American Union," or would she exert her influence to persuade other nations that the struggle was a noble one, "needful to the best interests of mankind?" If the requested concessions were made, would France still insist on the United States government maintaining its blockade "of every port on our seacoast of three thousand miles, or shall we be challenged when we proceed to close the ports usurped by our own disloyal citizens," on the ground that a nation might not close its own insurgent-held ports by municipal law, but only according to the strict rules of international law? Finally, Seward asked, did France intend, once the cotton trade was reopened to her, to cling to her position that "pirates preying upon our commerce [might] be sheltered, supplied and armed in the ports of nations to whom we have opened, at our own cost, a trade from which by the law of nations they had been rightfully excluded?"[32]

In closing his long dispatch, Seward held out for Thouvenel's consideration an alternative approach to those to which the Frenchman had alluded: (1) either relaxation of the Northern blockade for the benefit of European nations and the Southern rebels, to the injury of the United States, or (2) intervention of the European powers to break through the blockade by force. Although he could not, of course, "present our plan of operations" in detail, he wrote, he did feel free to suggest to the French foreign minister that "long before France or any other nation shall be brought to such distress as he apprehends by the privation of cotton from our insurgent ports, we expect to be in free possession of some or all of those ports. . . . Just as soon as that success shall have been attained it will be a pleasant duty to restore our own commerce . . . there."[33]

After thus carefully stalling Thouvenel with questions about the practical details of his proposition, and attempting to disconcert him with a warning of the possible unpleasant consequences of blockade-breaking, while yet simultaneously broaching to him the possibility of obtaining cotton from soon-to-be-reconquered Southern ports, Seward relaxed, momentarily, from the burdens of his office. "I have had two weeks," he wrote his wife, "of intense anxiety and severe labor." Not only had he performed the delicate task of responding to a French intervention threat in a way calculated to blunt it while yet maintaining amicable relations with Napoleon's government, but he had also been confronted once again with the ominous possibility of British recognition of the slaveholding confederacy—and he had met that challenge head-on by demanding the recall of her majesty's agent in the matter, Consul Bunch. Whether both the French and the British would yield to his stipulations remained to be seen. "The pressure of interests and ambition in Europe," he continued, ". . . have made it doubtful whether we can escape the yet deeper and darker abyss of foreign war. The responsibility resting upon me is overwhelming." However, he had "worried through, and finished my dispatches. They must go for good or evil. I have done my best."[34]

Europeans Invade North America

*The Mexican expedition is . . . foolish, and likely to
cause many complications. . . . It is one of the great
misfortunes caused by the folly and crime of the South
that now the European powers can resume their ancient
practice of interfering on your continent.*
JOHN BRIGHT TO CHARLES SUMNER,
20 November 1861.[1]

THE THREAT of European intervention in the struggles of the New
World soon spread south of the Rio Grande. During 1860 a longstanding revolution in Mexico had greatly expanded into a sanguinary civil war. The lives and property of foreigners in that hapless
land were jeopardized as the conflict intensified around them, and
stories of atrocities committed against Europeans and against citizens of the United States appeared with increasing frequency in the
world press. As offers extended by the governments of Great
Britain, France, and Spain to mediate between the warring factions
in Mexico were invariably rejected by the combatant leaders,
European patience visibly began to wear thin. Worried that great
power intervention might be contemplated, President Buchanan
sent an emissary to inform the European diplomats in Mexico that
the United States government would "resist any forcible attempt to
impose a particular adjustment of the existing conflict against the
will and sanction of the people of Mexico, and, also, any forcible
intervention, by any power, which looked to the control of the
political destiny thereof." Rather would the United States government, "to the extent of its power, defend the nationality and
independence" of Mexico. This was, of course, an empty statement, for on the very date on which it was issued the secession of
South Carolina signaled the breakup of the Union and the conse-

quent inability of the United States government to enforce any dictum whatever against European intervention in Latin America.[2]

Realizing this, Seward, on assuming his duties as secretary of state, began casting about for some effective method of keeping European powers out of Mexico, using persuasion and economic inducements, rather than by threatening to use force against them. Within one month after the Lincoln administration took office, he informed Lyons confidentially that he was considering "a new policy" for the nearest Latin American neighbor of the United States. He anticipated, he said, that the Southern insurgents would "endeavour by force or fraud to unite Mexico to the Southern Confederacy, and to force the institution of slavery upon that country." Moreover, he had heard of a plot to bring about the secession of California, followed by an invasion of Mexico, for the purpose of creating an independent Western empire out of the broken American Union. Meanwhile, the invasion of Santo Domingo by Spain foreshadowed possible similar action elsewhere in Latin America, making more imperative than ever the adoption of measures by the United States government to secure Mexico against "foreign invasion," for the smaller nation's "own interests and safety." Although no final decision had been made by the president's cabinet—indeed, Seward was merely presenting "ideas which had occurred to him at the moment in familiar conversation"—the secretary of state expressed a hope that when a policy in regard to Mexico was finally adopted by the Lincoln administration, the governments of Great Britain and France would assist in the furtherance of that policy.[3]

Even as Seward was hinting to Lyons that the Lincoln administration might be disposed to intercede economically in the Mexican civil war to protect the Mexican people from outside interference, the governments of Great Britain, France, and Spain were separately considering what action should be taken to protect the interests of their nationals in Mexico. By September they were negotiating with each other regarding an armed intervention there. As this negotiation proceeded, news reached the British Foreign

Office that the United States government had invited the Mexican government to sign a convention, by which, according to Lyons, the United States would pay the debts owed to the European creditors of Mexico in return for a mortgage on certain Mexican territories.[4]

The scheme to allow the United States to act as debt-collector for the European creditors of Mexico[5] represented a desperate attempt by the secretary of state to prevent foreign intervention in that country. In his initial instructions to Thomas Corwin, United States minister in Mexico City, Seward had merely asserted that, in regard to the large number of American "complaints against the Mexican government for violations of contracts and spoilations and cruelties" that had piled up in the State Department archives, President Lincoln planned to defer pressing these claims "until the incoming administration in Mexico shall have had time, if possible, to cement its authority and reduce the yet disturbed elements of society to order and harmony."[6]

Corwin warned, however, that England and France had broken off diplomatic relations with Mexico and were contemplating an invasion. "I beg the department to consider," the distraught American envoy wrote, "whether, *if it be possible*, our duty and interest do not require of us to prevent the consummation of this scheme." He assured Seward that he could "put a stop to every attempt of the kind" if he could sign a treaty with the Mexican government guaranteeing, for five years, the payment of 3 percent interest on the debt of about sixty-two million dollars owed to English bond-holders, with Mexico pledging "all her public lands and mineral rights in Lower California, Chihuahua, Sonora, and Sinaloa, as well as her national faith, for the payment of this guarantee. This," Corwin added, "would probably end in the cession of the sovereignty to us," but, most important of all, would ensure that "any further attempt in all time to come to establish European power on this continent would cease to occupy the minds of either England or continental Europe."[7]

It was this plan of Corwin's, then, which Seward adopted, and which, in an instruction dated September 2, he authorized his representative in Mexico to embody in a treaty, contingent upon the agreement of the British and French governments that they would "forbear from resort to action against Mexico on account of her failure or refusal to pay the interest in question until after the treaty shall have been submitted to the Senate, and, if ratified, then so long thereafter as the interest shall be punctually paid by the government of the United States."[8]

As soon as he received Seward's sanction to proceed with his treaty project, Corwin conferred with his British ministerial colleague and the appropriate Mexican authorities, and together they worked out an arrangement whereby the Mexican government would pay England slightly over one million dollars which allegedly had been confiscated by a previous regime from British residents, and British commissioners would be stationed in Mexican ports to divert a portion of future tariff revenues to foreign creditors, while simultaneously the United States government would lend Mexico several million dollars a year for from three to five years, with Mexican public lands serving as collateral as previously proposed by Corwin to Seward and approved by the latter. The negotiations necessary to complete this arrangement were prolonged well into November, and meanwhile preparations for armed intervention proceeded in Europe. Efforts to prevent this intervention were made by American diplomats, acting at Seward's behest, in Madrid, in Paris, and in London.[9]

Seward sent his minister in London a copy of his instruction to Corwin describing and approving the latter's debt-retirement project. He also directed Adams to find out whether the British government would refrain from attacking Mexico as long as the United States government paid British holders of Mexican bonds 3 percent interest on their investments, with the understanding that the entire undertaking would be subject to confirmation by the United States Senate when that body met the following December. If Russell approved the idea in principle, Adams was to discuss with him detailed arrangements for putting it into effect.[10]

Adams had to travel about five hundred miles to Abergeldie Castle in Scotland in order to deliver Seward's message to Russell.

He told the foreign minister that "great uneasiness" had been excited in the United States by a suspicion that several European powers contemplated an attack on Mexico and the imposition of a new government under their own control. This apparent "effort to introduce a new principle of action into American affairs, . . . in opposition to which the government of the United States had committed itself forty years ago, and which that of Great Britain had not favored then nor any time since," promised to have the gravest consequences. For if the intervention should prove successful, it would afterwards implicate

> America in all the struggles of Europe, from which it had always striven to keep aloof, and . . . bring on combinations not merely between the different States of North and South America, but also the formation of counter alliances by them all with the other States of Europe. This must be prompted by the instinct of self-preservation if by nothing else. For there was no telling, if such a project were executed in the case of one American State, how soon it might be repeated in another. And the United States might, in their present difficulties, be made the subject of a similar experiment.[11]

For all of these reasons, Adams had been commanded by his government to propose that Her Majesty's government "postpone action for the present" in regard to Mexico, until the United States representative in Mexico City could reach agreement there for the interest on Mexico's foreign debt to be paid for a certain period of time by the United States government, "and thus remove the immediate cause of dissatisfaction."[12]

"His lordship heard me very patiently to the end," Adams later reported, and then he drew from his pocket a dispatch from Lyons giving the exact particulars of the American proposal to assume the Mexican foreign debt. Unfortunately, Russell asserted, "the proposed arrangement did not, by any means, meet the cause of complaint. Great Britain had much more to object to in the action of Mexico than the mere suspension of the interest on her debt." English subjects had suffered great injuries to their lives and property there. Some had been murdered. Huge sums of money had been stolen. The ensuing protests had been deprecated or ignored by the Mexican government; so that the more recent act of suspending the payment of interest on the foreign debt was merely the "last straw," but by no means the only cause of complaint. Hence the proposal of the United States, confined to a single one out of a long list of wrongful acts against British subjects in Mexico, fell far short of meeting the demands of the case.[13]

Even had Seward's proposal been more comprehensive, Russell added, the additional categories of British claims against Mexico could hardly be transferred to the United States government

> without raising an infinite number of questions of detail upon which Great Britain and Mexico would have to appeal to the equity of the U.S. . . . I thought it the interest of our two countries to have as few entangling questions & clashing interests as possible. I should be afraid that our friendly relations might be endangered if we increased the number of points upon which we might come into collision.[14]

In order, however, as much as possible to assuage American fears, Russell said, he had proposed, through his representatives at Paris and Madrid, that, before any overt action was taken against Mexico, "the matter should be opened to the United States, and some plan, not of intervention, but of settlement, adopted with their co-operation." France, with some hesitation, had concurred in this opinion, but Spain had consented to wait only until the end of October or early November before applying force, either in concert with the other powers, or alone, to exact a suitable indemnity for the injuries sustained by her subjects in Mexico. The Spanish prime minister, however, had conceded (and here Russell took out a dispatch from Sir John Crampton, his envoy at Madrid,[15] to read the very words to Adams) that any effort to force a European-dominated government upon the Mexican people would be "open to grave objection." England "contemplated no domestic intervention in Mexico," and she was endeavoring to prevent such a movement on the part of France and Spain.[16]

In regard to the perplexing problem of what to do about Mexico, Russell continued, "the truth was that there was little hope of the establishment of any stable form of government at all" in that troubled land. So attempts to impose one by foreign powers were bound to fail. On the other hand, "some action" was necessary. Great Britain would go forward, with Spain and France, to seek redress of grievances. And the United States government, whose citizens also had claims against Mexico, would be welcome to participate in sustaining any effective "mode of government which the people of Mexico might themselves voluntarily establish."[17]

It "would be a great relief" to people in the United States, Adams declared, to learn that England contemplated no interference with the domestic institutions of Mexico. This assurance would probably cause the United States government not "to interpose objections to any ordinary mode of gaining redress for the commission of flagrant wrongs." On this note the conversation about Mexico ended.[18]

While Adams, after luncheon, went with Lady Russell on a carriage tour of the queen's Balmoral hideaway, which was located nearby, the foreign minister seems to have consulted a letter recently sent from the Foreign Office by one of his undersecretaries, saying that John Motley had been "excited to a degree I could scarcely have conceived about Mexico." "No American," Sir Henry Layard quoted Motley as saying, would be persuaded that the British were "not taking advantage of the difficulties of the United States, to raise a strong and hostile power in Mexico." Considered in the light of the "great gloom" exhibited by Adams "at the intentions of Spain, France & England to interfere in Mexico," these remarks of Motley's apparently caused the foreign secretary to conclude that a counterproposal should be tendered to the United States government, to show that a friendly desire existed in England to set at rest, as much as possible, American fears about British intentions in regard to Mexico. Somewhat the same thought appeared in a letter received that same afternoon from Palmerston, who had independently taken the same view of the American offer.[19]

"The Mexicans," the premier wrote, "have many Friends desirous of waiting upon them." England, France, and Spain all were ready to join in forcing payment of unsatisfied claims against Mexico.

But the Washington government, inspired by a chivalrous sense of justice, not satisfied with its own enormous expenditure on account of the civil war, proposes to undertake to pay the interest on the foreign debt of Mexico, I forget for how long, taking a mortgage upon all the mineral wealth of Mexico. This scheme . . . makes no provision for the satisfaction of the money claims of the Three European Powers, nor for the punishment of the Mexican murderers of the subjects of the Three Powers, and in the next place it lays the ground for foreclosure by this new creditor, and that raises a serious political question, and then it further tends to continue the present state of anarchy in Mexico; and indeed Motley complained that we and France are wanting to organize a strong government in Mexico to the detriment of the views of the United States. Perhaps the best answer to the Washington proposal would be a counter proposal to the U.S. govt to join the Three Powers, either morally or physically. Our action ought to begin in November, and the United States convention even if it were to cover the whole case would not be valid till it had obtained the approval of the Congress which does not meet till the 4th December and often amuses itself for weeks in discussing and voting about the choice of a speaker before it enters upon business. The Congress will probably have plenty to do about the war, and this Mexican Convention if concluded, might not be discussed and approved for some time after Congress had met.[20]

Therefore, before Adams departed for London the following morning, Russell drew him aside for a few moments to say that in his next dispatch to Lyons he would outline "a counter proposition" in response to Seward's proposal that the United States government assume the Mexican foreign debt. The American envoy said he "was glad to receive the announcement," and he would communicate it at once to his government. He "believed that it would be ready cheerfully to entertain any proposition which avoided as a basis the principle of domestic intervention." Adams carried back to London the distinct impression that the policy of the British government had become more conciliatory towards the United States. How long this might last, however, was "difficult to predict in the face of the ever recurring topics of irritation." Adams never knew whether a fresh set of dispatches from Washington might not "bring a torpedo to scatter to the winds all my feeble labors."[21]

While Adams waited, Russell composed a memorandum for the queen, saying that he was "now prepared to indicate the course which he thinks ought to be taken in reference to the affairs of Mexico." First, a naval force should be sent to Vera Cruz, "to batter and destroy the defences" of that place. England should continue coordinating her movements against Mexico with France and Spain, but it was also "absolutely necessary . . . to invite the co-operation of the U.S." and

> to declare openly that H.M.G. have no intention of interfering in the internal Govt of Mexico. To do so would be to meddle in a bitter struggle between two violent factions, equally cruel, unjust & un-principled; to depart from the principle of non-intervention which is our usual rule of conduct; to offend not only the Govt but the whole people of the U.S., who are opposed to any intervention in the internal affairs of America.[22]

As the queen considered Russell's recommendations about Mex-ico, Palmerston commented further on Seward's "curious pro-posal." On second thought, he did not oppose the American as-sumption plan, as far as it went, even though it involved "a mort-gage of Mexico to the United States," which "would certainly lead to foreclosing." Such an outcome, he had decided, would actually benefit England, because it "would secure probably the interests of the foreign creditors." Seward's scheme, however, fell short of acceptability insofar as it failed to provide redress for personal injury claims on behalf of British and French subjects, and reim-bursement for property "violently and unlawfully seized." Would the United States assume payment of "everything which is de-manded from Mexico"? If so, the prime minister wrote, "we might close with the offer," but the first order of business was to ask the Americans "whether they mean to place themselves fully in the shoes of Mexico and to adopt all her engagements & liabilities. If they mean this I don't see that we can object to it but if they do not they shud be told that England & France are obliged to make arrangements for employing force against Mexico to obtain satisfac-tion and redress, and that the employment of that force cannot be put off long enough to allow time for all the proceedings necessary for the proposed convention between the U.S. & Mexico." In the light of what Adams had told Russell about the American proposition, Palmerston could only assume that it fell far short of complete assumption of all foreign claims against Mexico; hence the European intervention would have to go forward, as previously contemplated.[23]

Throughout most of October and almost until the end of November, Seward waited anxiously for the British counter-proposition in regard to Mexico that Adams had written him would be sent by Russell; but Lyons presented no concrete proposals on the subject, because he received none from London. Rather did the British minister in Washington find in his mailbag, in mid-October, a dispatch instructing him to tell the American secretary of state:

> H.M.'s. govt are of opinion that if any combined operations are to be taken against Mexico they should be founded on these two bases: 1. The combined powers of France, Gt Bn, Spain & the U.S. feel themselves compelled by the lawless & flagitious conduct of the authorities of Mexico to seek from those authorities protection for the persons & property of their subjects & a fulfillment of the obligations contracted by the Republic of Mexico towards their govts. 2. The said combined powers hereby declare that they do not seek any augmentation of territory, or any special advantage, & that they will not endeavour to interfere in the internal affairs of Mexico or with the free choice of its form of govt by its people.

Lyons was commanded to invite the United States government to accept these two essential conditions to any British participation in an expedition against Mexico involving other powers, even as France and Spain had been invited to accept them; and then, when all parties had agreed to these simple conditions, the United States government was invited to participate in the intervention itself.[24]

Once more, as earlier during the Declaration of Paris negotiation, Seward understood that Lyons would be ordered to make a *definite, concrete proposition*, this time in regard to Mexico, and therefore the American secretary of state delayed transmitting further instructions to Adams on the subject; while Lyons, on his part, once more seems to have believed that Seward intended to channel his official correspondence regarding Mexico through Adams at London, rather than through him at Washington. In any case, the British minister at Washington thought, as he had earlier thought about the question of the Declaration of Paris, that a negotiation on the subject was useless. Consequently, he failed fully to carry out his instructions. In a conversation with the secretary of state on October 12, he confined his official overture to the obscure observation that the British government favored the participation of the United States, along with Spain, France, and Great Britain, "in a course of action the objects and limits of which should be strictly defined beforehand." With nothing more definite than this to go on, Seward, according to Lyons, preferred instead to favor an enlarged version of "his own plan," which he said he had already transmitted to the American ministers in London and Paris, "and which would enable them to engage that the United States should provide not only for the interest on the Mexican foreign debt, but also for "the general claims of Great Britain, France, and Spain, upon Mexico." Agreement on this latest plan, Seward declared, would "have the advantage of rendering all interference on the part of European powers in the affairs of Mexico entirely superfluous." Derisive, as usual, Lyons asserted that what Seward really sought was to manufacture "expedients for postponing any active proceedings for the settlement of [the Mexican question] . . . in the hope that a favourable turn in its domestic affairs may enable [the United States government] to revert to its old tone of defiance towards Europe." Moreover, the American secretary of state also desired to forestall "any concert of the great European Powers with regard to the affairs of this continent, lest their union on minor questions be the precursor of a simultaneous recognition by them of the independence of the Seceded States." Hence Seward's overtures were hardly to be taken seriously by the Great Powers of Europe.[25]

It appears doubtful whether Seward mentioned any specific enlarged "plan" for American brokerage of the Mexican question to Lyons, especially since he was still hopefully awaiting the arrival of one from Russell. The American secretary of state had written

Adams, two days before talking with the British minister in Washington, only that he desired his London representative to consult

> the spirit rather than the letter of my previous instructions, and considering them enlarged so as to embrace the new danger with which Mexico is threatened, you will confer with him and ascertain whether any . . . proposition we can make . . . would receive the favorable consideration of the British government and engage its good offices to secure a forbearance of those three powers from hostile designs against the Mexican republic. . . . Operations may be definitively matured on the other side of the Atlantic while we are considering how we can most effectually and properly engage in preventing the necessity for them. I shall therefore expect you to consider carefully the whole case as you find it, and rather to propose to me what this government shall do than to wait for new suggestions from me. . . .

Seward's "plan," then, consisted of nothing more than a plea for Adams to find out specifically what price the United States would have to pay to prevent the British and their European allies from proceeding with their armed expedition into Mexico. Implied in the language of the secretary of state's instruction to Adams was the intention, if possible, to pay that price.[26]

Seward's latest instruction brought forth an answer from Adams on November 1. As yet unaware that on the previous day representatives of the British, Spanish, and French governments had signed a treaty committing themselves to a Mexican expedition,[27] Adams reported that "rumors continue to fly about in the newspapers of the adoption of a scheme of co-operation between the three governments, which, in my belief, are as yet the offspring of the wishes of interested parties rather than of established facts." Yet there was little doubt that a diplomatic negotiation was "actively in progress for the attainment of some positive result," a result which Adams thought himself entirely unable to influence, as Russell had not even thought "fit to make me acquainted with the nature of the plan he was about to submit to your consideration through Lord Lyons." Therefore, Adams believed that it was "utterly out of my power to propose a course of action for the government of the United States." This notwithstanding, he then proceeded to offer some observations on Seward's earlier plan, which really amounted to tactful suggestions for a new approach to the Mexican question. First, Adams asserted, the condition of Mexico seemed "such as positively to invite interference from abroad, and the great obstacle to it interposed by the ordinary position of the United States is so far diminished by their existing divisions as to give full play to the revival of ambitious national dreams in Spain." It was possible, Adams thought, that Great Britain "proposes to take a part in order to retain a right to control the result. Considering who her associates are and how little she herself trusts them, all that I can say is that the game is a dangerous one."[28]

To the extent that the United States government was also interested in trying to "control the result" of the intervention movement, Adams thought it very important to appear

to divest the United States of any personal and selfish interest in the action it may think proper to adopt. The view customarily taken in Europe is that their government is disposed to resist all foreign intervention in Mexico, not upon any principle, but simply because it is itself expecting, in due course of time, to absorb the whole country for its own benefit. Hence any proposal like that which I had the honor to receive, based upon the mortgage of portions of Mexican territory as security for engagements entered into by the United States, naturally becomes the ground of an outcry that this is but the preliminary to an entry for inevitable foreclosure. And then follows the argument that if this process be legitimate in one case, why not equally in all. . . . Great Britain and France . . . have of late years been disposed to give more and more weight to the doctrine of non-intervention in the internal government of nations where there may be a conflict with the general sentiment of the population. . . . [If the small nations of the Western Hemisphere should] fail in performing their honest engagements, they make themselves liable in their property, but not in their persons or their political rights. Any attempt to transcend that broad line of distinction is a mere appeal to force, which can carry with it no obligation one moment beyond the period when it may be successfully overthrown. And the principle is broad enough to make the maintenance of it in one country equally the cause of all the rest.[29]

When he received this advice from Adams, hinting (as the American minister at London wrote more bluntly to Dayton) that since Russell had "disclaimed all purpose of domestic intervention" in Mexico, the course the British had committed themselves to "would be of more value to the United States than their own plan," Seward heard almost simultaneously that the convention between Great Britain, France, and Spain establishing the bases of intervention stipulated "against any political designs, and confines the expedition merely to the redress of grievances." Moreover, the *unofficial* news from Europe (which Lyons, acting against his chief's orders, had refrained from communicating officially) was that the United States would be invited to become a party to this agreement, so that it might be unnecessary to act positively upon Adams's advice. It was difficult, however, for Seward to accept the idea that the European powers would not content themselves with an American guarantee of the Mexican debts and were apparently going to proceed hastily with "concerted hostilities" without waiting further for word from Washington. This, he wrote Adams, was a "very unsatisfactory state" of affairs, and he found himself "unable to see at this moment what course we can take to afford relief or security to Mexico." As the situation stood, however, he supposed that neither he nor Adams could do more than they already had done "for the benefit of Mexico to assure her peace." Rather must they "only be watchful for occasions for that purpose, and jealous of our own rights and interests."[30]

Seward and Adams were both worried that the European intervention in Mexico might turn out to be a warm-up exercise for a more elaborate demonstration further north, for the purpose of aiding in the permanent destruction of the American Union. As Adams put it, Spain appeared to be "creeping out of her shell again, and striving to weave once more her web over her ancient possessions in America," while the French "expedition to the city of

Mexico may not stop until it shows itself in the heart of the Louisiana purchase." Meanwhile, Great Britain, Adams said, was "holding the door" in Mexico, "whilst her two associates, with her knowledge, go in, fully prepared, if they can, to perpetuate the act which she, at the outset, made them denounce, at the same time that she disavowed every idea of being made to participate in it." To the American minister in London, the policy of Russell in regard to Mexico had been so equivocal that it had indicated a great and "growing danger of European intervention" in the domestic affairs of the United States.[31]

Although Seward, too, was fully conscious of the potential dangers that the United States faced because of the Mexican intervention, which began officially when a Spanish advance force took possession of Vera Cruz on December 17, he had hanging over him, by that time, an even more serious threat of a much more direct and distinct character—the *Trent* affair. Hence he could only repeat to Adams that the United States would confine itself to a policy of watchful waiting in regard to Mexico, and would try not to "indulge apprehensions" based upon distrust of European good faith. Once the Southern insurrectionists had been suppressed and the Union fully restored, there would be plenty of time to consider altering the United States policy toward Mexico from one of cautious sympathy to one of overt action.[32]

As the year 1861 ended, therefore, the presence of British military forces on Mexican soil, operating in open concert with the armed forces of France and Spain, seriously shook the already wobbling edifice of Anglo-American understanding. The United States government had made an offer in good faith to satisfy the claims of British creditors against Mexico, in order to prevent armed European intervention there. Not only had the British government rejected the American offer, but also the counteroffer promised by Russell was never received. Instead the British foreign minister seemed to have used the weeks during which Seward vainly awaited its arrival to make final preparations for the Great Power invasion of Mexico. And, although Russell had appeared to insist that the European expedition should be punitive only, and that it must not lead to any permanent European presence in Mexico, it seemed nevertheless clear enough to American statesmen that, whatever England might do, France and Spain had territorial ambitions in Latin America that would not be deflected by any such preliminary promise—and it seemed obvious, furthermore, that men as sagacious as Palmerston and Russell were reputed to be must have realized this at the time they assured the United States government that no permanent outside occupation of Mexico would follow the three-power intervention. From the American point of view, then, British behavior in regard to Mexico during 1861 had been, at best, deceitful, and at worst it inspired suspicions that the armed invasion against Mexico might have been initially designed, or might eventually prove, to be a trial run for later movements further North. Even if British motives were pure, once European warships had been assembled into a powerful armada in Western waters, and once European troops had been landed in large numbers on the North American continent, their use outside Mexico, sooner or later, might readily come to mind in London or in Paris.

From the British point of view, however, the situation appeared very different. The military occupation of the ports of small nations, in which her majesty's subjects and their property had not been treated with proper deference by local rulers, was an old story to British statesmen: and such a course of action, to them, was sufficient unto itself. Apparently the thought that the Mexican intervention might have any relation at all to a future armed intervention in the war between the United States government and the Southern rebels never occurred to them. Nor did they encourage in any way the French and Spanish wish to gain permanent political footing in Mexico. Seward's attempts to buy them off, particularly the provision contained in his original plan for an American mortgage on Mexican lands, seemed to them to indicate a desire to keep Europeans out of Mexico until the United States could settle its own domestic problems, after which American armies might occupy Mexico in leisurely fashion, and a despised figure like the American secretary of state might at length dictate terms to British creditors.

Hence the Mexican intervention episode, by enhancing the corrosion of confidence on both sides—English and American—in the motives and aims of the other party, served further to widen the gulf of trans-Atlantic misunderstanding as the year 1861 drew to a close.

England Becomes the Armory of the Confederacy

The activity and success of the insurgents in getting military and naval stores and munitions out of Europe, and especially out of Great Britain, are a subject of deep concern.

SEWARD TO ADAMS,
November 27, 1861.

ANGLO-AMERICAN DISCORD over the Mexican intervention, aggravated by the suspicions engendered by the cotton supply question and the Bunch affair, was further fueled by a controversy over the outfitting of Confederate ships in England with supplies for the South. Confederate agents, from the very beginning of the Civil War, were hard at work in Great Britain purchasing munitions and providing for their shipment to the South. Captain James D. Bulloch, a veteran mariner still in his thirties who had served under Farragut on the *Decatur*, arrived in Liverpool on June 4 with instructions from the Confederate Navy Department to buy or have built six steam cruisers for use against Union commerce. While awaiting the construction of these vessels, he was also ordered to purchase naval cannons, shells, large quantities of small arms, ammunition, powder, parts, cutlasses, and naval clothing. In this procurement work he kept in close touch with Major Edward C. Anderson and Captain Caleb Huse, who were charged with purchasing supplies in Europe for the Confederate Army. And he soon found the means to transport all these supplies to the shores of the Confederacy. For, as early as June, 1861, the Liverpool banking and commercial firm of Fraser, Trenholm and Company, a branch of the South Carolina banking house of John Fraser and Company, put all their vessels under the British flag and began to send them out with cargoes for the Confederacy.[1]

Information about such voyages began to reach the London

legation of the United States from Freeman Morse, the new American consul in the British capital. It was Morse who first discovered the *Bermuda*, a fast steamer under construction for Fraser, Trenholm and Company at Stockton on the River Tees about thirty miles south of Newcastle. He informed Vice Consul Henry Wilding at Liverpool of the whereabouts of the vessel, and Wilding had her watched while she was being loaded with Confederate supplies.[2]

In mid-August, armed with information gathered by Morse and Wilding that an armed steamer was about to be sent out from Liverpool to make war against the United States, Charles Francis Adams asked the British foreign minister to determine whether a violation of British law was taking place. For the half-century-old Foreign Enlistment Act did in fact prohibit, "without leave or license of his Majesty," British subjects from (1) entering foreign military service, (2) aiding anyone else to enlist in a foreign military unit, (3) "equipping, furnishing, fitting out, or arming of any ship or vessel" for foreign service, "in order that such ship or vessel shall be employed . . . as a transport or store-ship, or with attempt to cruise or commit hostilities . . . against the subjects or citizens of any prince, state, or potentate . . . , with whom his Majesty shall not then be at war, . . ." (4) "or by the addition of any equipment for war," from "augmenting the warlike force of any . . . armed vessel, which at the time of her arrival in any part of the United Kingdom, or any of his Majesty's dominions, was [an] . . . armed vessel in the service of any foreign . . . state." In the Queen's Neutrality Proclamation, issued in May, the provisions of this act, and the penalties of fines and imprisonment provided in it, were extended specifically to include any endeavor either to break a lawful blockade, or to carry "officers, soldiers, dispatches, arms, military stores, or materials, or any article or articles considered and deemed to be contraband of war."[3]

The fitting out of the *Bermuda* as a transport vessel for munitions to be run through the blockade to the Southern insurgents seemed to Adams a flagrant violation of the British Foreign Enlistment Act. His complaint about it to Russell, however, elicited only the sparse statement that the case would be looked after. "This means," Legation Secretary Benjamin Moran concluded, "that she will be let off."[4]

Moran was right. On August 18, with no hindrance from the British government, the *Bermuda* put out to sea. All Federal efforts to intercept her were in vain. On September 16 the *Bermuda* successfully ran the blockade into Savannah, Georgia, where she delivered into the hands of Confederate authorities huge quantities of cannons, rifles, cartridges, gunpowder, shot, shoes, blankets, and medical stores, as well as many other articles badly needed by the Southern soldiers. The total cost of her cargo in Liverpool had been almost one million dollars. From a Confederate point of view, Adams wrote Seward, the dispatch of the *Bermuda* was "the most effective thing that has been done here," and if her cargo should reach the South, "it would be a most important agent in continuing the war."[5]

Meanwhile, Adams received a note from the British foreign minister declaring that the crown law officers had advised Her Majesty's government "that there is not sufficient evidence" to warrant any interference with the clearance or the sailing of the vessel. Although the Foreign Enlistment Act prohibited equipping a vessel for foreign service "as a transport or cruiser," Russell wrote, it had "no reference to the mere nature of the cargo on board, and there is at present no proved intention that the vessel itself is to be employed for a warlike purpose." Adams was disgusted at this narrow legalistic position. He advised Seward "that no assistance can be expected from the government here, in preventing the transmission of these supplies. The true reliance must be upon the activity of our own officers and the energy of our own administration."[6]

Other ships followed the *Bermuda* out of British ports, crammed with supplies for the Confederacy. Among them were the *Thomas Watson*, the *Fingal*, and the *Gladiator*. Adams could think of no effective means to stop these shipments. He was well informed of the activities of Huse, Bulloch, and many other Southern emissaries and their British friends. But he had little confidence in any attempt to impede them by applying to the British government. His lack of success in preventing the departure of the *Bermuda* was a clear indication of his helplessness. "No stronger case," he wrote Seward, "is likely to be made out against any parties than this. The activity of our Consuls . . . furnished me with very exact information attending the equipment of this vessel, and yet Her Majesty's Government on being apprised of it disclaimed all power to interfere." He had alerted the American consuls at most of the British ports to be on the watch for suspicious activities, and to report all such movements promptly to the State Department, so that Union naval vessels might be given an opportunity to intercept the supplies before they reached the Southern coast. That, and a hint that "the presence of a few vessels of war in the European waters would be very wholesome," seemed to be his only recourse.[7]

By late summer Adams despaired of any attempt whatever by the Palmerston ministry to cut off supplies for the Confederate armies and navies. As for all the warnings and descriptions of ships and cargoes sent by the consuls and by himself to Washington, Adams had little hope that they would avail to bring about the capture of the Confederate supply vessels. Moreover, the "cunning and profligate" Southern emissaries had accomplished much more than sending out huge quantities of supplies from England. Bulloch had also supervised the keel-laying of two vessels destined to become the Confederate cruisers *Florida* and *Alabama*. Besides, as Morse lamented, the rebel agents had labored hard to influence British opinion against the United States, and had been able to "infect many minds with their heresies." Adams attributed the "precipitate" queen's neutrality proclamation at least partly to pressure brought on the British government by the cotton manufacturers and shippers—pressure which had been initiated by the Confederate commissioners.[8]

For their part the Southern emissaries were satisfied that their cause was inexorably gaining ground in England. Seward's conduct was considered "offensive" there, they reported, and Adams apparently did not get along with the leading members of the British cabinet. "Both in his diplomatic and social relations," the Confederate commissioners gloated, Adams had proved himself "a blunderer." He had been assisted by pro-Union men who had attempted to influence English public opinion by publishing speeches and letters in the press, without doing more, however, than to injure their own cause and "excite British antagonism." By contrast, the commissioners declared, they had confined themselves to quiet attempts privately to inspire "correct views . . . in the minds of persons . . . we thought would be most likely to bring to bear a favorable influence on the British Cabinet." For example, William S. Lindsay, wealthy shipowner and influential member of Parliament, had been persuaded to make several speeches favorable to the Confederacy and to act as an intermediary between the Southern commissioners and the British ministry. Meanwhile, those same commissioners were content to "allow the blunders of our enemies to have full effect on the public mind, and not to divert attention from them by any public movements."[9]

Aware that the Southern agents had gained some influence over public opinion in England and France, Adams yet saw no way whereby he, in his official capacity, could effectively counteract their machinations. His best tactic was "patience." All would right itself in good time, he believed, provided only that the Northern armies won victories in the field. His confidence in this respect was supported by the testimony of the Confederate agents. They complained that although they were widely supported and entertained by British commercial leaders, they were unable to gain "the least notice or attention, official or social, from any member of the Government." Moreover, only Northern newspapers were received in England, so that Confederate sympathizers had no reliable organ to serve as a source of palatable information about events in America. Anxiously, they awaited the arrival in London of a young Mobile journalist, Henry Hotze, who had been assigned to start a newspaper, the "Index," the object of which would be to influence public sentiment in England to favor the Confederate cause.[10]

Henry Sanford did not intend that the United States should lack its own propagandists in Europe to combat those laboring for the

Confederacy. For several months he had been pleading with Seward and other influential Americans for "good speaking and writing" in England, directed toward winning the sympathies of the English masses—"a Union crusade among them." While the rebel agents had "been infernally active," he wrote, ". . . a lot of deaf and dumb officials" representing the United States were apparently "incapable of doing anything. We need active useful men over here." Late in September, Sanford wrote Seward that there was much reason to regret "that no means have been adopted to act on public opinion in Europe." Southern agents had been so successful in appealing to the selfish political and commercial interests of the British governing classes that "a great change" had been wrought in public opinion to the detriment of the United States. It was "indispensable" that the impression among the lower and middle classes of Great Britain "that there was something vital to their common interests & rights at stake in this contest" be strengthened, so that the great weight of their opinion would be brought to bear against interference.[11]

Sanford's recommendation was reinforced by Navy Captain William Walker, the State Department's top secret agent in Europe. Walker wrote that while some of the Confederate government's agents in England "were occupied in conducting its purchases and making its shipments—others *highly* gifted in their social qualities and mingling in various grades of society, adroitly enforced their views and opinions . . . , all collecting and distributing such intelligence as might best advance [their] . . . cause." It had been largely as a result of these influences, Walker asserted, that "a material change had been wrought in [British] public sentiment within a very brief period; and there was reason to apprehend that this adverse current would increase in depth and strength."[12]

In Walker's opinion official diplomatic representatives, "however eminent for their abilities, are not the persons to meet such adversaries." A United States minister would only hurt his public character by trying to encounter the Southerners on their own ground. Walker suggested meeting the "assaults of the enemy by the employment of means similar to his own." He urged "the presence in London of *several gentlemen* altogether in the confidence of the Govt, but ostensibly without any connexion with it, competent to discuss American affairs in conversation or in writing, & occupying such a position in society as would ensure their friendly reception into any circles." The dispatch of such a mission, Walker concluded, "almost certainly would be productive of immense benefit."[13]

Walker's recommendations were vigorously reinforced by such trusted envoys as George Marsh, who wrote from Turin:

> The public opinion of continental Europe on all American questions is manufactured by a few leading journals in England and France, and by the Paris and London correspondents of what may almost be called the *provincial* European press. I have no doubt that, so far as that opinion is erroneous, it might be in a great degree corrected by the employment of proper means to influence European journalism.

One such means, Marsh wrote, especially in England, would be "popular lectures or addresses by eminent American speakers."[14]

Seward's reaction to suggestions of this sort was to send off to Europe his New York political associate, Thurlow Weed; Roman Catholic Archbishop John J. Hughes of New York; and the Reverend Charles P. McIlvaine, Episcopal bishop of Ohio. Others, among them former Massachusetts Senator Robert C. Winthrop and former Secretary of State Edward Everett, declined Seward's invitations to undertake unofficial missions to England. Everett wrote Charles Francis Adams that such a mission seemed superfluous to him, for everything that he had heard and read indicated that the official duties of the American minister in London were performed by Adams "in a manner which leaves nothing to desire"; moreover, all anyone could expect to be accomplished through social influences was being effected "with equal skill and success." Everett questioned the wisdom of sending "out half a dozen *volunteers* when the *regular* service is so efficient." In this opinion James E. Harvey, American minister in Portugal, concurred. He wrote Adams that "if the gentlemen who have volunteered in these British lists could understand that the Government

& people of the United States consider themselves abundantly well represented in England, it would save many mortifications."[15]

Seward's plan "of operating on society" in London by sending unofficial emissaries seemed to Adams "of no value, and based upon a very superficial notion of the influences that go to form opinion here." Members of English upper-class society based their attitudes toward the American conflict almost exclusively on their domestic concerns. Most Englishmen of rank, Adams wrote Everett, were "oppressed with a fear of the growth of democracy mainly through the success of the American example." From this point of view, the war in the United States offered a long-awaited opportunity to destroy the specter of democracy, perhaps for many years to come. Adams doubted that British opinion in regard to the American war would "be bettered by any effort on the part of officers of the Government to amend it." Such efforts could only make matters worse.[16]

Adams was nevertheless capable of speaking out publicly in behalf of his country on the rare occasions when such speeches seemed advisable. In November, for example, he addressed almost twelve hundred persons at the London Guildhall banquet celebrating the installation of a new lord mayor. Asked at the last minute to respond on behalf of the *corps diplomatique* when the appropriate toast was drunk, Adams centered his extemporaneous remarks around the idea of "the uses of diplomacy to perpetuate peace." As one who believed that all diplomats should practice "plain straightforward dealing in good faith," he asserted, he was ever ready to "explain mistakes, to correct misrepresentations, and to retract errors in season," so that he might accomplish the primary object of his mission, which was to "perpetuate the friendly relations that have so long existed between the two countries."[17]

The reaction to Adams's first attempt at speech-making in England was almost universally favorable. His purpose of counteracting the impression, reinforced by Confederate emissaries and sympathizers, that the people of the United States were greatly hostile to England, seemed to have been at least partly attained. His address, so the Speaker of the House of Commons told him, had diminished the general impression in Great Britain "that the Americans were unreasonable in their anger with the government for the course they had taken in issuing the proclamation of neutrality." The London *Times* editorialized that "there was certainly nothing warlike about the speech by Mr. ADAMS." It had been "so highly complimentary that we could wish that America could speak to us more frequently by the mouth of her minister, and never at all in the tone common to her press and her SECRETARY OF STATE." From elsewhere in Europe came word that the speech had "been much commended for its good taste and excellent expression in the diplomatic circles." To some it seemed to have shamed Lord Palmerston into tempering his "sneering criticism" of the United States. Seward, too, approved. He wrote his London representative: "No minister ever spoke or acted more wisely in a crisis which excited deep public solicitude than you did on the occasion of the Lord Mayor's dinner."[18] The London *Times* to the contrary, Seward, too, favored peace.

XV

American "Amorality" and British Aggravation

〜✥〜

O Jonathan and Jefferson,
Come listen to my song;
   I can't decide, my word upon,
Which of you is most wrong.
      I do declare I am afraid
To say which worse behaves,
      The North, imposing bonds on Trade,
Or South, that Man enslaves.
                    PUNCH, XL (25 May 61), p. 209.

ADAMS WAS WISE in his first public address to an English audience to avoid touching on the key questions of Anglo-American relations. For powerful elements of the British press would probably have pounced on whatever he said to enhance the already serious trans-Atlantic irritation over such controversial matters as the new American protective tariff, which most Englishmen detested. During the last days of President Buchanan's administration, when the Republican tariff bill was still being debated in Congress, the British minister at Washington had been almost frantic with worry about the adverse effects it would have on English trade with the United States. At first Lyons and his German colleague, Rudolf Schleiden, minister from Bremen, had attempted to lobby against the "obnoxious" bill. After a few ineffectual gestures, however, they had limited themselves to lamenting the withdrawal from Congress of the Southern senators and representatives, which had opened the way for the easy passage of the tariff bill into law. They had decided that foreigners in Washington ought to be circumspect in opposing the measure. For in what seemed the current belligerent mood of the secretary of state, a strong official protest might have produced a diplomatic crisis. Reluctantly, Lyons had concluded that the Republicans seemed blinded by "protectionist bigotry" to the fact that not only would the new tariff act be "likely to force matters between the North and South to a crisis," but also that the maritime blockade of Southern ports, as one of the requisite results of that crisis, would put a strain on Anglo-American amity that might well become intolerable.[1]

When the details of the Morrill tariff became known in England, the British press was almost unanimous in condemning it, as were statesmen of all parties, including those otherwise friendly to the policies of the Lincoln administration. Richard Cobden, for example, wrote that "The news from America is indeed afflicting. . . . The new protectionist tariff argues an amount of ignorance and stupid suicidal selfishness such as we never dreamt of beholding triumphant in that educated community." And John Bright, blunt as always, wrote Sumner that "a more stupid and unpatriotic act was never passed than the Morrill Tariff," which had "all but destroyed" Anglo-American trade in many items, on which it had imposed additional marketing costs of up to 75 percent.[2]

During his first conversation with Adams, the British foreign minister made a special point of remonstrating against the new American tariff law; soon afterward, Prime Minister Palmerston told a prominent American banker that the whole British nation "dislike very much your Morrill tariff." As the clamor against the measure intensified throughout the United Kingdom, some leading merchants even considered that the American tariff, "having arbitrarily deprived us of the trade as it had been by custom & usage for a long time carried on with them," and considered in combination with the blockade of Southern ports, constituted "a justifiable cause for war." For Great Britain, as a manufacturing nation practically dependent upon free trade for prosperity, had a "right" to demand that her commerce not be unduly hindered by foreigners.[3]

Although a declaration of war was considered by the men of Her Majesty's ministry too extreme a response to make to the Northern tariff, they continued to be outspoken in their opposition to it. John Motley learned "on the very highest authority and from repeated conversations," as well as from reading English newspapers, "that there has been a change, a very great change, in English sympathy since the passing of the Morrill Tariff Bill. That measure has done more than any commissioner from the Southern Republic could do to alienate the feelings of the English public toward the United States. . . . If the tariff people had been acting in league with the secessionists to produce a strong demonstration in Europe in favor of the dissolution of the Union, they could not have managed better."[4]

It was the Morrill tariff that did most to undercut the arguments of those who insisted that the Civil War was a fight against Southern slavery. To many a British freetrader, there was little difference morally between slave-holding and protectionism. As *Punch* declaimed:

> We for North and South alike
>   Entertain affection;
> Those for negro slavery strike;
>   Those for forced protection.
> Yankee Doodle is the pot;
>   Southerner the Kettle;
> Equal morally, if not
>   Men of equal mettle.
> [Chorus:] Yankee Doodle, &c. . . .[5]

In reply to British and French criticism, the American secretary of state argued that the Morrill tariff act was designed by Congress to produce additional revenue rendered necessary by "new and peculiar circumstances," that the measure was not and could not be permanent, and that if it should "prove to be onerous to foreign commerce," it would, "of course, prove also to be unfruitful of revenue." In that case, he asserted, it would "be promptly modified." On the tariff issue, as on other topics, however, Seward was either disbelieved or misunderstood by most Englishmen.[6]

Such was also the case regarding the slavery question, long a topic of great interest in England.[7] For Englishmen, like American Southerners, had generally ignored the affirmations of the new Republican president, both while campaigning for election and later in his inaugural address, that he did not intend "directly or indirectly, to interfere with the institution of slavery in the States where it exists." He believed, Lincoln had asserted, that "I have no lawful right to do so, and I have no inclination to do so." Notwithstanding these disclaimers, most of the American abolitionists had supported Lincoln for election, and their support had apparently led many Englishmen to expect that, once the Republicans took office, the new administration would strike at slavery.[8]

Perhaps it would have been advantageous to American diplomacy in Europe if, once the struggle for the preservation of the Union began, it could have been made to seem primarily a war against slavery. "But to make immediate emancipation as a moral crusade the purpose of the war," Richard Henry Dana, Jr., wrote, and to "set aside the Constitution, and construct by force of arms a central government, which shall take upon itself the solution of the four million negro problem, without the assent or cooperation of the Southern whites—from that we should shrink." Most Northerners, including many of those who voted for Lincoln, apparently agreed with Dana throughout the year 1861.[9]

Adams, at first, apparently concurred in this opinion. At least he made no objection when Seward, in his initial instructions to his newly appointed minister at London, commanded that the latter "not consent to draw into debate before the British government any opposing moral principles which may be supposed to lie at the foundation of the controversy." Nor did Adams's colleague at Paris question Seward's declaration, contained in his first major instruction to Dayton, that the "condition of slavery in the several States will remain just the same," whether the slaveholders' rebellion should succeed or fail; "for the rights of the States, and the condition of every human being in them, will remain subject to exactly the same laws and forms of administration." Lincoln had "always repudiated all designs whatever . . . of disturbing the system of slavery as it is existing under the Constitution and laws." Indeed, "any such effort on his part would be unconstitutional, and all his actions in that direction would be prevented by the judicial authority, even though they were assented to by the Congress and the people."[10]

Other American diplomats in Europe, however, wanted the

Lincoln administration to announce a policy of emancipation, under the "war power," in order to win additional foreign support for the Union cause. As early as May 12, Henry Sanford wrote Seward from Paris that in order to fend off English aid to the newly formed Southern Confederacy, the United States government "MUST . . . COMMENCE AN ANTISLAVERY CRUSADE IN ENGLAND." Three months later, Cassius M. Clay wrote Seward from St. Petersburg, to advocate "treating *treason* as *treason*. . . . I declare that if a more rigid course is not adopted, we are lost! We must raise the tension of our martial courage, by a higher tone of principle —*Liberty for ourselves*—*Liberty for the slave*, in all the *rebel states*." One month later the ministers of the United States at The Hague and at Madrid both wrote Seward on the same day to plead for an overt policy of emancipation, as the only way of staving off European intervention in favor of the slaveholders' rebellion.[11]

The secretary of state, however, rejected these admonitions. While "not surprised," he wrote Carl Schurz, to learn that the United States government "might excite more fervent sympathies abroad by avowing a purpose . . . to extirpate at once an institution which is obnoxious to the enlightened censure of mankind," he indicated that the Lincoln administration did not intend to risk alienating any of the millions of loyal Americans who were staunch for the Union and the Constitution, but who would not support a war to eradicate slavery. Although the sympathy of foreigners was "eminently desirable," he wrote, "foreign sympathy, or even foreign favor, never did and never can create or maintain any State, while in every State that has the capacity to live, the love of national life is and always must be the most energetic principle which can be invoked to preserve it." Early in April, Seward had advised Lincoln that in order to hold the Union together, particularly in order to keep the border states loyal, the new administration ought to change "*the question before the Public from one upon Slavery, or about Slavery, for a question upon Union or Disunion.* In other words, from what would be regarded as a Party question to one of *Patriotism* or *Union.*" Since then the foreign policy of the United States had been based on that principle, and Seward was determined to postpone, until public opinion would sanction the step, the moment when the national government, by striking against the constitutional right of property in slaves, would supplement its basic objective, that of preserving the Union, with a second objective, that of freeing the slaves, which would necessarily involve instituting a far-reaching social and economic revolution.[12]

Perhaps the best statements about the slavery question by an American diplomat were made by John Motley. Not only did he publish an able analysis of the constitutional aspects of the problem in the London *Times* early in 1861, one which was widely respected by official England, but he followed up this public letter with private communications, both written and oral, which seem to have been given great weight among members of the British cabinet. He wrote the duke of Argyll, for example, that Lincoln's election had signaled an end to the expansion of slavery on the North American continent. Slavery would never gain another inch of territory. It was

dethroned forever from the dominion which it has exercised over American affairs for these forty years. It must remain a local, munici-pal institution henceforth, and the attempt to make it national, to spread it over the territories and over the free States, has been completely and forever foiled. But there is no intention of interfering with it in the States where it constitutionally exists, because to confiscate £400,000,000 sterling of property would be a stupendous crime, and to make such a compensation would be an impossibility.

We have gone to war to maintain the Constitution in its integrity, because we believe that, with a few trifling modifications, it would be difficult to improve upon it at present. But if the question be *death to the republic* or *death to slavery*, if the conspiracy makes a foreign alliance or protracts the anarchy and civil war into which it has plunged us beyond a reasonable time, then the great law of self-defence *will cause that sword to be drawn*, the unsheathing of which causes us all to shudder.[13]

Later, Motley told the British foreign minister that, "should there be a foreign combination against us, in the interest of cotton spinners & in defence of the slavery power, I had never heard of any person in the free states, whatever his politics, who doubted that general emancipation would be proclaimed." The protection given by the Federal Constitution to slavery in the states where it was already established would be withdrawn, and the war would be transformed into "a war to the knife, a struggle for existence," which would include an attempt to rouse the slaves against their masters. Such a servile uprising, as Motley well understood, was an idea almost as reprehensible to members of the English aristocracy as to American slaveholders. For as the earl of Clarendon put it, "a servile war might stop the cultivation of cotton & then what will become of 2 millions of people here & of our manufactures & our revenue?"[14]

Russell, like Clarendon and most other English aristocrats, did not believe that the Unionists would "ever reestablish their power." He could not comprehend why Northern abolitionists were "so anxious to restore the Union." For it was "evident that anti-slavery policy is separation policy & that if the Union is restored, all the schemes for the extension of Slavery will revive & gain fresh force. But I suppose the spirit of vengeance animates Sumner, Mrs. Stowe & all the party, & blinds them to the consequences of their acts." Gladstone, too, thought that the Union could not be restored by war. Furthermore, he was convinced that most Northerners, had they the same climatic and economic reasons to "recommend slavery in the North as now sustain it in the South," would have few qualms about reestablishing the peculiar institution "in the North itself, despite the opposition of a philanthropic minority." Hence the Civil War was *not* "a war for freedom," but only "a war without cause, . . . a foolish and wicked war," and Motley's arguments, though facile, did not remove this difficulty in the way of English sympathy for and assistance to the North.[15]

On the other hand, Argyll, who disputed Gladstone's contention that most Northerners were not antislavery in attitude, insisted that Motley was right that the Civil War *was* "one against slavery, & this is becoming progressively more evident." Cobden, also, thought that the war would result in "the freedom, sooner or later, of the slaves." The longer the conflict continued, the greater would be the "ascendency" of the abolitionist party in North America, which meant ultimately thrusting "the torch and the dagger into the negroes' hands, and the invoking of a servile insurrection on a tenfold scale of horrors to that of St. Domingo." And John Bright was likewise convinced that "the whole question is one of slavery. The North was divided between those who would abolish [it], those who would control it, and those who would tolerate it for the sake of Union. The South was and is against its abolition, and against its limitation, and prefers its perpetual existence to the Union itself." It was ridiculous, Bright added, to speak of the slaveholders as " 'Free Traders,' . . . as if the freedom of individual industry were not the basis of all freedom."[16]

Argyll, Cobden, and Bright, all three encouraged periodically by antislavery communications not only from Motley, but also from Senator Sumner, were, however, lonely voices in an England which had convinced itself, on the whole, that tariff protection in the North was morally equivalent to the existence of African Negro slavery in the South, with which, in any case, most Northerners had no desire to interfere. With the ideas and institutions of both slaveholders and Yankees equally odious, then, it had become the obvious duty of morally superior Englishmen to adopt a chilly "neutrality" between them—a "neutrality" which nevertheless seemed to Northerners often to favor their enemies.

From the point of view of the Lincoln administration, one of the most irritating aspects of British "neutrality" during the latter part of 1861 was the use of British colonies in the Western Hemisphere as depots for shipments of Confederate war supplies and as places where Southern warships found shelter and sympathy. On September 10, Seward wrote Adams that British authorities at Trinidad had allowed the C.S.S. *Sumter*, which had already captured and burned several American vessels, to remain one week in their harbor taking in provisions and coal. The British authorities had appeared "to be on amicable terms" with the insurgent officers. Adams was instructed to bring this "clear case of connivance" to the attention of the British foreign minister and ask him to promise to "prevent such occurrences in the future." In another instruction bearing the same date, the secretary of state sent Adams evidence that arms and gunpowder were being shipped from England to the British island of Nassau, thence to be run through the blockade into rebel ports. The American minister in London was ordered to request that the British foreign minister issue "proper instructions" sufficient "to prevent the exportation of contraband of war from British colonies near the United States for the use of the insurgents in the South."[17]

While awaiting a response from London, Seward spoke to Lyons about the annoyance produced in the loyal states by reports of the "friendly reception" given to the *Sumter* at Trinidad. He asked the British minister to help him ease the problem by disclaiming any intention on the part of Her Majesty's colonial authorities to give aid or sympathy to such insurgent vessels. Lyons replied, however, that he "did not know what the facts were." He told Seward that he assumed that the *Sumter* had met with the same reception that "would have been given to a United States Privateer or Man of War—and that to this we could not allow him to object."[18]

When Adams brought the two cases to the attention of the British foreign minister, he was told in reply, first, that the crown law officers had found no reason to believe that Her Majesty's Proclamation of Neutrality had been violated at Trinidad, and, second, that the British colonial secretary would be asked to investigate the allegations that Nassau was being used as a depot for the shipment of contraband of war to the Southern insurgents. Adams predicted that "the result of the promised investigation will be of much the same character with that of all its predecessors." For in response to all accusations regarding British assistance to the Confederates, "the responsibility for all Ministerial action" was "systematically devolved" upon the crown law officers, who were "seldom disposed to counsel active measures of repression, when a passive system is believed to be more agreeable." This policy, Adams added, "had the effect of rousing the selfish interests" of many Englishmen, who sought to turn the American tribulations into personal profits by trading in contraband of war. To some degree, of course, the Federal cause also benefited from this "stolid indifference" to aid rendered by British subjects to the American belligerents, but the South, lacking more, benefited more.[19]

When Seward learned that the British had again dismissed "our complaint from their consideration," he replied to Adams that "the United States cannot consent that pirates engaged in destroying it shall receive shelter and supplies in the ports of friendly nations." The Federal authorities would consider what steps ought to be taken to restore the security of American trade; meanwhile Seward hoped that the British would reconsider their stand, for, he told Lyons, England was the only nation which "admitted the enemies of the United States, without restriction, into its harbors." Other European governments "refused to allow privateers to remain for more than twenty-four hours in their ports." The secretary suggested that Lyons ask Russell to adopt the same rule for England. If "this matter could be satisfactorily settled," he told the British envoy, it would resolve "the only question we have against you," and would thus greatly improve Anglo-American relations. Lyons seemed little disposed, however, to endorse Seward's recommendation. Rather did he content himself with defending the practice of his government as doubtless following "precedents afforded by her own previous conduct in similar cases." Implied was the idea that "precedents" would rule British future behavior as well—an idea calculated to reflect the disposition of the elderly British foreign minister. For his part, Russell replied "that Mr. Seward never chooses to understand the position of Her Majesty's government." If the American secretary of state desired "that the ships of war of the Confederate States should not be allowed to stay more than twenty-four hours in a British port, he should declare it in plain terms," in which case he should also realize that any such rule should have to apply as well to the warships of the United States.[20]

That Seward did not appreciate the British position was true enough. Twice again during November he directed Adams "to recall the attention of Her Majesty's government to the question under the influence of a spirit of peace and friendship and with a desire to preserve what remains of a commerce mutually important to both countries." The secretary of state was determined to continue exerting all the pressure at his command to persuade the British to "exclude piratical vessels" from their ports—at least for longer than twenty-four hours. If the British government was "awake to the importance of averting possible conflict, and disposed to confer and act with earnestness to that end," he declared, they would take his protests seriously.[21]

The British, too, issued protests growing out of maritime activity of the American belligerents, but Seward's reactions to these protests were usually more accommodating than were Russell's frequently unobliging responses to American objections. One of the most widely publicized maritime incidents of the year involved the British merchant ship *Perthshire*, which, after being warned off Pensacola by a United States blockading vessel during May, sailed along the Gulf Coast to Mobile, where it loaded 2,240 bales of cotton and put back out to sea on June 30. Soon afterward the *Perthshire* was boarded by an officer from the U.S.S. *Massachusetts*, who took possession of the ship with a prize crew, hauled down the British flag, and sailed her back to Pensacola. There she was released by the senior naval captain present, who asserted that the ship's capture, performed by one of his subordinates, was illegal, as the *Perthshire* had sailed from Mobile before "the fifteen days allowed by the proclamation of the President of the United States for neutral vessels to depart" had expired. When the vessel finally reached her home port of Liverpool, her owner addressed a memorial to the British foreign secretary, claiming compensatory damages of £200 for the twelve days lost from the normal time of her voyage, owing to her temporary seizure by naval officers of the United States.[22]

Seward lost little time in acting to defuse British wrath over the incident. Ascertaining from the secretary of the navy that the facts alleged by the *Perthshire*'s owner were substantially correct, he promised, less than a fortnight after the British minister brought the case to his attention, that he would ask Congress to appropriate the full sum, "not an unreasonable one," claimed by the British as compensation for the vessel's interrupted voyage. At the same time he also assured Lyons that the president would admonish the

United States naval authorities "against a repetition of the errors of which you have complained." Lyons was noncommittal about the case at the time these notes were exchanged, but later, during December, after Congress had appropriated one thousand dollars to compensate the *Perthshire*'s owners for the delay in her voyage, the British minister wrote his chief in London that he supposed there was no point in objecting to the award "of such an insignificant sum in compensation for such a great injury."[23]

The *Perthshire* case was thus quietly settled out of court. This was not true of the case of the *Hiawatha*, which engendered the most intense diplomatic interest of all the so-called "prize cases" stemming from the Northern blockade of early 1861. The facts of the case were simple enough. The English bark *Hiawatha* was captured in Hampton Roads on May 20, 1861, by a Federal blockader. It had loaded a large cargo of cotton and tobacco at Richmond well after the blockade was declared for that portion of the Virginia coast on April 27 and had set sail for Liverpool after the deadline of the fifteen-day grace period granted by Seward for foreign vessels caught loading in Southern ports at the time the blockade went into effect. The vessel was sent as a prize to New York, where in due course it was condemned by a Federal district judge along with its cargo for breach of blockade. On appeal to the circuit court, the condemnation decision was affirmed, and after many months had passed it was ultimately upheld by the United States Supreme Court. Long before the final disposition of the case, however, it had produced a notable flurry of diplomatic communications across the Atlantic Ocean. At least sixteen separate dispatches, many of which were loaded with heavy enclosures, were exchanged between Lyons and Russell during the year 1861 alone regarding the *Hiawatha* case, besides considerable correspondence between those two gentlemen and the British consul at New York, who was charged with monitoring the proceedings of the prize court. Despite at least two separate opinions by the queen's advocate declaring the sentence of condemnation justified, a view supported even by the chauvinistic London *Times*, and despite a great reluctance on the part of Lyons to apply to Seward for the vessel's release, the

British foreign secretary nevertheless fired a continuous barrage of dispatches across the water to Washington repeatedly requesting his diplomatic representative there to seek the vessel's discharge "in equity," on the ground that the original blockade regulations had not been clearly enough stated to hold the *Hiawatha*'s captain at fault. Only the onset of a serious Anglo-American war scare at the end of the year brought an end to Russell's agitation of the question.[24]

Such maritime incidents as the *Hiawatha*'s seizure, as well as the Bunch affair, the port-closing act, the Mexican intervention, and many other vexatious diplomatic questions, large and small, all still being discussed early in November, led some members of the British cabinet to reconsider whether to ship more arms and troops to Canada. The prime minister worried that recent communications from Lyons had made it clear that the policy of the Washington government was "to heap indignities upon us" which the Yankees were encouraged all the more to do "by what they imagine to be the defenceless state of our North American Provinces." Palmerston called in the American minister to warn him against such further provocations, rumored to be intended by Seward, as sending a Northern warship to British waters to seize Confederate passengers from a British mail steamer. Such a step, he said, would be "highly inexpedient." Likewise, he added, the threatened dismissal of Consul Bunch would benefit no one, and would be sure to create added "agitation" in England against the United States. He could not, the premier concluded, "perceive the benefit that could ensue to either country from that."[25]

Adams countered Palmerston's remonstrance with one of his own. He "begged his Lordship to dismiss all idea that my Government was not as desirous as Her Majesty's Ministers could be to raise no needless questions of difference between the two countries. But we had a great many things to try our patience, as well as they." For example, Adams said, he was personally "vexed and annoyed" at witnessing, day by day, active English assistance to the Confederacy. Not only were there many instances of war supplies being sent to the Southern insurgents from England, but the major source of irritation, the mainstay of the slaveholders' conspiracy, "which had kept it in vigor down to this moment," was the hope of recognition by England and France. Had the United States been left utterly alone "to manage the domestic difficulty for ourselves," Adams said, "the rebellion would have burned out for want of fuel by this time. It was the faith in foreign aid that had kept it up. And the sense of this was the real and only source for what bad feeling had been roused toward England in America."[26]

When Seward read his London minister's report of his conversation with Palmerston, he wrote that he and President Lincoln were both "impressed very favorably" with Adams's expostulations. For the New Englander had spoken "the simple fact" in telling the British premier "that the life of this insurrection is sustained by its hopes of recognition in Great Britain and France. It would perish in ninety days if those hopes should cease." If a recognition of Confederate independence should ever come, Seward declared, the United States would "immediately" declare war on "all the recognizing powers." He did not suppose it possible "that the British government could fail to see this," but it had certainly appeared "inattentive to the currents that seem to be bringing the two countries into collision."[27]

A Historical Misunderstanding

*We entertain a good hope that by steadily practicing
good faith and all possible liberality towards foreign
states we shall avoid the dangers of foreign war.*
W. H. SEWARD TO NORMAN JUDD,
January 8, 1862.

SUDDENLY, collision was at hand. Two rebel diplomats, former
United States Senators James Mason and John Slidell, had been
ordered to Europe to seek diplomatic recognition in London and
Paris for the Richmond regime. Early in November, however, they
were abducted from the deck of a British mail steamer, as she lay
helpless under the guns of a Federal warship.

Outraged over this latest example of what they considered a long
series of deliberate insults, English leaders grimly prepared their
response to the American affront. From the Foreign Office an
ultimatum—demanding an apology and the restitution of the
Southern captives—sped across the Atlantic Ocean. Ordinary Englishmen, reinforced enthusiastically by an anti-American press,
stood solidly behind the hectic war preparations of their government. Meanwhile, a raging war cry reverberated across the Northern States in America, as the grandsons of the Revolutionary
generation, already in arms against the slaveholders' conspiracy,
demonstrated that their ancient Anglophobia was still very much
alive. The arrogant English had repeatedly violated their own
bogus Proclamation of Neutrality, as they struggled surreptitiously
to aid the Southerners in destroying the American Union. Now the
unofficial allies of the rebels would receive a well-deserved retribution; an Anglo-American war would be but a natural adjunct to the
American Civil War. If John Bull seemed anxious, all at once, for a
military test of strength, Brother Jonathan would demonstrate no
less eagerness for the trial.

The story of the *Trent* affair is well known. How the suspense heightened as the deadline drew near for an official American response to the British ultimatum; how military preparations in England continued at fever pitch; how Lincoln and a majority of his advisers seemed about to drift the United States into a terrible trans-Atlantic war; how the British demands were met and war avoided—all of this can be read about, at least in outline form, in almost every American history textbook.

Why did this essentially trivial misunderstanding impel the people of two great nations to ready their weapons of war? Why did the British leaders precipitately send an ultimatum to Washington without waiting for American explanations? Why did most Englishmen assume that the *Trent* seizure was a calculated official act of the American government? Why did they take it for granted that an Anglo-American war was inevitable? These are questions that most writers treating the *Trent* affair do not answer. I have answered them in this book by demonstrating that, as an editor for the *New York Times* perceived over a century ago, "the whole English press and a clique of his enemies" at home had spread the idea everywhere by the late summer of 1861 that William Henry Seward's diplomacy had been "unconciliatory and hectoring and that his aim was to unite parties at home by a war with England." Yet, as this same writer asserted, every missive sent abroad by Seward to London had been "marked by a singular forbearance and courtesy toward England." And throughout his diplomatic correspondence, Seward had unfailingly deprecated "in the strongest terms 'the evils of a foreign war.' "[1]

At the same time, his duty as secretary of state, in view of his conviction "that the life of this insurrection is sustained by its hopes of recognition in Great Britain and in France," was to do everything in his power to prevent such a recognition. Hence his deep concern over news from London that the British government, without even allowing Adams an opportunity to speak on the question, had recognized Confederate belligerent rights. As one of the British foreign minister's biographers recognized later, "We can hardly be surprised that Washington anticipated the worst consequences from the British government's action. The gulf that separates the mere rebel from the recognized belligerent is a broad one. But the line between the recognition of a belligerent and the recognition of his independence is a very thin line indeed." Hence, also, the serious nature of the Bunch case, which involved a British determination to press for American recognition of the legal right of Englishmen to deal directly with the Confederate authorities through official diplomatic channels. Fortunately, this case was resolved before it developed into a question of a defense of national *honor* on either side, but had the *Trent* affair not arisen just when it did, the Bunch matter, compounded by the seizure of additional British consular dispatch bags by American authorities on grounds similar to those on which Bunch's bag was taken from Robert Mure, might well have developed into a crisis as serious as that of the *Trent* affair, but one less capable of peaceful resolution. For the British foreign minister indicated on November 16, only eleven days before he learned of the *Trent* incident, that he was determined, with the strong support of his colleagues in the British cabinet, "to open a communication with the South." This, according to the lord chancellor, the British government had "a perfect right to do . . . where British persons & property are in question."[2]

By this time many British leaders had become exasperated with Seward, assuming (largely on the basis of misinformation forwarded by Lyons, Sumner, and W. H. Russell) that the American secretary of state was determined to goad them into a war with the United States. With such a conflict appearing progressively more inevitable, it was natural for men like Palmerston and Russell to adopt a relatively rigid stand regarding the Bunch matter, in which they considered themselves the aggrieved parties; so that if war came they would have the advantage of what they considered was a sound moral and legal position. That they did in fact intend—until the onset of the *Trent* crisis caused them somewhat to alter their attitudes—firmly to defend their "rights" in regard to the American rebellion can be demonstrated not only by recalling the positions of the leading members of the British cabinet in regard to the Bunch affair during October and November, but also by recollecting their attitudes toward the Northern blockade and toward the cotton supply question during the same period of time.

As Seward put it, there were also other "currents that seemed to be bringing the two countries into collision" toward the end of 1861. "The arms, munitions, and materials of war used by the insurgents came from Great Britain, and British merchants dispatch vessels with supplies for the insurgents to run the blockade," Seward complained. And "piratical vessels . . . preying upon our merchant marine, engaged in carrying bread to Europe" were supplied "with shelter, coal, and provisions" almost entirely in British ports. One such vessel, the *Nashville*, had received a friendly welcome in Southampton directly after destroying the Northern merchant vessel *Harvey Birch*—an incident that might itself have led to a war crisis had it not been eclipsed by the simultaneous explosion of British wrath over the *Trent* incident. Meanwhile, in England there was great indignation, and not a little bellicosity, over the imprisonment in the United States of British subjects accused of sedition and over the way in which the Federal blockade of Southern ports interfered with the British cotton trade. The evident determination of British leaders forcibly to resist the imposition of a Northern port-closing act on the Confederate cotton ports, even at the price of trans-Atlantic war, indicates the depth of resentment in commercial England over the decision of the Lincoln administration to employ blockade as a weapon of war against the slaveholding insurrectionists.[3]

Another source of Anglo-American contention as the year 1861 ended was the Mexican intervention, a prime example of the tendency of European governmental leaders to interfere in the affairs of less affluent and less powerful people all over the world. Such meddlesomeness was a typical trait among the leading English politicians, only a few of whom were likely to agree with the secretary for war, who wished for "somnolence" in the Foreign Office on the ground that the British "position abroad is an excellent one, if we did not spoil it by perpetual meddling." In the case of the Mexican intervention, however, the long-range impact on Anglo-American relations was probably advantageous to the United

States. For the English, the French, and the Spanish became so tightly entangled in an overseas enterprise (which began with the diplomats representing each of the three governments suspicious of the intentions of their foreign counterparts) that when the Triple Alliance eventually flew apart over Mexico, it was unlikely that it would be reconstituted for the purpose of aggression against the United States. And in the meantime the Mexican adventure probably consumed much of the interventionist enthusiasm and energy available in Europe for application in the New World during the early 1860s—not to mention military resources that in a moment of ill-feeling against the United States, Europeans might have been tempted to use against her. At the time of the *Trent* affair, for example, the British government had a considerable naval force fully occupied in the expedition against Vera Cruz, which it would have been inconvenient to redirect against New York or Boston.[4]

The *Trent* affair was a needless occurrence. It grew out of unwarranted prejudice and misunderstanding on both sides, and a hypersensitive tendency of British leaders to react with a show of military force to the slightest threat to the commercial interests of British subjects. To men like Palmerston, Russell, Newcastle, and Lyons, most Americans were bullies—brash, boorish, crafty, pushy, cowardly, and entirely unamenable to logical argument or conciliatory persuasion where British interests were concerned. Hence a display of superior force was thought to be the best device for coping with the Yankees, toward whose resources, especially cotton, the British tended to take a proprietary view. Meanwhile, the British aristocracy hungered for the demise of democracy in North America. From the vantage point of an American, the English seemed to have changed very little since 1775; Burke and Fox had given way to Bright and Cobden, who were no more influential in opposing the policies of Palmerston than the Whigs of almost one century before had been in resisting those of Lord North.

To men who seemed at times to view the United States as still practically a British colony, the refusal of a statesman like Seward to take dictation from London about how international aspects of the American economy—whether regarding tariff laws or regarding cotton exports—should be managed was considered irrational and the acme of "arrogance" or "belligerence." How could any American possibly conceive of his nation having interests contrary to those of Great Britain? Yankees, as Palmerston wearily observed, were "so difficult to deal with." They persisted in making "questions with foreign governments, and especially with the English government, subservient to party purposes." In other words, the Americans tended to give first priority to their own internal needs, rather than to the desires of foreign rivals. Truly mad behavior—from Palmerston's point of view.[5]

Palmerston's opinion of leadership in Washington was hardly improved by his reading of reports from his representative in the United States. During October, Lyons had "reminded" his superiors in London that the British were not dealing

> with a country in which a few Statesmen decided what was for the interest of the community, and guided public opinion by their superior wisdom, talents and authority. Here the government was in the hands of what are called in America "politicians," men in general of second rate station and ability, who aim at little more than at divining and pandering to the feeling of the mob of voters. . . . The present Congress, as well as the Cabinet, is composed of men whose political career has come to depend upon the prosecution of the war to extremities. . . . The party in power would be more likely to be overthrown by the disasters which must immediately follow a war with Europe, than to be drawn from their posts by public opinion, in time to prevent their imprudently engaging in one.[6]

From the time of his arrival in the United States, Lyons repeatedly reported that a "mob" dictated the decisions of the host government—which made it necessary to deal with that government cautiously but firmly—in the same way that a constable might quell a riot of London laborers. Lyons's letters from Washington reflect a vision of himself as a skillful diplomat successfully coping with irresponsible, half-educated semi-barbarians who constantly sought to trap or cow him and thus to injure his country through him. Persistent, cool, firm, and vigilant, he struggled on at his isolated post, honestly believing, as he told Chase on the first day of

1862, "that his conduct had always been that of a Peacemaker." Yet apart from his own vision of himself stands the reality—of an envoy who one year after his arrival in Washington testified to his sister that he did not get along well with Americans and had failed to make any friends at all—and of a diplomat who convinced his superiors in London that the American secretary of state was an insulting, arrogant warmonger, when nothing could have been further from the truth. Had the *Trent* affair erupted into war, Lyons—patient, courteous, dutiful, and intensely patriotic though he was—would have shared the responsibility for the debacle.[7]

Nor would Palmerston and Russell have been without their large share of responsibility for such a tragic culmination of a year of miscalculation and misunderstanding. Both cabinet leaders, it will be remembered, had created a rousing commotion about Seward's demand that Consul Bunch, after taking a first step toward opening diplomatic relations with the Confederate government, be removed from office at Charleston, and they had quickly endorsed Lyons's call for more troops and arms to be rushed to Canada in response. Yet, as Gladstone put it privately to a Cabinet colleague, "a Consul is not a diplomatic or political officer and does not represent his country; and if this be so I cannot readily understand how even an unreasonable request for the removal of a Consul can afford a ground of military movement of this critical kind."[8] Even assuming Seward had been wrong in thinking Bunch was up to mischief in carrying out his "negotiation" with the Richmond rebels, his act in recalling his exequatur hardly justified the great flourish of military might that followed. Yet the British public, conditioned by a venal press, continued to think of *Seward* as unduly bellicose and the English leaders as paragons of wisdom and self-restraint. Some Americans even found it possible to agree with them.[9]

"The government at Washington," wrote Lyons, "and indeed all the military commanders, assume and exercise the right all over the country to arrest any persons, to keep them in confinement without assigning any cause, and to impose such terms as they please as conditions of release. . . . The government appears to assume what powers it pleases; the judicial authorities to be submissive or helpless; and the people to look on with singular complacency." What Lyons objected to, of course, was not that the "liberties" of Americans were lessened by the wartime emergency, but that some British subjects were caught in the massive dragnet operation designed to take subversives and traitors out of circulation. The *Trent* affair was a sore point for Englishmen in part because it seemed to involve the most insulting variety of arbitrary arrest. Yet when one considers that Seward had eventually released every person claiming British protection whose case had been brought to his attention by Lyons, one wonders why the assumption was so widespread in England that the American secretary of state would reject the representations of the British minister in the case of Mason, Slidell, and their two secretaries.[10]

The Lincoln administration's practice of imprisoning persons suspected of sedition without allowing writs of *habeas corpus* seemed in England to confirm the existence of a pervasive militarism in the United States. In combination with the already present mob-rule democracy, this aroused blood-hunger appeared to point in only one direction—to Canada. Governor General Charles S. Monck and Colonial Secretary Newcastle traded letters in which the former warned of an American "intention of cherishing their grudge towards us with a view to a rupture at some more convenient season to themselves," while the latter cautioned that it was "of great importance that our North American possessions should not again allow themselves to be caught in a state of utter unpreparedness, especially now that their neighbours will be in possession of an organized army in at any rate a *certain* condition of discipline and order." Even the American minister in London admitted that he had more fear of the young men of the Northern States "becoming too good than too bad soldiers."[11]

Although some Englishmen still actually worried that the Northerners and Southerners might reunite for the purpose of a joint assault on British colonies in the New World, far more Britishers believed that the Civil War would end with the North unable "to reconstruct the Union upon its former footing," as Lewis put it, at which point the Yankees would redirect their huge hordes of soldiers northward to compensate themselves in Canada. It is difficult to find many Englishmen who realized, as did Cobden, that each major war tends to "be terminated by its own self-destroying & exhaustive process," and that, if not fueled from some outside source, the American Civil War would also run down of its own accord. Besides, if it was true that a Northern failure to subdue the slaveholders would automatically pose a threat to Canada, then why should Englishmen not support the Union cause, in order to ensure the conquest of the South, the reconstruction of which would fully engage all the remaining aggressive energies of the North?[12]

Instability on the Continent and the precarious political position of the Palmerston ministry were both restraining forces to hold back the British government from the kind of overt interference in the Civil War that would bring on a declaration of war from the United States, but once the *Trent* incident took place the anti-French psychosis that had fueled an armaments race with the government of Napoleon III helped to drive the British cabinet into a militaristic response, while their insecure political position made it difficult for cabinet leaders, even if they wished, to resist the public clamor for war.

As the British political leaders were militaristic, so were they legalistic in their approach to the "American Question." Prior to the seizure of Mason and Slidell this near-obsession with the literal application of law to Anglo-American controversies tended to prevent precipitation in dealing with the Yankees, as the law officers apparently had to be consulted in each case before a move could be made, but once these learned counselors had pronounced the *Trent* seizure an "*outrage*," it became very difficult to resist the subsequent rush to arms or to deal diplomatically with the crisis.

In his *Recollections*, the British foreign minister recounted what happened at the outset of the "calamitous" American Civil War. "Lord Campbell, then Lord Chancellor," Russell related, "was of opinion that the Government could not do otherwise than recognise the belligerent rights of the Southern States, . . . We, therefore, proclaimed neutrality." This was indicative of Russell's almost blind faith in the opinions of lawyers on what were essentially political questions. Russell was not alone in this. For one who closely scrutinizes the reactions of most of the members of Palmerston's ministry to changing events in America during 1861 soon discovers that at every crisis, indeed at almost every hint of any disagreement whatever between Americans and Englishmen, the British leaders seem instinctively to have solicited opinions from the crown law officers before deciding what course to take. Hence the policy finally adopted was invariably based on narrow (and often archaic) legalistic considerations rather than on those of either political realities or humanitarian concern.[13]

To almost every American complaint, Russell's characteristic reply was equivalent to what he told Adams in June; namely, "That in the present case, and in all others, Her Majesty's government would adhere strictly to the law," which the foreign minister believed was the policy "most likely to afford a solution of the difficult questions which might from time to time arise, and perhaps threaten to disturb the friendly relations of the two countries." Had these "difficult questions" pertained only to the well-established municipal laws of a single nation, perhaps Russell's formula would have worked reasonably well. But international disputes could not be settled solely by references to international law, a field of jurisprudence even more unsettled one century ago than today, in which many traditional precepts of maritime law in particular, formulated at a time when all ships were wooden and propelled by sails and oars, had limited application to situations involving steam-powered, screw-driven, iron-clad vessels. This tendency to cling blindly to precedents out of the past, without considering political realities and changing technologies, was one of the major causes of Anglo-American diplomatic tension during 1861.[14]

The greatest mistake derived directly from this attitude was the precipitate issuance of the queen's neutrality proclamation on May 13, 1861. Probably it would have been necessary to issue such a proclamation later on. But the unseemly haste with which that document was composed and announced, despite the lack of adequate information from America on which to base it, was what irritated the great majority of Northerners and caused them to suspect that ulterior motives lay behind the apparent eagerness of the English to grant the Southern secessionists full belligerent status. Having been issued as a matter of *policy*, the queen's proclamation afterwards was binding upon all her subjects as a matter of law. As an ordinance designed to prevent Her Majesty's subjects from aiding either side in the American Civil War, it was shot through with loopholes, as Confederate agent James D. Bulloch soon delightedly discovered. But as a barrier preventing any flexibility in carrying on Anglo-American diplomatic relations, at a time when the need for ingenuity in making adjustments was crucial, the queen's proclamation was remarkably effective.

Yet in regard to a proposed Northern port-closing act, which the British vehemently opposed, Lyons wrote that if Lincoln and Seward really desired to maintain a legitimate blockade under international law, despite possible congressional legislation requiring the substitution of a port-closing law, "they will find the means of overcoming any legal impediment to doing so." Neither the British minister in Washington, nor his superiors in London, ever seemed to consider that this attitude of "where there is a will, there is a way" justified Seward's assumption that if the British really *wanted* to stop shipments of munitions from England to the Southern Confederacy, and the building of Confederate warships in British ports, their officials could easily find the means of terminating these activities, irrespective of the technicalities of the British Foreign Enlistment Act revived by the queen's neutrality proclamation.

The political leaders of Great Britain were, however, not the only statesmen of the period who lacked the necessary imagination to deal adequately with the international aspects of the American Civil War. Toward the end of 1861, Adams wrote disconsolately from London:

> What has become of our civilians? Is there not one who is willing to raise this controversy to its proper level? I see in the newspapers nothing but the wretched details of the immediate conflict. The President has never yet placed before the country the question in any

other light than that of a construction of law. . . . This conflict, if it means anything at all, involves the theory of the rights of man. It touches the interests of all the generations yet unborn. It justifies or it condemns the whole theory of human freedom. People in Europe open their eyes in wonder and ask what it means. . . .

The truth is that there is a want in America of some clear-spoken voice on this subject. We are befogged with constitutional questions, that only obscure the vision of people outside of the ring.[15]

Of course there *had* been all along one "clear-spoken voice" on the "irrepressible conflict," who almost one dozen years before had warned those who treated the great sectional controversy over slavery as basically a legal question that there was a "higher law" than the man-made American Constitution. Early in 1861, while expressing opposition to the queen's neutrality proclamation, Seward explicitly declined to offer "any argument of fact or of law in support of the position we have thus assumed." Rather, he said, was the basic Union position derived from "the instinct of self-defense, the primary law of human action, not more the law of individual than of national life." Repeatedly he informed the British that in its struggle the United States stood "simply on the principle of self-preservation, and . . . our cause will involve the independence of nations and the rights of human nature." The question was one "of the integrity, which is nothing less than the life, of the republic itself."[16]

The United States government, Seward asserted, was doing "just what Great Britain . . . would do if a domestic insurrection should attempt to detach Ireland, or Scotland, or England from the United Kingdom." The policy of the United States government, therefore, was "based on interests of the greatest importance . . . , while the policy [toward the United States] of foreign States rests on ephemeral interests of commerce or of ambition merely." Such nations would "do wisely by leaving us to manage and settle this domestic controversy in our own way." Should the British, in particular, side with the Southern insurrectionists, a war "not unlike" the one that occurred "between the same parties . . . at the close of the last century" would ensue. The "fountains of discontent" lay deep beneath the temporarily placid surface of European society. "If they should be reached" by the expansion of the American Civil War into a trans-Atlantic clash, no man could "tell how or why they could be closed. It was foreign intervention that opened and that alone could open similar fountains in the memorable French revolution."[17]

Even should foreign intervention make possible "permanent dismemberment of the American Union," such an eventuality would only mean "perpetual war" between the Northern and the Southern states. Meanwhile, the so-called "confederacy . . . must, like any other new state, seek to expand itself northward, westward, and southward. What part of this continent or of the adjacent islands would be expected to remain in peace?" International trade would be permanently disrupted. In a hitherto quiet and relatively isolated sector of the world, great standing armies and navies would threaten stability and continually portend a renewal of trans-Atlantic conflict.[18]

Historically, it had long been an "injurious trait" of civil wars "to subvert the good understanding and break up the relations between the distracted state and friendly nations, and to involve them, sooner or later, in war." The British were already aiding "pirates" engaged in waging war against the United States by granting them shelter and supplies, and they were also allowing contraband of war and ships of war to originate in England for use against that same friendly country. "The inefficiency of the British laws," Seward declared, "to prevent violations of our rights is deeply to be regretted." If Great Britain wished for the restoration of peace and prosperity on the North American continent, so that current disruptions of her trade might end, she could "most effectually contribute to their restoration by manifesting her wishes for the success of this government in suppressing the insurrection as speedily as possible." When a civil war broke out in Canada in 1838, the secretary of state added, the United States government enacted legislation "which effectually prevented any intervention . . . by American citizens." Now it was time for the British government to enact similar "special legislation."[19]

As for himself, Seward was willing to let history judge his behavior as secretary of state. He had long believed that it was

> a popular fallacy about diplomatists, as about lawyers, that they gain their ends by deceit and chicanery. On the contrary, the best and highest diplomacy is marked by extreme frankness. No man has to weigh his words so carefully as the diplomatist. He must say nothing that he does not mean. He must say nothing that his Government and his people are not prepared to stand by. To utter even a sentence, in the way of deception or initimidation, which his country will not maintain at the cannon's mouth, is to pave the way for his own or his country's humiliation.

In conducting the diplomatic relations of the United States with Great Britain during 1861, Seward wrote, he had been "under the necessity of consulting the temper of parties and people on this side of the water, quite as much as the temper of parties and people in England." He could not have maintained his credibility at home if he had been too "tame" in dealing with the British. Nevertheless, he was "willing to let my treatment of the British nation go on record with the treatment of this nation by the British Ministry, and abide the world's judgment of the question on which side greater forbearance and courtesy have been exercised."[20]

By the end of 1861 those of Seward's contemporaries who were not his political enemies were prepared to concede his great diplomatic ability. Admiringly, the youngest of the president's private secretaries scribbled what *should* have been a prophetic ode

To WILLIAM H. SEWARD
. . . And so, a generous people, at the last
Will hail the power they did not comprehend,
Thy fame will broaden through the centuries;
As storm, and billowy tumult overpast,
The moon rules calmly o'er the conquered seas.

JOHN HAY
Washington, December, 1861[21]

Abbreviations

ALP	Papers of Abraham Lincoln
AP	Papers of Adams family
AT	Archives of the *Times*
BM	British Museum
BPCUS, G&B	Belgian Political Correspondence, United States, General and Bound
CP	Papers of George William Frederick Villiers, 4th earl of Clarendon
ESD	Dispatches of Edouard Stoeckl
FMAE, AD	Archives of the French Ministry of Foreign Affairs, including "Archives diplomatiques, Angleterre"
FMAE, MD	Archives of the French Ministry of Foreign Affairs, including "Memoires et Documents, Papiers de Thouvenel"
FO	British Foreign Office
GCLP	Papers of Sir George Cornewall Lewis
HL (or HM)	Manuscripts of Charles Sumner, Francis Lieber, and Thomas Dudley, Huntington Library
HSSP	See SaP
HWLP	Papers of Henry W. Longfellow
JBP	Papers of John Bigelow
JMMP	James Murrary Mason Papers
JSPP	James Shepherd Pike Papers
LC	Library of Congress
LP	Papers of Richard Bickerton Pemell Lyons, 1st earl Lyons
MHSP	Massachusetts Historical Society *Papers*
MLN	Papers of Sir Alexander Milne
NA	National Archives
NeC	Papers of Henry Pelham Fiennes Pelham Clinton, 5th duke of Newcastle

Abbreviations

ORA	*War of the Rebellion: Official Records of the Union and Confederate Armies*
ORN	*Official Records of the Union and Confederate Navies in the War of the Rebellion*
OsC	Papers of John Evelyn Denison, viscount Ossington
PP	Papers of Henry John Temple, 3d viscount Palmerston
PRO	Public Record Office, London
RCP	Papers of Richard Cobden
RCSA	Records of the Confederate States of America
RHDP	Papers of Richard Henry Dana, Jr.
RSD	Dispatches of Rudolf Schleiden
SaP	Papers of Henry Shelton Sanford
SeP	Papers of William H. Seward
WP	Papers of Thurlow Weed

Notes

PREFACE

*Frederick W. Seward, *Seward at Washington* II, 475.

CHAPTER I: EUROPE INTERFERES

1. The most recent full-scale biography of Seward is by Glyndon Van Deusen. It is a much better work than the biography by Frederick Bancroft, long the standard life. See also the three-volume biography of his father by Frederick W. Seward, which includes an autobiographical sketch by Seward himself. Short studies of Seward's life have been written by George Baker; Edward Hale, Jr.; Thornton Lothrop; Henry Temple (published in vol. 7 of the series: "The American Secretaries of State and Their Diplomacy," ed. by Samuel F. Bemis); and Gordon Warren (published in vol. 1 of *Makers of American Diplomacy*, ed. by Frank Merli and Theodore Wilson).

2. Seward no. 14 to Adams, 3 June 61, NA; Schleiden no. 30 to Bremen Senate, 4 Mar 61, RSD, LC. Lincoln told a visitor who attempted to influence his thinking about Anglo-American relations that "it does not so much signify what I think; you must persuade Seward to think as you do." (*Correspondence of Motley* II, 159.)

3. "Every friend of despotism," wrote an English journalist to an American friend, "rejoices at your misfortune; it points the moral and adorns the tale in every aristocratic salon. . . ." The "immortal smash" of Southern secession had finally demonstrated "the failure of republican institutions in time of pressure." (W. H. Russell to J. Bigelow, 4 Feb and 14 Apr 61, JBP, NYPL.)

4. Moran, Journal, 820; Adams, Diary, 27 May 61, R76, AP; *Hansard's*, 3d Ser., CLXIII, 134.

5. Maxwell, *Clarendon* II, 237; Bell, *Palmerston* and Guedalla,

Palmerston, both of which allude frequently to Palmerston's free-trade sympathies.

6. *Seward at Washington* I, 435.

7. Bigelow, *Retrospections* I, 365; Moran, *Journal*, 417, 419, 495n, 769n, 774n, 808; Seward to Gen. A. Porter, and Seward to G. Harrington, both 19 Dec 61, in "Letters Sent Regarding Prisoners of War and Intercepted Messages, Aug. 1861–Feb. 1863," RG59, NA; *New York Times*, 8 Apr 61, p. 4; Owsley, *King Cotton Diplomacy*, 521; *Illustrated London News* XXXIX, no. 1106 (31 Aug 61), p. 209; Sanford to Seward, 16 Aug 61, SeP; and R. H. Dana III, *Hospitable England*, 126–27.

8. Moran, *Journal*, 799, 806, 808, 837; and C. L. Wilson to Seward, 11 Sept 61, SeP. But see also Newcastle to Head, 25 Mar 61, NeC.

9. A few examples are referred to in ORN, Ser. 2, III, 385; and Moran, *Journal*, 157n, 796, 799, 903, 1330–31, 1361.

10. *New York Times*, 26 Apr 61, p. 2.

11. *Message of the President*, 31–33; Stoeckl nos. 11, 15, 18 to Gortchakov, 26 Feb and 12 and 25 Mar 61, ESD, LC; Cuelebrouck no. 148 to de Vrière, BPCUS, G&B, roll 6; Mercier nos. 19, 23, 25, 29 to Thouvenel, 7 Jan and 11 and 25 Feb and 29 Mar 61, vol. 124, FMAE, AD, EU; and Lyons no. 123 to Russell, 30 Mar 61, FO115/252, substantially corroborated by Stoeckl no. 23 to Gortchakov, 2 Apr 61, ESD, LC, and Cuelebrouck no. 148 to de Vrière, BPCUS, G&B, roll 6. See also Lyons nos. 15, 32, 78, 94, 101, 126 to Russell, respectively, 15 and 29 Jan, and 26 Feb, and 12 and 18 Mar, and 1 Apr 61, all in FO115/251–52; and Lyons to Russell, 6 May 61, PRO30/22/35; Head to Lewis, 17 and 24 Feb and 25 Mar 61, GCLP; and Head to Newcastle, 1 Mar 61, NeC; W. H. Russell, *My Diary*, 40, 55, 60; M. Morris to J. C. B. Davis, 18 Apr 61, AT; *Correspondence of Motley* II, 143; F. Lieber to S. B. Ruggles, 24 May 61, Lieber Papers, LC; and Stoeckl no. 23 to Gortchakov, 2 Apr 61, ESD, LC. Anyone who scans the Washington and New York newspapers for the month of March, 1861, finds both ideas—that the restoration of the Union was not probable, and that Lincoln lacked a policy for meeting the secession crisis—reflected in issue after issue.

12. Lincoln's *Works* IV, 316; *Albany Evening Journal*, 30 Mar 61, p. 2; Lyons no. 125 to Russell, 1 Apr 61, FO115/252.

13. Faulkner no. 108 to Black, 4 Mar 61, NA; *New York Times*, 2 and 3 Apr 61, both p. 1. See also *Albany Evening Journal*, 3 Apr 61, p. 2.

14. Mercier no. 29 to Thouvenel, 29 Mar 61, vol. 124, FMAE, AD, EU;

Lyons no. 123 to Russell, 30 Mar 61, FO115/252; Stoeckl no. 23 to Gortchakov, 2 Apr 61 ESD, LC; and Cuelebrouck no. 148 to de Vrière, 30 Mar 61, BPCUS, G&B, roll 6; Thomas R. R. Cobb to Marion Cobb, 18 Feb 61, T. Cobb Papers, Special Collections, University of Georgia.

15. Bancroft, *Seward* II, 135n; Stoeckl nos. 20, 23 to Gortchakov, 28 Mar and 2 Apr 61, ESD, LC.

16. Moran, *Journal*, 804.

17. Russell to Lyons, 16 Feb 61, LP.

18. Lyons to Russell, 18 Mar 61, PRO30/22/35.

19. W. H. Russell, *My Diary*, 40. Russell, already famous as the first professional British "war correspondent" for his dispatches from the Crimean War theater, was sent to America by his managing editor to tour the country and supplement the reports of the *Times*' regular correspondent in New York, who was thought to be too pro-Northern for true objectivity. (M. Morris to J. C. B. Davis, 22 Feb 61, AT.)

20. Schleiden no. 23 to Bremen Senate, RSD, LC. Lyons and Seward occasionally used Schleiden as a go-between. (See, for example, Schleiden to Lyons, 11 Feb and 21 Apr 61, LP.)

21. Newton, *Lyons* I, 15–16; *Seward at Washington* I, 345, 377; Van Deusen, *Seward*, 257; cf. Mercier no. 22 to Thouvenel, 1 Feb 61, vol. 124, FMAE, AD, EU.

22. Lyons no. 40 to Russell, 4 Feb 61, FO115/251; Newton, *Lyons* I 15–16; Lyons to Russell, 4 and 12 Feb 61, PRO30/22/35; cf. Mercier no. 22 to Thouvenel, 1 Feb 61, vol. 124, FMAE, AD, EU.

23. Lyons to Russell, 2 May 61, PRO30/22/35; Mercier no. 29 to Thouvenel, 29 Mar 61, vol. 124, FMAE, AD, EU; Stoeckl no. 35 to Gortchakov, 11 May 61, ESD, LC. The peculiar story of Sumner's relations with Seward during 1861 has been alluded to most fully in Donald, *Sumner* II, 18–39, *passim*, but I am unable to agree with such statements as "under Sumner's watchful eye [Seward] grew 'mild and gentle' in his conduct toward foreign powers." Donald's two most important sources for his account of the Seward-Sumner relationship during this period are Sumner's letter to R. H. Dana, Jr., 14 Apr 61, RHDP, and the "Journal" of Henry W. Longfellow, 29 Apr and 13 May 61, HWLP. Both of these sources show that Sumner criticized the new secretary of state for "insincerity" in dealing with foreign powers, but they do not deal with Seward's alleged bellicosity. For evidence of Sumner's extensive influence on Lyons, see W. H. Russell, *My Diary*, 54, 68; Lyons nos. 206, 209 to Russell, 20 and 23 May 61, both FO115/253, and Newton, *Lyons* I, 41. I

have dealt with aspects of the Seward-Sumner relationship elsewhere in this book.

24. Lyons no. 59 to Russell, 12 Feb 61, FO115/251.

25. Lyons to Russell, 26 Mar 61, PRO30/22/35.

26. *Ibid.*; Stoeckl no. 20 to Gortchakov, 28 Mar 61, ESD, LC. Most historians accept Lyons's account of Seward's behavior during his first few months as secretary of state and consequently describe the secretary of state as discourteous and belligerent. The after-dinner conversation of Mar. 25 is frequently cited as a case in point, and Lyons's description of that occasion is presented as evidence of Seward's violent tendencies. It was then, according to Lyons, that Seward announced a "paper blockade" of the Southern ports, and afterwards "went off into a defiance of Foreign Nations, in a style of braggadocio. . . . Finding he was getting more and more violent and noisy, and saying things which it would be more convenient for me not to have heard, I took a natural opportunity of turning, as host, to speak to some of the ladies in the room." In Mercier's report of the same incident, Seward "boasted" to Lyons, Stoeckl, and himself "that the most felicitous event for America, at this moment," would be for the European powers to dare to involve themselves in the internal struggle in the United States. If, as a consequence of such activities, Seward asserted, "the Union were dissolved, not a government in Europe would remain standing." (Mercier to Thouvenel, 26 Mar 61, vol. 13, Papiers de Thouvenel, FMAE, MD.) Mercier's unhappiness in his current diplomatic assignment and his avid desire to be recalled from Washington, as well as his strong anti-Northern bias (see Blumenthal, *France and the United States*, 87–90), hardly had him in a frame of mind to draw any but the most unfavorable conclusions from Seward's words. Happily, testimony is available from another witness to this conversation between Seward and Lyons. According to Stoeckl, it was *Lyons* who was vehement and threatening, while Seward remained calm. The Russian minister, who had no particular liking for Seward, wrote his government that when the American secretary of state announced a probable blockade of the Southern coast, a "rather spirited discussion took place between him and the English Minister." Seward said: " 'I tell you, gentlemen, that if civil war should break out, all commercial relations with the Southern ports will be interrupted.' " Lyons complained that such a step " 'would be injurious in the highest degree to the English commerce,' " whereupon Seward replied: " 'We are sorry, but you will have to do without commerce and cotton for a while.' " Lyons then "abandoned his habitual

reserve, and answered that England could not do without cotton and that she would have it, one way or the other. Mr. Seward gave no reply but allowed these words to bombard him without evoking the least show of emotion." The only other report of this conversation which I have seen —that of the Belgian envoy—seems to have come originally from Mercier. Cuelebrouck wrote that when Seward announced "a blockade of all the Southern ports," Lyons replied "loudly: 'the only thing that I can say to you is that we must have cotton and we shall have it!' " It only remains to inquire: was it Seward or was it Lyons who was bellicose in this conversation? (Lyons to Russell, 26 Mar 61, PRO30/22/35; Stoeckl no. 20 to Gortchakov, 28 Mar 61, ESD, LC; Cuelebrouck no. 152 to de Vrière, 7 Apr 61, BPCUS, G&B, roll 6.)

27. Lyons no. 123 to Russell, 30 Mar 61, FO115/252; Mercier no. 29 to Thouvenel, 29 Mar 61, vol. 124, FMAE, AD, EU. The British consul at Charleston, S. C., advised Lyons that the Southern commissioners should *not* be warmly welcomed in England. "They go," Robert Bunch wrote, "believing in their inmost hearts that we cannot do without their confounded cotton—and that we will do anything or yield anything to get it. This is not a flattering estimate of us." (Bunch to Lyons, 31 Mar 61, LP.)

28. Russell, *My Diary*, 61.

29. *Seward at Washington* I, 534.

30. Lincoln's *Works* IV, 317–18.

31. *Ibid.*, 318.

32. *Ibid.*

33. *Ibid.*, 316–17. Lincoln allegedly told John Hay about this time: "My policy is to have no policy." (Quoted repeatedly in Donald, *Lincoln Reconsidered*, e.g., 18, 131.)

34. Seward's object in persuading Lincoln and the rest of the cabinet to establish the blockade, the secretary of the navy quoted him as saying, was to *avoid* complications that might involve the United States in a foreign war. (Welles, *Lincoln and Seward*, 122–24.) A press dispatch from Washington, dated Apr. 4, and headlined "A GOVERNMENT POLICY AT LAST," asserted that "the President has come slowly up to realize the necessity of decisive and vigorous action. . . . Every port of importance, south of Charleston, which has inland communication, will be blockaded. . . . By order of the President all further appointments of Consuls are postponed for several weeks." (*New York Times*, 5 Apr 61, pp. 1, 4.)

35. Lyons no. 169 to Russell, 2 May 61, FO115/253; Lyons to Russell, 23 Apr 61, PRO30/22/35; Russell to Lyons, 4 May 61, PRO30/22/96.

36. Lyons nos. 171, 206 to Russell, 2 and 20 May 61, both FO115/253; Lyons to Russell, 15 and 27 Apr and 2 May 61, PRO30/22/35. The colleague was probably Senator Sumner.

37. Lyons to Russell, 6 May 61, PRO30/22/35; *New York Times*, 15 May 61, p. 9, and 22 May 61, p. 1, and 23 May 61, p. 5, and 26 May 61, p. 5, and 31 May 61, p. 1; Washington *Evening Star*, 15 May 61, p. 1, and 6, 8, and 24 June 61, all p. 2.

38. Lyons no. 183 to Russell, 6 May 61, FO115/253; Mercier no. 33 to Thouvenel, 26–27 Apr 61, vol. 124, FMAE, AD, EU. Lyons and Mercier were close personal friends and their relationship was based more on mutual trust than is usual among diplomats representing rival nations. (Lyons to his sister, 10 June 61, LP.)

39. Seward nos. 21, 42 to Adams, 19 June and 21 July 61, NA.

CHAPTER II: WARNINGS OF WAR FROM WASHINGTON

1. Palmerston to Russell, 19 Jan 1841, PRO30/22/4.
2. Palmerston to Russell, 10 Mar 61, PRO30/22/21.
3. Palmerston to Russell, 18 Feb 61, PRO30/22/21; Palmerston to Newcastle, 24 May 61, Add. MS 48,582, BM; Russell to Lyons, 6 and 20 Apr 61, both PRO30/22/96; Stacey, *Canada and the British Army*, 118. Reports from Sir Edmund Head, who had been governor general of Canada since 1854, reinforced Lyons's warnings. (Head to G. C. Lewis, 17 Feb 61, GCLP; Head to Newcastle, 18 Feb 61, NeC; Newcastle to Head, 25 Mar 61, NeC; Newcastle minute dtd. 14 May 61 on F.O. to C.O., 13 May 61, CO42/629.)
4. Russell to Lyons, 21 and 25 May 61, both PRO30/22/96.
5. Palmerston to Newcastle, 24 May 61, and Palmerston to Somerset, 26 May 61, both Add. MS 48,582, BM; Palmerston to Russell, 31 May 61, PRO30/22/21; Palmerston to Russell, 23 May 61, PRO30/22/35.
6. Palmerston to Newcastle, 24 May 61, Palmerston to Herbert, 24 May 61, and Palmerston to Somerset, 26 May 61, all in Add. MS 48,582, BM; Russell to Palmerston, 21 May 61, PRO30/22/35; Newcastle to Palmerston, 25 May 61, NeC.
7. Faulkner no. 119 to Seward, 15 Apr 61, NA.
8. Dallas no. 330 to Seward, 9 Apr 61, NA; Russell no. 89 to Lyons, 12 Apr 61, FO115/240/I.
9. Seward no. 4 to Adams, 27 Apr 61 and Seward no. 7 to Dayton,

4 May 61, both NA; Lyons no. 170 to Russell, 2 May 61, FO115/253; *New York Times*, 6 May 61, pp. 1, 4, and 8 May 61, p. 1.

10. Appleton (St. Petersburg) no. 16 to Seward, 8 Apr 61, and Dallas no. 333 to Seward, 2 May 61, both NA; *New York Times*, 17 May 61, p. 5.

11. Faulkner no. 119 to Seward, 15 Apr 61; Sanford to Seward, 19 and 25 Apr 61, both NA; Thouvenel no. 6 to Mercier, 25 Apr 61, vol. 124, FMAE, AD, EU.

12. Woldman, *Lincoln and the Russians*, 23; Stoeckl nos. 15, 35 to Gortchakov, 12 Mar and 23 May 61, both ESD, LC; *Daily National Intelligencer*, 23 Apr 61, p. 3; Lyons to Russell, 23 May 61, PRO30/22/35; Lyons no. 209 to Russell, 23 May 61, FO115/253; Cuelebrouck no. 172 to de Vrière, 20 May 61, BPCUS, G&B, roll 6.

13. Mercier no. 37 to Thouvenel, 20 May 61, vol. 124, FMAE, AD, EU; Lyons no. 209 to Russell, 23 May 61, FO115/253.

14. *Seward at Washington* I, 575–76; Sanford to Seward, 25 Apr 61, NA.

15. Seward to Sanford, 20 May 61, SeP. That Seward's apprehensions were based on something more than a gloomy interpretation of his diplomatic correspondence is shown, to give only one further example, in the following news story filed by a Washington journalist on May 24. All mail received from Europe, this reporter warned, indicated "a prevalent belief throughout Europe that the dissolution of the American Union is a fixed fact and that European governments are acting upon such a theory." (*New York Times*, 25 May 61, p. 1.) Of course an American secretary of state does not normally receive his best impressions of the policies and activities of foreign governments from newspaper stories. But one must keep in mind that, at this particular moment, either most of Seward's own official representatives had not yet had time to file their initial reports from Europe, or these reports were based on no more than sketchy initial impressions. The Buchanan holdovers in Europe were almost all not to be trusted. Hence it was logical to consult the reports of the experienced journalists who acted as European correspondents or as European experts for the leading American newspapers to learn what normally would have been derived from ministers or consuls on the scene.

16. *Seward at Washington* I, 576.

17. Lincoln's *Works* IV, 376–80; Seward no. 10 to Adams, 21 May 61, NA; A. T. Rice, "A Famous Diplomatic Despatch," entire article plus a facsimile of the dispatch showing Lincoln's emendations, which also appeared as part of the introduction to Rice, ed., *Reminiscences of Abraham*

Lincoln, and in which Rice declares that the president's alterations "without question . . . saved the nation from a war with England."

18. Seward no. 10 to Adams, 21 May 61, NA.

19. *Ibid.*

20. *Ibid.*; see also Belmont, *A Few Letters and Speeches*, 32–39.

21. Lyons no. 206 to Russell, 20 May 61, FO115/253. Sumner arrived in Washington on May 18 from his Boston home, and he apparently had a protracted conference with Lincoln on the evening of May 19. (*New York Times*, 20 May 61, p. 1; Sumner to the duchess of Argyll, 4 June 61, HM25970.) That Lincoln may have been assisted in editing Seward's instruction of May 21 to Adams, not by Sumner alone, but rather by the entire cabinet with Seward himself present and participating, is hinted in contemporary dispatches by foreign envoys in Washington, cited hereafter, and also in testimony by Edward Everett, to whom Sumner later described his role in the affair, quoting Seward as saying of England and France: "God damn them. I'll give them hell." (Frothingham, *Everett*, 432–33.) Another version of this episode, apparently also emanating from Sumner, has the Massachusetts senator warning Seward: "The issues of peace and war between England and America do not rest with you, and henceforth every statement put forth from Washington concerning European powers will be carefully watched." Sumner then allegedly went to the White House and told Lincoln what he had said to Seward, urging: "You must watch him and overrule him." Sumner spread variations of this story all over Washington. Apparently, he was asked to intervene with the president by Lyons and by Mercier, the latter of whom wrote "that the report that I have expressed to some influential men on the subject of the tone of Mr. Seward's despatches," as well as efforts he had made to bring his objections to the personal attention of President Lincoln, "have had a good effect." (Conway, *Autobiography* I, 350–51; Rice, *Reminiscences of Abraham Lincoln*, 579–80; Schleiden no. 64 to Bremen Senate, 24 May 61, RSD, LC; Lyons no. 209 to Russell, 23 May 61, FO115/253; Mercier no. 39 to Thouvenel, 26 May 61, vol. 124, FMAE, AD, EU.)

22. Lyons no. 206 to Russell, 20 May 61, FO115/253; Lyons to Russell, 23 May 61, PRO30/22/35.

23. Lyons no. 209 to Russell, 23 May 61, FO115/253. Lyons later wrote Russell that he had since discovered that means had been "found of alarming the President and the more reasonable members of the Cabinet" about Seward's instruction of May 21, which in draft form had been "all but a direct announcement of war"; whereupon, the British envoy as-

serted, "sentences and even pages [were] scored out in the draft, and strong expressions altered in the President's own hand, and . . . a special injunction added by the President" for Adams "to consider the Despatch as intended for his own eye only," and "on no account to communicate it to anyone." (Lyons to Russell, 24 June 61, PRO30/22/35.)

24. Head to Newcastle, 18 May 61, and Newcastle to Head, 5 June 61, both NeC. I believe that the principal factor in frightening Lyons at this time was an article that appeared in the New York *Herald* of 22 May 61, entitled "OUR RELATIONS WITH FOREIGN POWERS." This article, which the Belgian minister reported had "caused a great sensation," because all the foreign diplomats in Washington believed that it was "inspired by the Secretary of State," began by declaring that "Any act of intervention which affords direct advantage to the insurgent States, and which tends to hamper or obstruct the action of our government, will lead to the most decisive measures on the part of the administration. . . . They are quite resolved not to deliberate for a single moment should England manifest any such insane disposition [to aid the Confederates], but to launch against her the thunderbolts of a war that would not cease till every Power in Europe was involved. On this vital matter the President, the Secretary of State and all the Cabinet entertain but one view. . . . They feel . . . the nation . . . will sustain them at every sacrifice against England and all the world." It was "consoling to think that while the portfolio of the State Department is in [Seward's] hands there will be no blunders to regret, and certainly no timidity to deplore." Lyons reported that this article was "well known to have been written under Mr. Seward's own eye, and to express the sentiments he desires to be believed to entertain. . . . The eulogy of himself at the end is by no means looked upon as intrinsic evidence to the contrary by those who are accustomed to listen to his conversation." And Mercier wrote that he knew that the *Herald* article had been "proofread" by Seward before publication. I do not believe that these statements are correct. I think that a *Herald* reporter, along with reporters for other newspapers, obtained copies of Seward's instruction no. 10 to Adams, discussed above, and wrote his story from it, exaggerating considerably, and throwing in the tribute to Seward at the end for some personal reason of his own. It is ridiculous to suggest that the *Herald* was a mouthpiece for the Lincoln administration. Constantly, at least until after the first battle of Bull Run, James Gordon Bennett and his newspaper opposed the Lincoln administration with as much vehemence and vigor as any major newspaper in the United States. Long an organ of the Democratic party, the

Herald was traditionally opposed to Seward and to his policies, and in an editorial during June, the month following the publication of the article cited above, it called for his removal from the cabinet. Yet foreign statesmen persisted in assuming that its strident anti-British articles were planted by Seward for the Lincoln administration. (Cuelebrouck no. 180 to de Vrière, 27 May 61, BPCUS, G&B, roll 6; Lyons nos. 210, 211, both 23 May 61, FO115/253; Mercier no. 37 to Thouvenel, 20 May 61, vol. 124, FMAE, AD, EU; Weed, *Autobiography*, 615–19; Randall, *Lincoln the President* I, 313, 370; Harper, *Lincoln and the Press*, 319–20; Seitz, *The James Gordon Bennetts*, 173–76, 182.)

25. Palmerston to Herbert, 3 June 61, Add. MS 48,582, BM.

26. Palmerston to Somerset, 23 June 61, *ibid.*

27. Lyons to Head, 22 May 61, LP. See also the endorsement of Lyons's clamor for military reinforcements in Head to Newcastle, 25 May 61, CO42/626.

28. *Letters of Queen Victoria. 1st Ser.* III, 562.

29. Apparently, the official decision to send the additional troops to Canada was made at a cabinet meeting held on June 12. (Russell to Palmerston, 11 June 61, GC/RU/661, PP.)

30. Verner, *Military Life of the Duke of Cambridge* I, 312; Dugan, *Great Iron Ship*, 96–101; London *Times*, 10 June 61, p. 8, 11 June 61, p. 5, and 12 June 61, p. 5; Lewis, *Letters of Sir George Cornewall Lewis*, 397–98.

31. London *Times*, 17 June 61, p. 8.

32. *Hansard's* 3d Ser., CLXIII, 1517–23.

33. *Ibid.*, 1524–27.

34. Russell to Lyons, 8 June 61, PRO30/22/96; Russell no. 43 to Lyons, 20 Feb 61, FO115/239/II; Russell no. 185 to Lyons, 21 June 61, FO115/243/I.

35. Lyons nos. 253 and 263 to Russell, 6 and 8 June 61, FO115/254. The British minister's panic may have been partly inspired by the following note received by him from "Alice" on June 7, 1861, at 8:30 P.M., LP. "I am not much educated," it read, "but I cannot trust anyone else to give you this information. I am employed by Mr. Lincoln's family, and I overheard something that concerned you. Some of the party said you was secretly in favor of the South, when Mr. Seward said your Queen expected to get the Southern States away from this government, but you couldn't come it [*sic*], and Mr. L[incoln] said you ought to have been put out of the way long ago. You had a bad effect on the Parliament by privately expressing your opinion of his Administration. I am afraid from what they said that

something will happen to you, and I hope you will excuse me, and keep a watch out. These dreadful times, they stop at nothing, *poison*, nor anything. Please be particular, and don't be deceived by fair appearances. I am an English woman, and therefore sympathize."

36. Lyons no. 263 to Russell, 8 June 61, FO115/254.

37. Lyons nos. 265, 276, 311 to Russell, 10 and 13 June and 1 July 61, all in FO115/254; Seitz, *The James Gordon Bennetts*, 173–82 and *passim*.

38. Lyons to Russell, 24 June 61, PRO30/22/35; Russell to Palmerston, 25 June 61, GC/RU/663, PP; Palmerston to Russell, 9 July 61, PRO30/22/21.

39. *New York Times*, 26 May 61, p. 4.

CHAPTER III: REBELS BECOME "BELLIGERENTS"

1. R554, AP.

2. E. D. Adams, *GB & Amer. CW* I, 38–39; Jordan and Pratt, *Europe and the American Civil War*, 6; London *Times*, 29 Nov 60, p. 8, and 9 Jan 61, p. 6; *Punch* XL (30 Mar 61), p. 129; Cobden to Sumner, 23 Feb 61, Add. MS 43, 676, BM. See also extracts from London press printed in *New York Times*, 1 Apr 61, p. 1; 12 May 61, p. 5; 14 May 61, p. 5; 15 May 61, p. 4, all tending to show that virtually the entire daily press of the British capital sympathized early in 1861 with the North against those whom the *London Chronicle* labeled "those enslavers of humanity whose ferocity has so long invited the vengeance of the world."

3. Lincoln's *Works* IV, 263. See also W. C. Ford, "Goldwin Smith's Visit . . . ," *MHSP* XLIV, 45; Lewis to Clarendon, 19 Jan 61, CP.

4. E. D. Adams, *GB & Amer. CW* I, 38–57.

5. London *Times*, 22 Jan 61, p. 6.

6. Maxwell, *Clarendon* II, 237.

7. Russell to Lyons, 10 Jan 61, PRO30/22/96; Lyons no. 197 to Russell, 12 May 61, FO115/253.

8. C. F. Adams, Jr., "British Proclamation," 211–12; Encl. to Russell no. 84 to Lyons, 10 Apr 61, FO115/240/I; *Illustrated London News* XXXVIII (4 May 61), 408; L. M. Sears, "The London Times' American Correspondent in 1861," 252; Gladstone to the duchess of Sutherland, 29 May 61, Add. MS 44, 531, BM.

9. E. D. Adams, *GB & Amer. CW* I, 50–51. Even Radicals like Richard Cobden and John Bright shared the general desire of Englishmen for

"peaceful but prompt separation" of North and South. (Cobden to J. Slagg, 4 Feb 61, and Cobden to Sumner, 23 Feb 61, both in Add. MS 43, 676, BM; Cobden to Bright, 25 Mar 61, RCP; Bright to Sumner, 6 Sept 61, "Bright-Sumner Letters," MHSP, LXVI, 93.)

10. Palmerston to Russell, 11 and 30 Dec 60, both in PRO30/22/21; Russell no. 89 to Lyons, 12 Apr 61, FO115/240/I. See also the disagreement between Lord Russell and J. L. Motley over the question of separation, in C. F. Adams, Jr., "Trent Affair," 77; *Correspondence of Motley* II, 191–92, 200.

11. Near the end of his life, Gladstone recalled that: "Lord Palmerston desired the severance [of the American Union] as a diminution of a dangerous power, but prudently held his tongue." (Morley, *Gladstone* II, 82.)

12. Dallas nos. 330, 333 to Seward, 9 Apr and 2 May 61, NA; London *Times*, 30 Apr 61, p. 5; Palmerston to Russell, 27 Apr 61, PRO30/22/21.

13. Lyons to Russell, 15 Apr 61, PRO30/22/35; Lyons nos. 146, 156 to Russell, 15 and 22 Apr 61, FO115/252 and 253.

14. Lyons no. 101 to Russell, 18 Mar 61, FO115/252.

15. Dallas no. 333 to Seward, 2 May 61, NA. The maneuver of a common Anglo-French policy on the question of recognizing the Confederacy had been advised by Lyons as early as February, and he had repeated this suggestion several times subsequently. (Lyons to Russell, 12 Feb and 26 Mar 61, PRO30/22/35; Lyons no. 123 to Russell, 30 Mar 61, FO115/252.)

16. *Case of Great Britain* III, 12; Russell nos. 89, 115 to Lyons, 12 Apr and 2 May 61, FO115/240/I & VI; London *Times*, 3 May 61, p. 5; *Hansard's*, 3d Ser., CLXII, 1378–79.

17. C. F. Adams, Jr., "British Proclamation," 208–10; Lyons no. 77 to Russell, 26 Feb 61, FO115/251; Russell no. 128 to Lyons, 11 May 61, FO115/241/II; *ORN*, Ser. 2, III, 214–16.

18. Lyons to Bunch, 12 Dec 60, LP; London *Times*, 22 Mar 61, p. 9.

19. E. D. Adams, *GB & Amer. CW* I, 86–87; Russell no. 121 to Lyons, 6 May 61, FO115/241/I; *Claims v. GB* I, 48–49; *Hansard's*, 3d Ser., CLXII, 1566; Russell to Lyons, 4 May 61, PRO30/22/96. Newton, *Lyons* I, 37–38, has misdated this letter; it should be May 4 rather than May 6.

20. *Hansard's*, 3d Ser., CLXII, 1763; London *Times*, 15 May 61, p. 5; *Correspondence of Motley* II, 123; Argyll, *Memoirs* II, 169–70.

21. Adams, Diary, 13 May 61, R76, AP; *Hansard's*, 3d Ser., CLXII, 1378–79, 1564–67; Adams no. 1 to Seward, 17 May 61, NA.

22. Adams, Diary, 18 May 61, R76, AP; Adams no. 2 to Seward, 21 May 61, NA.

23. Adams no. 2 to Seward, 21 May 61, NA.

24. *Ibid*.

25. *Ibid*.

26. *Ibid*. A comparison of Adams's original dispatches, found in the National Archives, with the printed compilations issued by the State Department annually, beginning in Dec. 1861, upon which historians like E. D. Adams, C. F. Adams, Jr., and Frank Owsley relied heavily, if not entirely, shows that not only did typographical errors creep into the edited versions, but also that some of the most significant portions were edited out of the published documents, sometimes with no indication that omissions had been made. Confidential dispatches and instructions containing sensitive (and hence important) information were, of course, even less likely to be printed; and most of them were not. (Cf. *Message of the President* for 1861. Adams's dispatch no. 2 is extracted on pp. 90–96 of this volume.)

27. Seward no. 15 to Adams, 8 June 61, NA.

28. Seward nos. 14, 15 to Adams, 3 and 8 June 61, NA.

29. Adams no. 4 to Seward, 31 May 61, NA; Lyons to Russell, 14 June 61, PRO30/22/35; Cuelebrouck no. 187 to de Vrière, 13 June 61, BPCUS, G&B, roll 6.

30. Mercier nos. 41, 42 to Thouvenel, 10 and 14 June, vol. 124, FMAE, AD, EU.

31. Russell no. 136 to Lyons, 18 May 61, FO115/241/II; Lyons no. 282 to Russell, 17 June 61, FO115/254; Seward no. 21 to Adams, 19 June 61, NA.

32. Lyons no. 282 to Russell, 17 June 61, FO115/254.

33. Lyons no. 282 to Russell, 17 June 61, FO115/254; Lyons to Russell, 18 June 61, PRO30/22/35; Mercier no. 43 to Thouvenel, 18 June 61, vol. 124, FMAE, AD, EU.

34. Lyons to Russell, 24 June 61, PRO30/22/35; Stoeckl no. 41 to Gortchakov, 10 June 61, ESD.

35. Seward no. 21 to Adams, 19 June 61, NA; Lyons no. 282 to Russell, 17 June 61, FO115/254.

36. For Gladstone's view of the American question at this time, see Gladstone to Dowager Lady Wenlock, 13 June 61, Add. MS 44,396, BM.

37. Adams to Seward, 6 June 61, R165, AP; Adams, Diary, 5 June 61, R76, AP; Adams no. 5 to Seward, 7 June 61, NA; Moran, *Journal*, 825. The British cabinet's decision to close British overseas ports to prizes taken

by the vessels of either American belligerent was inspired by a telegram from Lyons. See Lyons no. 201 to Russell, 17 May 61, FO115/253; Russell no. 162 to Lyons, 1 June 61, FO115/242/I; Russell to Lyons, 8 and 22 June 61, both PRO30/22/96; *Letters of Queen Victoria*, 1st Ser., III, 561–62.

38. Adams no. 5 to Seward, 7 June 61, NA.

39. Adams no. 5 to Seward, 7 June 61, NA; Adams, Diary, 7 June 61, R76, AP; Moran, *Journal*, 827–28; *ORN*, Ser. 2, III, 221.

40. Seward no. 10 to Adams, 21 May 61, NA.

41. Adams, Diary, 10 June 61, R76, AP; *Letters of Henry Adams, 1858–1891*, 93.

42. *Correspondence of Motley* II, 142; *New York Times*, 21 and 22 May 61, both p. 4, and 23 May 61, p. 1. On May 23 Seward told a German diplomat that he no longer feared "a break with England." (Schleiden no. 65 to Bremen Senate, 27 May 61, RSD.)

43. London *Times*, 10 June 61, p. 8; Lyons to Head, 22 May 61, LP; C. F. Adams, Jr., "British Proclamation," 228; Ashley, *Palmerston*, II, 226; *Letters of Queen Victoria*, 1st Ser., III, 562.

44. Adams no. 8 to Seward, 14 June 61, NA.

45. *Ibid.*

46. *Ibid.*

47. *Ibid.* See also Sanford to Seward, 15 June 61, SeP.

48. Adams, Diary, 12 June 61, R76, AP.

CHAPTER IV: MISUNDERSTANDINGS PROLIFERATE

1. *New York Times* and Washington *Evening Star*, both May and June 61, *passim*.

2. Lyons to his sister, 29 Feb 60, LP. See also *Letters of Mrs. Edward Twisleton, 1852–62*, 310.

3. C. F. Adams, Jr., "British Proclamation," 218; Adams, Diary, 1 and 6 June 61, R76, and Adams to Seward, 6 June 61, R165, both AP.

4. Seward to Adams, 21 June 71, R554, AP.

5. Lyons no. 246 to Russell, 3 June 61, FO115/253. On the following day, Lyons wrote his sister that the "new people," meaning Seward and the other Republicans, were "particularly civil." Unfortunately, he added, he had little in common with them *socially*. (Lyons to his sister, 4 June 61, LP.)

6. Adams, Diary, 12 June 61, R76, AP.

7. Lyons to Russell, 21 May and 24 June 61, both PRO30/22/35; Sum-

ner to J. Andrew, 24 June 61, Andrew Papers, Mass. Hist. Society; Pierce, *Sumner* IV, 31. The document which Lyons thought was almost a "declaration of war" was, of course, Seward's instruction no. 10 to Adams, with which Sumner had apparently familiarized Lyons. (Lyons no. 206 to Russell, 20 May 61, FO115/253.)

8. C. F. Adams, Jr., *Richard Henry Dana* II, 258–59. Lyons was doubtless a recipient of the slander against Seward. (Russell, *My Diary*, 54, 68; London *Times*, 22 Oct 61, p. 6.)

9. Adams to C. F. Adams, Jr., 21 June 61, R554, AP.

10. Adams to Seward, 21 June 61, R165, AP; Adams no. 9 to Seward, 21 June 61, NA.

11. Seward to Adams, 9 July 61, R554, AP; Seward nos. 32, 35 to Adams, 1 and 9 July 61, both NA. But see Sanford to Seward, 5 Nov 61, NA.

12. London *Times*, 20 May 61, p. 9.

13. *Ibid.*, p. 8.

14. *Ibid.*, 3 June 61, p. 12; Crooks, *M'Clintock*, 302.

15. The *Times* rejected for publication still another letter, this one by Horatio J. Perry, U. S. secretary of legation at Madrid, on the ground that it contained nothing especially new. (Jordan and Pratt, *Europe and the American Civil War*, 14; London *Times*, 3 June 61, p. 12, and 1 Nov 61, pp. 8–9, and 14 Nov 61, p. 8; *Letters of Henry Adams*, 1858–1891, p. 92; Clarendon to Adams, 6 June 61, R554, AP. See also J. S. Pike to W. P. Fessenden, 7 June 61, JSPP-LC; Clay to Adams, 1 Jan 62, R557, AP; Bayard Taylor to Horace Greeley, 5 July 62, Greeley Papers, N. Y. Public Library; Clay to F. Lieber, 30 June 61, LI1105, HL; Sanford to Weed, 18 and 31 May 61, both WP; and Cobden to Bright, 23 May 61, RCP.)

16. *Illustrated London News* XXXVIII (25 May 61), 484; *Punch* XL (29 June 61), p. 61; Hobson, *Cobden*, 347–49; C. F. Adams, Jr., "Trent Affair," 128–30.

17. Adams to C. F. Adams, Jr., 2 July 61, R554, and C. F. Adams, Jr., to A. B. Adams, 29 Sept 61, R555, and Everett to Adams, 30 Sept 61, R555, and Adams to Everett, 25 Oct 61, R166,—all in AP; Weed to Seward, 31 Dec 61, SeP; Sumner to the duchess of Argyll, 4 June and 11 Nov 61, HM25970–71, HL; Pierce, *Sumner* IV, 48–49. Everett judged from the tenor of a diatribe that Sumner delivered against Seward in his presence that the senator planned "to supplant Seward " in the cabinet. (Frothingham, *Everett*, 432–33.)

18. Adams to Everett, 25 Oct 61, and Adams to Seward, 1 Nov 61, both R166, AP.

19. Adams, Diary, 18 Nov 61, and 22 Oct 61, R76, AP.

20. London *Times*, 23–24 May 61, both p. 9; Clay to Adams, 1 Jan 62, R557, AP.

21. Lyons no. 171 to Russell, 2 May 61, FO115/253; "Correspondence Regarding Prisoners of War, 1861–62, Parr-Sullivan," Box no. 9, folder no. 75, "Civil War Papers," RG59, NA.

22. Lyons no. 171 to Russell, 2 May 61, FO115/253.

23. *Ibid.*

24. *Ibid.*

25. *Ibid.* Lyons to Seward, 1 May 61, and Seward to Lyons, 1 May 61, both NA.

26. Lyons no. 171 to Russell, 2 May 61, FO115/253; Lyons to Russell, 2 and 6 May 61, both PRO30/22/35; Lyons to Seward, 1 May 61, NA.

27. Russell to Palmerston, 17 May 61, GC/RU/658, PP.

28. Ashmun, from Springfield, Mass., had been for six years an anti-slavery Whig member of Congress, as well as the president of the Republican national convention of 1860, and he was, as Seward later described him to Lyons, "a most respectable man." (Lyons no. 286 to Russell, 17 June 61, FO115/254.)

29. Lyons nos. 153, 181, 194, 195 to Russell, 22 Apr and 4, 11 and 12 May 61, FO115/253; New York *Herald*, 17 Apr 61; Seward to Ashmun, 13 Apr 61, "Instructions to Special Agents," vol. 21, RG59, NA.

30. Lyons no. 206 to Russell, 20 May 61, FO115/253.

31. Russell no. 135 to Lyons, 15 May 61, FO115/241/II.

32. Seward to Ashmun, 18 Apr 61, "Instructions to Special Agents," vol. 21, RG59, NA.

33. Lyons no. 286 to Russell, 17 June 61, FO115/254; Lyons to Head, 2 Aug 61, LP.

34. Adams no. 8 to Seward, 14 June 61, NA.

35. Adams, Diary, 12 June 61, R76, AP Adams no. 8 to Seward, 14 June 61, NA.

36. Seward no. 32 to Adams, 1 July 61, NA.

37. *Ibid.*; Head to Newcastle, 26 Apr 61, NeC. The Ashmun and *Peerless* cases are discussed in Winks, *Canada and the United States: The Civil War Years*, 38–41, 45–47, from the usual pro-Lyons, anti-Seward, point of view. According to Winks (p. 47): "The fate of the *Peerless* remains un-

known." What happened to the vessel, however, seems clear enough. John Murray Forbes telegraphed Seward that he believed "she is bought by our friends" in the War Department, which Lyons later confirmed, writing Russell: "it turned out that the ship had all the time been purchased by the United States government itself." More details about the movements of the *Peerless* may be found in Northern newspapers during May and June, including word of the ship's arrival in New York on June 17, sailing under the American flag. (Forbes telegram to Seward, from Boston, 25 May 61, "Correspondence Regarding Prisoners of War, 1861–62. Parr-Sullivan," Box no. 9 folder no. 75, "Civil War Papers," RG59, NA; *Letters and Recollections of John Murray Forbes* I, 219; Lyons no. 740 to Russell, 6 Dec 61, FO5/776, PRO; Washington *Evening Star*, 11 May 61, p. 1 and 11 June 61, p. 3, and 18 June 61, p. 2.) From New York the *Peerless* sailed southward, joining the Northern expedition sent to capture Port Royal early in November. In a heavy gale off the coast of North Carolina, the *Peerless* went to the bottom, with all persons on board saved by the crew of the *Mohican*. (Miller, *Photographic History of the Civil War* VI, 270; *New York Daily Tribune*, 14 Nov 61, p. 5; *New York Times*, 14 Nov 61, pp. 4–5; *Charleston Mercury*, 21 Nov 61, p. 4; and *Frank Leslie's Illustrated Newspaper* XIII (30 Nov 61), 17.

38. Lyons no. 740 to Russell, 6 Dec 61, FO5/776, PRO. But see also Head to Newcastle, 26 Apr 61, NeC.

39. Palmerston to Russell, 30 Dec 60, PRO30/22/21; Lyons to Russell, 4 Feb and 27 Apr 61, both PRO30/22/35; Lyons no. 159 to Russell, 23 Apr 61, FO115/253; Palmerston to Russell, 5 May 61, GC/RU/1138/1, and Palmerston to Edward Ellice, 5 May 61, GC/RU/1138/2, both PP.

40. Russell no. 136 to Lyons, 18 May 61, FO115/241/II; Lyons no. 262 to Russell, 8 June 61, FO115/254; Seward no. 21 to Adams, 19 June 61, NA. The British foreign minister's *real* feelings about America shine forth from some of his most private communications. In his mind, he had already recognized Confederate sovereignty. (Russell to Clarendon, 23 May 61, CP.)

41. Lyons to Russell, 27 Apr 61, PRO30/22/35; Palmerston to Edward Ellice, 5 May 61, GC/RU/1138/2, PP.

CHAPTER V: THE DECLARATION OF PARIS NEGOTIATION

1. I have written more extensively about the Declaration of Paris

negotiation in a *festschrift* in honor of Bell I. Wiley, currently awaiting publication.

2. Russell no. 136 to Lyons, 18 May 61, FO115/241/II; Russell no. 139 to Lyons, 18 May 61, FO115/241/III; John B. Moore, ed., *A Digest of International Law* VII, 562–63.

3. Russell no. 139 to Lyons, 18 May 61, FO115/241/III. See also Case and Spencer, *US & France: CW Diplomacy*, 77–85; E. D. Adams, *GB & Amer. CW* I, 156–58; Thouvenel no. 75 to Flahault, 14 May 61, and Flahault no. 37 to Thouvenel, 16 May 61, both vol. 719, FMAE, AD, Angleterre.

4. Seward no. 3 to Adams, 24 Apr 61; Lincoln's *Works* IV, 339; *ORN*, Ser. 2, III, 96–97, and Ser. 1, I and IV, *passim*; Robinson, *Confederate Privateers*, 25–26. See also Dalzell, *Flight From the Flag*, and Argyll, *Memoirs* II, 170.

5. Seward no. 3 to Adams, 24 Apr 61, NA.

6. *Ibid.*

7. Lyons to Russell, 27 Apr 61, PRO30/22/35; Lyons no. 169 to Russell, 2 May 61, FO115/253. See also Mercier no. 33 to Thouvenel, 26 Apr 61, vol. 124, FMAE, AD, EU; and Thouvenel no. 75 to Flahault, 14 May 61, vol. 719, FAME, AD, Angleterre.)

8. Adams no. 2 to Seward, 21 May 61, NA; Russell no. 141 to Lyons, 21 May 61, FO115/241/III.

9. Adams no. 8 to Seward, 14 June 61, NA; Russell no. 187 to Lyons, 22 June 61, FO115/243/I and encl.; Lyons nos. 280, 283 to Russell, 14 and 17 June 61, FO115/254; London *Times*, 4 June 61, p. 5; *ORN*, Ser. 2, III, 241; and Adams to Dayton, 2 July 61, R165, AP.

10. Lyons nos. 251, 253, 259, 262, 263 to Russell, 4, 6, and 8 (3) June 61, FO115/254; Mercier to Thouvenel, 2 June 61, vol. XIII, Papiers de Thouvenel, FMAE, MD; Mercier no. 41 to Thouvenel, 10 June 61, vol. 124, FMAE, AD, EU.

11. Lyons nos. 262, 278, 282 to Russell, 8, 13 and 17 June 61, FO115/254; Mercier nos. 41, 42 and 43 to Thouvenel, 10, 14 and 18 June 61, vol. 124, FMAE, AD, EU; F. W. Seward, *Reminiscences*, 179–80; *Seward at Washington* I, 580–82; Wodehouse to Lyons, 29 June 61, LP.

12. Lyons no. 282 to Russell, 17 June 61, FO115/254.

13. Lyons to Russell, 10 and 18 June and 8 July 61, all PRO30/22/35; Lyons no. 284 to Russell, 17 June 61, FO115/254; Mercier no. 43 to Thouvenel, 18 June 61, vol. 124, FMAE, AD, EU; Russell no. 195 to

Lyons, 26 June 61, FO115/243/II; and Lyons no. 347 to Russell, 16 July 61, FO115/255.

14. Lyons to Bunch, 5 July 61, encl. to Lyons no. 324 to Russell, 8 July 61, FO115/254. Lyons persisted in using the word "negotiation" to describe the approach to the Confederate government for many weeks thereafter. (See, for example, Lyons to Russell, 27 Sept and 14 Oct 61, both PRO30/22/35.) Mercier also used the same unfortunate language, in referring to "the identical instructions for the consuls which we shall charge with the negotiation." (Mercier no. 43 to Thouvenel, 18 June 61, vol. 124, FMAE, AD, EU.)

15. Seward no. 4 to Dayton, 24 Apr 61, and Dayton nos. 5, 6, 8, 9, 10 to Seward, 22, 27 and 30 May and 7 and 12 June 61, respectively, all in NA. It seems probable that H. S. Sanford, by misrepresenting Adams's views on the subject to Dayton, helped to persuade him to delay the Declaration of Paris negotiation. (Dayton no. 8 to Seward, 30 May 61, NA.)

16. Palmerston to Queen Victoria, 12 June 61, Connell, *Regina vs. Palmerston*, 344; Lyons to Russell, 27 May and 4 June 61, both PRO30/22/35; Russell to Palmerston, 11 June 61, GC/RU/661, PP; Russell nos. 185, 195 to Lyons, 21 and 26 June 61, FO115/243/I-II; Lyons no. 262 to Russell, 8 June 61, FO115/254.

17. Adams no. 17 to Seward, 19 July 61, NA; Russell no. 708 to Cowley, 13 July 61, encl. to Russell no. 230 to Lyons, 13 July 61, FO115/244/I; Cowley nos. 865, 869, 883 to Russell, 15, 16, and 19 July 61, FO519/11; Cowley no. 871 to Russell, 16 July 61, encl. to Russell no. 240 to Lyons, 20 July 61, FO115/244/III; Russell no. 729 to Cowley, 17 July 61, FO27/1378/729; E. D. Adams, *GB & Amer. CW* I, 167.

18. Lyons no. 325 to Russell, 8 July 61, FO115/254.

19. *Ibid*.

20. Palmerston to Russell, 13 Aug 61, endorsed by Russell, PRO30/22/21; Russell to Lyons, 24 Aug 61, PRO30/22/96; Cowley no. 1031 to Russell, 20 Aug 61, encl. to Russell no. 287 to Lyons, 24 Aug 61, FO115/245/IV; *Claims v. GB* I, 88; Moran to Adams, 19 Aug 61, R554, AP; Adams no. 32 to Seward, 23 Aug 61, NA.

21. Adams no. 34 to Seward, 30 Aug 61, NA.

22. Seward announced in September that the United States would nevertheless abide by the last three articles of the Declaration of Paris "according to our traditional principles." (Seward nos. 83, 88 to Adams, 7

and 14 Sept 61, both NA; Russell to Palmerston, 26 Aug 61, GC/RU/667/1–2, PP.)

23. Even worse was the climate of mutual distrust that had arisen in Paris between Dayton, who spoke no French, and Thouvenel, who spoke no English.

Chapter VI: The Blockade as a Dangerous Issue

1. Lyons nos. 156, 157, 165, 169 to Russell, 22 (2) and 27 Apr and 2 May 61, all FO115/253; Welles, *Lincoln and Seward*, 122–24; *ORN*, Ser. 1, V, 617–18, 621–26.

2. Lyons nos. 191, 205, 222 to Russell, 20 and 25 May 61, all FO115/253.

3. Besides citations in previous notes, see Lyons nos. 214, 241 to Russell, 23 May and 3 June 61, both FO115/253, and Lyons no. 268 to Russell, 11 June 61, FO115/254; and Russell nos. 168, 178, 182 to Lyons, w/encls., 8, 13, and 15 June 61, all in FO115/242/I and III; and Russell no. 253 to Lyons, 27 July 61, FO115/244/V; and Russell no. 271 to Lyons, 9 Aug 61, FO115/245/I.

4. Adams no. 8 to Seward, 14 June 61, NA.

5. Lyons no. 263 to Russell, 8 June 61, FO115/254.

6. Russell to Palmerston, 25 June 61, GC/RU/663, PP; Palmerston to Russell, 25 June and 9 July 61, both PRO30/22/21; Russell to Lyons, 13 July 61, PRO30/22/96.

7. Russell no. 207 to Lyons, 4 July 61, w/encl., FO115/243/III.

8. Seward nos. 15, 21 to Adams, 8 and 19 June 61, NA; Russell no. 708 to Cowley, 13 July 61, encl. 4 to Russell no. 230 to Lyons, 13 July 61, FO115/244/I-II; Russell draft to Lyons, 10 July 61, FO5/756, inserted in FO115/243/V; Russell no. 237 to Lyons, 19 July 61, FO115/244/II.

9. Russell no. 243 to Lyons, 20 July 61, FO115/244/IV; Russell to Lyons, 24 July 61, FO5/756, inserted in *ibid.*; Russell to Lyons, 6, 13, and 20 July 61, all in PRO20/22/96. For the parallel French dispatch, see Billault no. 20 to Mercier, 18 July 61, vol. 124, FMAE, AD, EU. For the British insistence on sending such a dispatch, see Cowley nos. 848, 871, 874, 881 to Russell, 12, 16, 17, and 19 July 61, all FO519/11, as well as Flahault no. 50 to Thouvenel, 9 July 61, vol. 720, FMAE, AD, Angleterre.

10. Lyons nos. 326–28, 332 to Russell, 8, 11, 12, and 13 July 61, all FO115/254; Lyons nos. 345, 357 to Russell, 15 and 19 July 61, FO115/255; Lincoln, *Works* IV, 444.

11. Lyons no. 363 to Russell, 20 July 61, FO115/255; Mercier no. 48 to Thouvenel, 21 July 61, vol. 124, FMAE, AD, EU; Cowley no. 968 to Russell, 8 Aug 61, encl. 14 to Russell no. 280 to Lyons, 16 Aug 61, FO115/245/III; Russell no. 211 to Lyons, 6 July 61, FO115/243/IV; Browning *Dairy* I, 488–89.

12. Seward no. 42 to Adams, 21 July 61, NA.

13. Seward no. 42 to Adams, 21 July 61, NA; Lyons to Russell, 30 July and 1 and 16 Aug 61, PRO30/22/35; Mercier no. 48 to Thouvenel, 21 July 61, vol. 124, FMAE, AD, EU.

14. Cabinet memoranda on this topic are in PRO30/22/27. See also Russell nos. 237, 264, 265, 269, 270, 280, 292, 294 and 316 to Lyons, 19 July and 3(2), 8, 9, 16, 27 and 29 Aug, and 19 Sept 61, FO115/244/II–FO115/246/III; Cowley nos. 932, 933 and 939 to Russell, 1(2) and 2 Aug 61, FO519/II; Lyons nos. 422 and 423 to Russell, 12 Aug 61, FO115/255; Russell to Lyons, 16 and 24 Aug 61, PRO30/22/96.

CHAPTER VII: THE PRESSURE FROM LONDON INCREASES

1. "Bright-Sumner Letters," MHSP, XLVI, 93.

2. Adams no. 9 to Seward, 21 June 61, NA; Lyons to Russell, 20 July 61, PRO30/22/35.

3. Lyons to Russell, 20 July 61, PRO30/22/35.

4. Seward nos. 46, 49, 58 to Adams, 26 and 29 July and 12 Aug 61, and Seward no. 30 to Marsh, 30 July 61, and Adams no. 29 to Seward, 16 Aug 61, all NA.

5. Adams no. 29 to Seward, 16 Aug 61, NA; Adams to R. H. Dana, Jr., 28 Aug 61, R165, AP.

6. Seward no. 78 to Adams, 2 Sept 61, NA.

7. Lyons to Russell, 22 July 61, PRO30/22/35; Newton, *Lyons* I, 47, 50; Lyons no. 38 to Russell, 30 July 61, FO115/255; Palmerston to Newcastle, 1 Sept 61, Add. MS 48,582, BM; Russell to Lyons, 16 Aug 61, PRO30/22/96; Hammond to Palmerston, 5 Sept 61, GC/HA/245, PP.

8. Lyons no. 423 to Russell, 12 Aug 61, FO115/255; Adams to Russell, 23 Aug 61, encl. to Adams no. 34 to Seward, 30 Aug 61, NA; Russell to Palmerston, 26 Aug 61, GC/RU/667/1–2, PP; London *Times*, 7 Aug 61, p. 8; Palmerston to Lewis, 26 Aug 61, and Palmerston to Newcastle, 1 Sept 61, Add. MS 48,582, BM.

9. Lewis to Palmerston, 27 Aug 61, GC/LE/141/1–2, PP.

10. Bourne, *Britain and the Balance of Power*, 218; Lewis to Palmerston, 3 and 8 Sept 61, GC/LE/142–43, PP.

11. Argyll to Gladstone, 13 Sept 61, Add. MS 44,099, BM.

Chapter VIII: The Bunch Affair Begins

1. No. 109, NA.

2. Lyons no. 29 to Russell, 28 Jan 61, FO115/251; C. F. Adams, Jr., "British Proclamation," 216.

3. Lyons no. 83 to Russell, 2 Mar 61, FO115/252.

4. Russell no. 6 to Lyons, 10 Jan 61, FO115/238/I.

5. Lyons no. 294 to Russell, 21 June 61, and Lyons no. 300 to Russell, 24 June 61, both FO115/254; Lyons no. 413 to Russell, 12 Aug 61, FO115/255; *ORA*, Ser. 2, II, 46, 644.

6. *ORA*, Ser. 2, II, 415–24; Seward to Lyons, 5 and 17 Aug 61, LP; Lyons nos. 310, 317 to Russell, 1 and 6 July 61, FO115/254; Lyons nos. 344, 389, 390, 399, 400, 405, to Russell, 15 July and 1, 4 and 5 Aug 61 variously, FO115/255.

7. *ORA*, Ser. 2, II, 123, 1006, 1049, 1056.

8. Lyons, too, thought that the Mures were related, but he later learned otherwise. (Lyons nos. 433, 438 to Russell, 16 and 19 Aug 61, both FO115/255; *ORA*, Ser. 2, II, 645; Lyons no. 574 to Russell, 21 Oct 61, FO115/257.)

9. *ORA*, Ser. 2, II, 645; Lyons no. 433 to Russell, 16 Aug 61, FO115/255.

10. Lyons to Russell, 16 Aug 61, PRO30/22/35.

11. Adams, Diary, 2 Sept 61, R76, AP; Moran, *Journal*, 872–73; Seward nos. 63, 64 to Adams, 17 Aug 61, NA; *Seward at Washington* I, 628; "Prisoners of War, 1861–2," Folder 70, Box 8, RG59, NA; Trescot, "Confederacy and the Declaration of Paris"; *ORN*, Ser. 2, III, 230–32; *ORA*, Ser. 2, II, 643–65. Trescot to Sanford, 1 Dec 67, Box 132, HSSP.

12. Adams (2) to Russell, 3 Sept 61, both encl. to Adams no. 41 to Seward, 9 Sept 61, NA; Moran, *Journal*, 873, 877–78; Adams, Diary, 3, 7, and 10 Sept 61, R76, AP; Russell no. 227 to Lyons, 12 July 61, FO115/244/I.

13. Hammond to Palmerston, 5 and 6 Sept 61, GC/HA/245–46, and Russell to Palmerston, 6 Sept 61, GC/RU/669, both PP.

14. Russell to Lyons, 6 Sept 61, PRO30/22/96; Hammond to Palm-

erston, 5 and 6 Sept 61, GC/HA/245–46, PP; Palmerston to Russell, 9 Sept 61, PRO30/22/21.

15. Russell, *Later Correspondence* II, 320; Russell to Palmerston, 11 Sept 61, GC/RU/670/1–2, PP.

16. Russell (2) to Adams, 9 Sept 61, both encl. to Adams no. 44 to Seward, 14 Sept 61, NA.

17. *Ibid.* "The Queen," Russell wrote Palmerston, "wishes me to modify the phrase about not being prepared to recognize the Southern govt, but I do not feel disposed to do so." (Russell to Palmerston, 11 Sept 61, GC/RU/670/1–2, PP.)

18. Adams no. 44 to Seward, 14 Sept 61, NA; W. C. Ford, *Cycle* I, 45.

Chapter IX: The Bunch Affair Reaches Crisis Proportions

1. Russell to Palmerston, 14 and 19 Sept 61, both GC/RU/671–72/1–2, PP; Palmerston to Russell, 17 Sept 61, PRO30/22/21; Argyll to Gladstone, 17 Sept 61, Add. MS 44,099, and Gladstone to Lewis, 21 Sept 61, Add. MS 44,236, and Lewis to DeGrey, 29 Aug 61, Add. MS 43,533, all BM; Lewis to Clarendon, 7 and 15 Sept 61, both CP; Head to Newcastle, 11 July and 1 and 7 Aug and 12 and 21 Sept 61, and Newcastle to Head, 27 Aug and 28 Sept 61, and Newcastle to Lewis, 5 and 24 Sept 61, and Newcastle to Palmerston, 3 Sept 61, and Lewis to Newcastle, 25 Sept 61, all in NeC.

2. Palmerston to Russell, 9 Sept 61, PRO30/22/21; Russell to Lyons, 13 Sept 61, PRO30/22/96.

3. Lyons nos. 267, 492 to Russell, 31 Aug and 14 Sept 61, FO115/255–256.

4. Lyons nos. 499, 542, 543, 562 to Russell, 19 Sept and 12 (2) and 17 Oct 61, all FO115/256; Lyons nos. 573, 608 to Russell, 21 and 28 Oct 61, both FO115/257.

5. Russell no. 400 to Lyons, 7 Nov 61, FO115/247/VI; Lyons to Russell, 27 Apr and 29 Nov 61, both PRO30/22/35; Lyons nos. 713, 767 to Russell, 29 Nov and 16 Dec 61, FO115/258 and 259; Lyons to Russell, 23 Dec 61, PRO30/22/14C.

6. Lyons to Russell, 14 Oct 61, PRO30/22/35.

7. *Ibid.*

8. *Ibid.*; Lyons to Russell, 28 Oct 61, PRO30/22/35.

9. Lyons no. 622 to Russell, 4 Nov 61, FO115/257.

10. *Ibid.*

11. Seward had been quick to release Robert Mure from custody, as soon as he promised "on his honor" that he would neither re-enter any of the rebellious Southern states nor hold any correspondence with anyone there residing without permission from the secretary of state. And when couriers carrying dispatch bags from British consuls both at Richmond and at Norfolk were seized and found to be carrying private letters as well, Seward, in Lyons's own words, "behaved properly" about these cases. If the consuls could not be counted upon to heed his instructions forbidding them to forward private letters, the British minister wrote Russell, "I am afraid I shall be obliged to ask you to support me by some severe act." (Lyons nos. 571, 572, 574, 598, 599 to Russell, 21–25 Oct 61, all in FO115/257; Lyons nos. 696, 697, 711, 712, 721, 722 to Russell, 25–29 Nov 61, all in FO115/258; Lyons no. 784 to Russell, 21 Dec 61, FO115/259; Russell no. 406 to Lyons, 8 Nov 61, FO115/248/I; Russell no. 466 to Lyons, 10 Dec 61, FO115/250/II; Russell no. 486 to Lyons, 20 Dec 61, FO115/250/IV; Lyons to Russell, 25 Oct and 25 Nov 61, both PRO30/22/35.)

12. Lyons to Russell, 14 Oct 61, PRO30/22/35; Lyons no. 605 to Russell, 26 Oct 61, FO115/257; Seward no. 109 to Adams, 23 Oct 61, NA.

13. Russell to Palmerston, 12 Nov 61, GC/RU/680, PP.

14. Adams, Diary, 12–13 Nov 61, R76, and Adams to Seward, 15 Nov 61, R166, both AP; Adams no. 71 to Seward, 14 Nov 61, NA.

15. Adams, Diary, 20 Nov 61, R76, AP.

16. Adams to Russell, 21 Nov 16, encl. to Adams no. 74 to Seward, 22 Nov 61, NA.

17. Russell to Adams, 26 Nov 61, encl. to Adams no. 81 to Seward, 29 Nov 61, NA.

18. Adams to Russell, 29 Nov 61, encl. to Adams no. 81 to Seward, 29 Nov 61, NA.

19. Palmerston memo dtd. 30 Nov 61, PRO30/22/14C.

20. Adams, Diary, 6 Dec 61, R76, AP; Russell to Adams, 4 Dec 61, and Adams to Russell, 6 Dec 61, both encls. to Adams no. 84 to Seward, 6 Dec 61, NA.

21. Lyons no. 814 to Russell, 31 Dec 61, FO115/259; Russell no. 30 to Lyons, 18 Jan 62, FO115/284/II. Acting on orders from Lyons, who anticipated great embarrassment if Federal soldiers should suddenly land at Charleston and discover Bunch still there, the former consul left abruptly on a British ship for England on February 7, 1863. He was replaced by Pinckney Walker, "Acting Consul." (Walker no. 19 to Russell,

7 Feb 63, FO5/906.) Up to the time of his departure, Bunch apparently continued to exercise the full authority of the Charleston consular office. (See, for example, Bunch no. 15 to Russell, 31 Jan 63, FO5/906, and Bunch to J. P. Benjamin, 30 Jan 63, Pickett Papers, LC.)

22. For a curious interpretation of the Bunch affair, see L. M. Sears, "The London *Times*' American Correspondent in 1861 . . . ," 255.

23. Russell no. 416 to Lyons, 16 Nov 61, with encl., FO115/248/II; Russell no. 458 to Lyons, 6 Dec 61, FO115/249/V; Lyons no. 810 to Russell, 31 Dec 61, FO115/259; Lyons to Russell, 27 Dec 61, PRO30/22/35.

CHAPTER X: SEWARD JAILS BRITISH SUBJECTS

1. PRO30/22/21.

2. Lyons to Russell, 2, 5, 23, and 27 Aug 61, all PRO30/22/35.

3. Russell to Palmerston, 8 Oct 61, GC/RU/675/1–2, PP; Russell no. 321 to Lyons, 21 Sept 61, FO115/246/IV.

4. Lyons nos. 472, 473 to Russell, both 6 Sept 61, FO115/256; Lyons to Russell, 6 Sept 61, PRO30/22/35.

5. Russell no. 328 to Lyons, 28 Sept 61, FO115/246/IV.

6. Lyons nos. 483, 484, 485, 489, 498, 502 to Russell, 10 (2), 12, 13, 14, 19, and 23 Sept 61, all in FO115/256; *ORA*, Ser. 2, II, 627–35; Lyons to Russell, 10 and 23 Sept 61, both PRO30/22/35.

7. Lyons to Russell, 30 Sept 61, PRO30/22/35.

8. Russell no. 339 to Lyons, 3 Oct 61, FO115/246/VI; Lyons nos. 472, 473 to Russell, both 6 Sept 61, FO115/256.

9. Russell no. 328 to Lyons, 28 Sept 61, FO115/246/IV; Lyons no. 587 to Russell, 22 Oct 61, FO115/257; Lyons to Seward, 14 Oct 61, NA.

10. Seward to Lyons, 14 Oct 61, NA; *Daily National Intelligencer*, 19 Oct 61, p. 2.

11. Lyons no. 587 to Russell, 22 Oct 61, FO115/257.

12. Russell no. 391 to Lyons, 2 Nov 61, FO115/247/VI; London *Times*, 5 Nov 61, p. 7, and 6 Nov 61, p. 8; London *Herald*, quoted in *Daily National Intelligencer*, 25 Nov 61, p. 2.

13. Russell no. 426 to Lyons, 22 Nov 61, FO115/248/V.

14. Lyons no. 756 to Russell, 13 Dec 61, FO115/259.

15. Russell no. 497 to Lyons, 27 Dec 61, FO115/250/IV; Seward to Lyons, 13 Jan 62, NA.

16. Lyons nos. 504, 505, 524, 525, 530 to Russell, 23 (2), 28 and 30 Sept, and 3 Oct 61, all FO115/256; Russell nos. 353, 355, 356 to Lyons, all

10 Oct 61, FO115/247/II; Russell no. 368 to Lyons, 17 Oct 61, FO115/247/IV; Russell no. 403 to Lyons, 8 Nov 61, FO115/248/I; Russell no. 409 to Lyons, 8 Nov 61, FO115/248/II.

17. Lyons to Seward, 28 Oct 61, NA.

18. See, for example, Seward to Lyons, 14 Oct 61, NA.

19. Lyons nos. 503, 609, 618 to Russell, 23 Sept and 28 Oct and 4 Nov 61, FO115/256–257; Russell no. 354 to Lyons, 10 Oct 61, FO115/247/II; Russell no. 415 to Lyons, 14 Nov 61, FO115/248/II; Russell no. 456 to Lyons, 6 Dec 61, FO115/249/V; *ORA*, Ser. 2, II, 544–55.

20. Lyons nos. 604, 619, 636, 648, 649, 650, 666, 687, 753 to Russell, 26 Oct and 4, 9, 14 (3), 18, and 22 Nov and 12 Dec 61, all in FO115/257–259; Russell no. 422 to Lyons, 22 Nov 61, FO115/248/III, *ORA, Ser.* 2, 11, 711–21, 829–57, 897–904, 909–13, 982–1008; *Hansard's*, 3d Ser., CLXV, 89–92, 102–13.

Chapter XI: England Edges Toward Intervention

1. R165, AP.

2. Palmerston to Gibson, 7 June 61, Add. MS 48,582, BM.

3. *Ibid.*

4. Gibson to Palmerston, 9 July 61, GC/GI/12/1–2, PP.

5. Cobden to Richard, 12 July 61, Add. MS 43,659, BM; Buchanan, *Works* XI, 218; Bright to Sumner, 6 Sept 61, "Bright-Sumner Letters," MHSP, XLVI, 93. Bright's constant watchfulness on the subject of the Lancashire cotton supply is exemplified in Bright to Cobden, 6 Sept 61, RCP, and Bright to Denison, 5 Aug 61, OsC.

6. Adams to G. B. Ruggles, 5 July 61, R165, and Adams to C. F. Adams, Jr., 7 Sept 61, R555, both AP.

7. *ORN*, Ser. 2, III, 191–95, 238–46.

8. *ORN*, Ser. 2, III, 238–48.

9. *Ibid.*, 278–80. As early as mid-June, Henry Sanford reported from London that the Southern commissioners there "are assured by Palmerston that they will be probably recognized a few months hence—and name October as the fortunate month." (Sanford to Seward, 15 June 61, SeP.)

10. *ORN*, Ser. 2, III, 247–48; Russell to Palmerston, 1 Oct 61, GC/RU/674, PP; Russell endorsement on Layard to Russell, Memo on "United States," 20 Sept 61, Add. MS 38,987, BM.

11. Palmerston to Russell, 6 Oct 61, PRO30/22/21. A Northern banker, talking with Palmerston late in July, had received the distinct impression

that the prime minister awaited only a suitable pretext for breaking the blockade. "We do not like slavery," Palmerston allegedly told his visitor, "but we want cotton, and we dislike very much your Morrill tariff." (Belmont, *A Few Letters and Speeches*, 63–64.)

12. Layard to Russell, Memo on "United States," 20 Sept 61, Add. MS 38,987, BM; Russell to Palmerston, 8 Oct 61, GC/RU/675/1–2, PP; Palmerston to Russell, 12 Oct 61, PRO30/22/14B; *ORN*, Ser. 2, III, 591; Lindsay to Cobden, 21 Oct 61, Add. MS 43,670, BM; Russell to Lyons, 24 Aug 61, PRO30/22/96; Cobden to Slagg, 18 Oct 61, Add. MS 43,676, and Forster to Layard, 18 Sept 61, Add. MS 39,101, both BM; Cobden to Bright, 14 Oct 61, and Bright to Cobden, 3 Oct 61, both RCP.

13. Adams to R. H. Dana, Jr., 28 Aug 61, R165, AP.

14. *Ibid.*; Adams to Everett, 6 Sept 61, R165, AP.

15. Adams to C. F. Adams, Jr., 14 Sept 61, R555, and Adams, Diary, 10 Sept 61, R76, both AP.

16. Adams, Diary, 18 Sept 61, R76, and Adams to W. W. Story, 6 Sept 61, R165, and Adams to C. F. Adams, Jr., 14 Sept 61, R555, all AP; Adams nos. 38, 43 to Seward, 6 and 14 Sept 61, both NA. The pro-Confederate secretary to Palmerston was Charles Cavendish Clifford, M.P., who had served the premier in that capacity since 1854. (Adams no. 38, 6 Sept 61, NA).

17. Adams to Everett, 5 Oct 61, R165, AP; *Quarterly Review* CX (July 1861), 282. Cecil was later, as Lord Salisbury, to be prime minister during much of the period between 1885 and 1902.

18. London *Times*, 26 Sept 61, p. 7.

19. *Ibid.*, 18 Sept 61, p. 8, and 19 Sept 61, p. 6; *Punch* XLI (28 Sept 61), 126.

20. Perhaps the most influential report of this kind, aside from the letters of W. H. Russell published in the London *Times*, was written by Sir James Fergusson. Both Derby and Palmerston studied it closely and noted Fergusson's "irresistible" conclusion that the North would never be able "to crush the newly won independence of a resolute and united people." Palmerston, however, also was acquainted with Lyons's warning that Fergusson was too partisan in favor of the South "to give impartial opinions." (Fergusson report, 11 Nov 61, encl. to Derby to Palmerston, 13 Nov 61, GC/DE/70/1–7; Lyons to Russell, 22 Oct 61, PRO30/22/35.)

21. E. D. Adams, *G. B. & Amer. C.W.* I, 93; Lyons no. 183 to Russell, 6 May 61, FO115/253; C. F. Adams, Jr., "Trent Affair," 177–78; Russell

to Lyons, 24 Aug 61 and 2 Nov 61, both PRO30/22/96; Palmerston Memo dtd. 20 Oct 61, Add. MS 38,987, BM.

22. W. H. Russell, *My Diary*, 36–40, 172–76; Bigelow, *Retrospections* I, 369.

23. "Bright-Sumner Letters," MHSP, XLVI, 93, 97; Pierce, *Sumner* IV, 48; Seward to Sumner, headed "private for yourself and Mr. Bright," 11 Oct 61, Add. MS 43,390, BM. What seemed to many Europeans the most likely result of the American war was aptly expressed by a Russian diplomat, who declared during September that "the separation must be considered as an accomplished fact. [It] . . . will be completed when the North, exhausted in men and money, will yield to a sad necessity." (Stoeckl no. 57 to Gortchakov, 9 Sept 61, ESD.)

24. Adams no. 25 to Seward, 8 Aug 61, NA. Other U. S. diplomats were sending Seward the same warning. J. S. Pike wrote from The Hague, for example, that European public opinion was convinced "that a dismemberment of the Union was inevitable." (Pike no. 17 to Seward, 18 Sept 61, NA.)

25. Motley to Layard, 8 Sept 61, Add. MS 38,987, BM; *Correspondence of Motley* II, 204–207, 215; *Motley and His Family*, 122, 126.

26. Russell to Lyons, 16 and 17 Aug 61, LP; Argyll, *Memoirs* II, 171; Russell to Palmerston, 8 Oct 61, GC/RU/675/1–2, PP. The opposition leaders appear at this time to have been considering an attack on the Palmerston ministry during the forthcoming session of Parliament, based on what the conservative organ, the *Herald*, termed a policy of "drift" in the face of an impending cotton famine. The British government, said the *Herald*'s writer, should offer its "friendly offices" to try to end the American Civil War. (Quoted in *Daily National Intelligencer*, 11 Oct 61, p. 2.)

27. Lyons to Russell, 4 Oct 61, PRO30/22/35; Mercier to Thouvenel, 9 Sept 61, vol. 13, Papiers de Thouvenel, FMAE, AD; Cowley no. 1153 to Russell, 24 Sept 61, FO519/11.

28. Lyons to Russell, 4 Oct 61, PRO30/22/35; Russell to Palmerston, 17 Oct 61, GC/RU/676/1–2, PP; London *Times*, 15 Oct 61, p. 9. In reporting the British foreign minister's Newcastle address, the editors of the *Times* seem deliberately to have altered its wording. Whereas Russell had been reported in an early edition of that newspaper as saying that the North was fighting for "empire" and the South for "power," which implied no *moral* choice between them, someone appears to have gone to work on the transcript of the speech for the next morning's issue, and the new version

237

quoted the foreign minister as asserting that the belligerents were contending, "the one side for empire, and the other for independence." This phrase, which had originated in a *Times* editorial almost one month before, was thus apparently put into Russell's mouth by the editors of that journal, who then proceeded to suggest editorially that it was "the duty of this country to see whether this sanguinary contest cannot be put an end to." (London *Times*, 19 Sept 61, p. 6, and 15–17 Oct 61, pp. 9, 8, and 8 respectively.) The *Times*'s editor, John T. Delane, had by this time abandoned all pretense of neutrality toward the American combatants. He had been delighted at the Northern "*debacle* . . . at Bull's Run," and had boasted that if the American "scoundrels" dared to fight Great Britain, "the pretty little fleet we already have in those waters acting in concert with Mr. Jeff Davis, would raise their paltry blockade & turn all the tables against them in a week." (Delane to W. H. Russell, 6 Aug 61, AT.)

29. Russell to Palmerston, 17 Oct 61, GC/RU/676/1–2, PP; Dayton no. 5 to Seward, 22 May 61, and Seward nos. 10, 13 to Dayton, 30 May and 8 June 61, both NA.

30. Palmerston to Russell, 18 Oct 61, PRO30/22/14B.

31. Russell to Gladstone, 30 Oct 61, Add. MS 44,292, BM; Russell to Lyons, 2 Nov 61, PRO30/22/96.

Chapter XII: European Intervention Averted

1. Mercier no. 67 to Thouvenel, 28 Oct 61, vol. 125, FAME, AD, EU.

2. Rumors were floating about in British and continental newspapers, as the editors of one prominent journal put it, that "the Cabinet of St. James is said to have solicited France to combine with England in an effort to end the conflict in the United States, by demanding an armistice between the belligerent parties." (*Daily National Intelligencer*, 18 Oct 61, p. 2.)

3. Adams no. 61 to Seward, 18 Oct 61, NA.

4. Adams "Very Confidential" to Seward, 1 Nov 61, NA; London *Morning Post*, 19 Oct 61, quoted in *Daily National Intelligencer*, 7 Nov 61, p. 3; London *Times*, 21 Oct 61, p. 6.

5. H. W. Hayman–E. Hammond correspondence, 29 Aug–2 Oct 61, *passim*, reprinted in *Daily National Intelligencer*, 7 Nov 61, p. 2.

6. Adams "Very Confidential" to Seward, 1 Nov 61, NA; London *Times*, 29 Oct 61, p. 9.

7. Manchester *Examiner*, 30 Oct 61, quoted in Washington *Daily Na-*

tional Intelligencer, 20 Nov 61, p. 2; London *Morning Post*, 30 Oct 61, p. 5; Adams "Very Confidential" to Seward, 1 Nov 61, NA.

8. A quarter amounted to about eight bushels.

9. Adams to C. F. Adams, Jr., 29 Aug 61, R554, and Adams to Everett, 5 Oct 61, R165, and Adams to C. F. Adams, Jr., 18 Oct 61, R555, and Adams to R. C. Winthrop, 10 Oct 61, R166, all AP; W. C. Ford, *Cycle* I, 184; Adams no. 61 to Seward, 18 Oct 61, and Adams "Very Confidential" to Seward, 1 Nov 61, both NA; Cobden to J. Slagg, 8 Nov 61, Add. MS 43,676, BM; Cobden to Bright, 6 Nov 61, RCP. Karl Marx was another observer who stressed the British need for American wheat as a peace factor during the last months of 1861. (*New York Daily Tribune*, 14 Oct 61, p. 7, and see also Marx and Engels, *Civil War*, 16.) While it is true that Seward, in at least one instruction to Dayton (no. 75, dated 30 Oct. 1861), used the idea of a wheat scarcity as an argument against European threats of intervention for cotton, the historian Frank Owsley is mistaken in asserting that Adams received the idea from the American secretary of state. (Rather was the reverse true.) He also errs in dismissing the "wheat famine" threat as "Federal propaganda" which "had little if anything to do with preventing English intervention in the American Civil War." His contention, largely a restatement of one first made by E. D. Adams, echoes the latter's assumption that because the leaders of the British government did not make the subject of a wheat famine a matter for grave official consideration, as they did the cotton famine, they were not influenced by the possibility of losing the American supply of breadstuffs. (Owsley, *King Cotton Diplomacy*, 70–71, 547–49, and E. D. Adams, *G.B. & Amer. C.W.* II, 13n–14n.) This is faulty reasoning. The British leaders were deeply concerned about the cotton famine *because one already existed.* The wheat famine was merely potential—dependent upon a war with the United States. By staying neutral in regard to the American Civil War, British statesmen hoped to avoid such a contingency. But this is precisely why more perceptive historians have realized that the threat of a wheat shortage in case of an Anglo-American war helped to fend off British intervention in favor of the South. There *was* widespread awareness expressed in contemporary British newspapers of the danger of a wheat famine in case of a war with the United States. (See, for example, newspaper sources cited in J. H. Park, "English Workingmen and the American Civil War," 455–56.) Moreover, private letters exchanged among British statesmen *do* exhibit a concern for the scarcity of the 1861 wheat harvest and a consciousness of the importance of American wheat.

(See, for example, a series of letters from J. E. Denison, Speaker of the House of Commons, to Gladstone, 16 June, 13 and 20 Aug, and 19 Sept 61, all in Add. MS 44,261, BM.) Moreover, American newspapers, which were widely extracted in English newspapers, repeatedly raised the specter of a British wheat famine. (See, for example, articles with such titles as "CORN AND COTTON: WHICH IS KING?", "BREAD VS. COTTON," and "KING CORN," which appeared, either as quoted matter from other U. S. newspapers, or [in one case] as an editorial, in the *Daily National Intelligencer*, 16, 19, and 25 Oct 61, all p. 2, and *ibid.*, 13 Nov 61, p. 3.) For the "wheat thesis," to which Owsley and E. D. Adams object, but in support of which more good evidence from English sources is advanced than Owsley produces for his own "war profits" thesis, and which is based solidly on the fact that the United States supplied 41.5 percent of Great Britain's wheat imports for 1861, and the next year even more, see Schmidt, "Influence of Wheat and Cotton on Anglo-American Relations During the Civil War," 400–39. It is perhaps extravagant, however, to say that during "this time of crisis wheat proved itself more powerful even than King Cotton." (Trimble, "Historical Aspects of the Surplus Food Production of the United States, 1862–1902," 223.)

10. Adams to C. F. Adams, Jr., 14 Sept 61, R555, and Adams, Diary, 30 May 61, R76, both AP; Adams nos. 58, 61 to Seward, 11 and 18 Oct 61, NA.

11. Adams no. 58 to Seward, 11 Oct 61, NA; Adams, Diary, 9 Nov 61, R76, AP.

12. The Schleswig-Holstein question was re-opened by King Frederick VII of Denmark early in 1863, and war with Prussia and Austria followed before another year had passed.

13. In 1863 the Poles finally rebelled against Russia, an event which provoked diplomatic intervention by the governments of England, France, and Austria.

14. Adams, Diary, 9 Nov 61, R76, and Adams to C. F. Adams, Jr., 29 Aug 61, R554, and 7 Sept 61, R555, and Adams to Everett, 6 Sept 61, and Adams to R. H. Dana, Jr., 28 Aug 61, both R165, all AP; Adams no. 58 to Seward, 11 Oct 61, NA; W. C. Ford, *Cycle* I, 39. Although Palmerston professed himself to have "no fear of any blow up this year in Europe" in considering what military measures should be taken in regard to the defense of Canada against the United States, he was still warily watching developments on the continent, especially in regard to Italy and Poland. Moreover, the prime minister believed that Napoleon was waiting only for

the opportune moment "to launch his thunders and satiate his long pent up and craftily concealed enmity against England." The French people, he assumed, hated England "from the bottom of their hearts, and would make any sacrifice to inflict a deep humiliation upon England," in order to gain revenge for past humiliations. The British government, therefore, had to be very careful not to allow itself to become embroiled in a serious quarrel with the United States *to which France was not also a party on the side of England.* (Palmerston to Herbert, 3 June 61, and Palmerston to Newcastle, 1 Sept 61, and Palmerston to Lewis, 26 Aug 61, all in Add. MS 48, 582, BM; Palmerston to Russell, 9 Sept 61, PRO30/22/21; Ashley, *Palmerston* II, 224–25.)

15. Adams no. 58 to Seward, 11 Oct 61, NA; Adams to Everett, 25 Oct 61, R166, AP.

16. *Seward at Washington* I, 621; Dayton no. 56 to Seward, 3 Oct 61, NA; Cowley no. 797 to Russell, 2 July 61, FO519/11, and also encl. to Russell no. 213 to Lyons, 6 July 61, FO115/243/IV.

17. Seward no. 75 to Dayton, 30 Oct 61, NA; Lyons nos. 584, 606 to Russell, 21 and 28 Oct 61, both FO115/257; Thouvenel no. 27 to Mercier, 3 Oct 61, and Mercier no. 67 to Thouvenel, 28 Oct 61, both vol. 125, FMAE, AD, EU.

18. Thouvenel to Mercier (copy), found in Lyons no. 584 to Russell, 21 Oct 61, FO115/257. See also Thouvenel no. 27 to Mercier, 3 Oct 61, vol. 125, FMAE, AD, EU.

19. Lyons no. 606 to Russell, 28 Oct 61, FO115/257; Mercier no. 67 to Thouvenel, 28 Oct 61, vol. 125, FMAE, AD, EU.

20. Lyons no. 606 to Russell, 28 Oct 61, FO115/257, confirmed by Mercier no. 67 to Thouvenel, 28 Oct 61, vol. 125, FMAE, AD, EU.

21. According to Lord Lyons.

22. Lyons no. 606 to Russell, 28 Oct 61, FO115/257.

23. *Ibid.*

24. *Seward at Washington* I, 627, 633, 635.

25. *New York Times*, 17 Oct 61, p. 6; *Daily National Intelligencer*, 17 Oct 61, p. 3. Seward's coastal-fortification circular was probably inspired by a prior British gesture. Early in September, Lyons had learned from Russell that information had recently been received in London that both the tonnage and the armament of the American naval force on the Great Lakes appeared to be in excess of the amount permitted by the Rush-Bagot agreement of 1817 between Great Britain and the United States. The British minister in Washington was commanded to make a representation

to Seward on the subject, which he accordingly did. After inquiring at the Navy Department whether there was any basis to the charge, Seward replied that the total American naval force on the Great Lakes consisted of one small steamer mounting a single eight-inch gun, used "exclusively for purposes of recruiting for the Navy, with artillery practice for the newly recruited seamen." He did not believe that the United States government had committed any violation of the armaments limitation agreement of 1817, but if the British government thought otherwise, he wrote, "we shall be happy to consider their views in that respect." Apparently, this answer satisfied the British foreign minister, for he made no response; but the exchange of notes seems to have drawn Seward's attention to the vulnerability of the United States to attack along its northern coastlines, which when viewed in the light of recent large movements of British troops to Canada and the sudden British interest in the state of American naval strength on the Great Lakes, appeared possibly to have an ominous significance. (Russell no. 278 to Lyons, 15 Aug 61, FO115/245/II; Lyons nos. 465, 486 to Russell, 31 Aug and 12 Sept 61, FO115/255-256; Lyons to Seward, 31 Aug 61 and Seward to Lyons, 12 Sept 61, both NA; G. V. Fox to Seward, 9 Sept 61, "Miscellaneous Letters of the Department of State," RG59, NA.) Another version of the Great Lakes fortification incident suggests (somewhat obscurely) that the initiative for the issuance of Seward's circular came from certain Northern governors. (Bigelow, *Retrospections* I, 349-53, 446n.)

26. *New York Times*, 17 Oct 61, p. 1; Lyons nos. 568, 606 to Russell, 18 and 28 Oct 61, FO115/257; London *Times*, 5 Nov 61, p. 6; Adams [Confidential] to Seward, 15 Nov 61, R166, AP. Nothing much came of Seward's gesture, even though Lincoln did incorporate it into his annual message to Congress in December, which Lyons took "as a sign of a return to the policy of endeavouring rather to appeal to the fears of foreign nations by menaces, than to conciliate their good will." Congress did not act positively on the request for funds to fortify the Great Lakes region, nor did the governors pay much attention to it. (Lyons no. 742 to Russell, 6 Dec 61, FO115/259; Winks, *Canada and the United States*, 77.)

27. Lyons nos. 540, 623 to Russell, 8 Oct and 4 Nov 61, FO115/256-257; Russell to Gladstone, 30 Oct 61, Add. MS 44,292, BM; Russell to Lyons, 16 Nov 61, PRO30/22/96; Bates, *Diary*, 194-95; Charleston *Courier*, 30 Nov and 9 Dec 61, p. 2 and p. 1, respectively.

28. Lyons nos. 585, 623, 634 to Russell, 21 Oct and 4 and 8 Nov 61, all FO115/257.

29. Lyons no. 634 to Russell, 8 Nov 61, FO115/257; Russell no. 435 to Lyons, 26 Nov 61, FO115/248/VI; Russell to Lyons, 2 Nov 61, PRO30/22/96.

30. Seward no. 75 to Dayton, 30 Oct 61, NA.

31. *Ibid.* Even after Seward thus threatened war should France attempt to break the blockade to obtain cotton, Mercier advocated that the attempt should be made. He believed that in the end the United States government would "give way." (Frothingham, *Everett*, 436.)

32. Seward no. 75 to Dayton, 30 Oct 61, NA.

33. *Ibid.*

34. *Seward at Washington* I, 627. Seward wrote Adams: "Paris instead of London has lately been prominent as a scene of discontent with our blockade. We are looking with no little anxiety in that direction." (Seward no. 125 to Adams, 14 Nov 61, and Seward "private" to Adams, 27 Nov 61, both NA.)

CHAPTER XIII: EUROPEANS INVADE NORTH AMERICA

1. "Bright-Sumner Letters," MHSP, XLVI, 98.

2. *Present Condition of Mexico*, 17–18. Russell expressed "great surprise" at Buchanan's proclamation and found it difficult to believe that he meant it seriously. (Russell no. 28 to Lyons, 2 Feb 61, FO115/239/I.)

3. Lyons nos. 112, 125 to Russell, 25 Mar and 1 Apr 61, FO115/252; Russell no. 10 to Lyons, 16 Jan 61, FO115/238/I.

4. Lyons no. 481 to Russell, 10 Sept 61, FO115/256; *Present Condition of Mexico*, 307–308. Wyke first sent Lyons an outline of the Corwin-Seward proposals in June. (Wyke to Lyons, 23 June 61, LP.)

5. This idea later became known as the Roosevelt corollary to the Monroe Doctrine. But it had antecedents as far back as 1856, when John Forsyth, American minister to Mexico, endorsed the proposal of certain "intelligent Mexicans," apparently including Foreign Minister de la Fuente, that the United States ought to undertake "an American Protectorate" of Mexico. This project was abandoned, however, until Seward revived it. (Forsyth nos. 5, 23, 24 to Marcy, 8 Nov 56 and 2 and 10 Feb 57, and Forsyth no. 29 to Cass, 4 Apr 57, all NA.)

6. Seward no. 2 to Corwin, 6 Apr 61, NA.

7. Seward nos. 8, 16 to Corwin, 3 June and 24 Aug 61, and Corwin nos. 2 and 3 to Seward, both 29 July 61, all NA.

8. Seward no. 17 to Corwin, 2 Sept 61, NA.

9. *Present Condition of Mexico*, 383–85, 398–408; Corwin nos. 7, 8 to Seward, 21 Oct and 29 Nov 61, NA. At first Sir C. Lennox Wyke worked to thwart Corwin in getting his debt payment plan accepted by the Mexican authorities, but ultimately they worked closely together. (Wyke to Lyons, 29 Sept and 27 Oct 61, both LP.)

10. Seward no. 71 to Adams, 24 Aug 61, NA.

11. Adams, Diary, 25 Sept 61, R76, AP; Adams no. 50 to Seward, 28 Sept 61, NA; Russell no. 1023 to Cowley, 27 Sept 61, encl. in Russell no. 327 to Lyons, 28 Sept 61, FO115/246/IV, and also in *Present Condition of Mexico*, 308–309.

12. Adams no. 50 to Seward, 28 Sept 61, NA; Russell no. 1023 to Cowley, 27 Sept 61, encl. in Russell no. 327 to Lyons, 28 Sept 61, FO115/246/IV.

13. Adams no. 50 to Seward, 28 Sept 61, NA; Russell no. 1023 to Cowley, *Present Condition of Mexico*, 308–309.

14. Russell no. 1023 to Cowley, *Present Condition of Mexico*, 308–309.

15. *Present Condition of Mexico*, 302–303.

16. Adams no. 50 to Seward, 28 Sept 61, NA, and Russell no. 1023 to Cowley, *Present Condition of Mexico*, 308-309. For evidence of the French "hesitation" mentioned by Russell, see Thouvenel, *Le Secret de l'Empereur* II, 167–69.

17. Adams no. 50 to Seward, 28 Sept 61, NA, and Russell no. 1023 to Cowley, *Present Condition of Mexico*, 308–309.

18. Adams no. 50 to Seward, 28 Sept 61, NA, and Russell no. 1023 to Cowley, *Present Condition of Mexico*, 308–309.

19. Adams, Diary, 25 Sept 61, R76, AP; Layard to Russell, Memo on "United States," 20 Sept 61, Add. MS 38,987, BM; Palmerston to Russell, 24 Sept 61, PRO 30/22/21; Stanley of Alderley to Granville, 27 Sept 61, PRO30/29/31.

20. Palmerston to Russell, 24 Sept 61, PRO30/22/21.

21. Adams no. 50 to Seward, 28 Sept 61, NA; Adams, Diary, 25 Sept 61, R76, AP; W. C. Ford, *Cycle* I, 48–49.

22. Russell to Victoria, 27 Sept 61, PRO30/22/14B.

23. Palmerston to Hammond, 28 Sept 61, Hammond Papers, PRO391/7. Thouvenel opposed Seward's plan. (Cowley nos. 1157 and 1166 to Russell, 24 and 27 Sept 61, FO519/11; Cowley to Russell, 24 and 27 Sept 61, FO519/229; Dayton no. 51 to Seward, 27 Sept 61, NA.)

24. Russell nos. 327, 329 to Lyons, both 28 Sept 61, with encls.,

FO115/246/IV, V; Russell no. 342 to Lyons, 5 Oct 61, with encls., FO115/247/I; Seward no. 128 to Adams, 21 Nov 61, NA.

25. Lyons no. 553 to Russell, 14 Oct 61, FO115/256.

26. Seward no. 99 to Adams, 10 Oct 61, NA.

27. The text of the three-power convention may be found in *Present Condition of Mexico*, 185–87. The European negotiations antedating the signing of the convention are ably traced in Corti, *Maximilian and Charlotte of Mexico* I, 73–114.

28. Adams no. 66 to Seward, 1 Nov 61, NA.

29. *Ibid.*

30. Adams to Dayton, 2 Oct 61, R165, AP; Seward nos. 119, 128 to Adams, 9 and 21 Nov 61, NA.

31. Adams, Diary, 18 Oct 61, R76, AP; Adams nos. 106, 115 to Seward, 24 Jan and 14 Feb 62, NA. The author of a pamphlet published in France in 1863 congratulated Napoleon III for allegedly embarking upon the Mexican intervention as a first step toward aiding the Confederate States to win their independence. (Chevalier, *France, Mexico, and the Confederate States*, 16 pp.)

32. Seward nos. 119, 191 to Adams, 9 Nov 61 and 19 Feb 62, NA. Seward and Adams were not the only observers who suspected that the Mexican intervention had long-range implications for the security of the United States. See Bright to Cobden, 3 Oct 61, RCP.

CHAPTER XIV: ENGLAND BECOMES THE ARMORY
OF THE CONFEDERACY

1. *ORN*, Ser. 2, II, 64–65, 71, 82–87; *ORA*, Ser. 4, I, 220, 332–33, 343–46; Bulloch, *Secret Service* I, 47–48, 51–53; Adams no. 13 to Seward, 9 July 61, NA.

2. Morse nos. 5, 9, 10 to Seward, 14, 19, and 22 June 61, *London Consular Despatches*, vol. 29, NA; Sanford to Seward, 15 and 18 June and 23 July 61, all SeP; Morse to Sanford, 29 June and 12 July 61, Box 139, HSSP; Wilding to F. S. Seward, 13 Aug 61, *Liverpool Consular Despatches*, vol. 19, both NA; Adams, Diary, 14 Aug 61, R76, and Wilson to Adams, 14 Aug 61, R554, both AP; Moran, *Journal*, 861–62; and *ORN*, Ser. 1, VI, 213–14. For a good general treatment of Sanford's secret service activities, see H. C. Owsley, "Henry Shelton Sanford and Federal Surveillance Abroad, 1861–1865."

3. Adams, Diary, 14 and 15 Aug 61, R76, AP; Adams to Russell, 15 Aug 61, encl. to Adams no. 27 to Seward, 16 Aug 61, NA; *Claims v. GB* I, 41–44.

4. Adams no. 27 to Seward, 16 Aug 61, NA; Adams, Diary, 16–17 Aug 61, R76, AP; Moran, *Journal*, 863.

5. Moran, *Journal*, 865; Moran to Adams, 18–20 Aug 61, R554, AP; *ORN*, Ser. 1, VI, 171, 190–91, 203, 279, 286; *Illustrated London News* XXXIX (26 Oct 61), 417.

6. Adams no. 30 to Seward, 23 Aug 61, NA, and its encl., Russell to Adams, 22 Aug 61.

7. *ORN*, Ser. 1, VI, 101, 213–14, 272, 305, 323–28; Huse, *Supplies for the Confederate Army*, 19–20; Adams, Diary, 24 Aug 61, R76, AP; Wilding to F. W. Seward, 23 and 31 Aug 61, *Liverpool Consular Despatches*, vol. 19, NA; Adams nos. 21, 24, 26, 30, 35, 38 to Seward, 2, 6, 8, 23, and 30 Aug and 6 Sept 61, all NA.

8. Adams nos. 58, 59 to Seward, 11 and 17 Oct 61, NA; Adams, Diary, 3 Nov 61, R76, and Adams to C. F. Adams, Jr., 14 Sept 61, R555, and Adams to Dayton, 2 July 61, R165, all AP; Pierre Rost to Jefferson Davis, 20 July 61, Special Collections, Emory University.

9. *ORN*, Ser. 2, III, 214, 222–23, 291.

10. Adams to C. F. Adams, Jr., 14 Sept 61, R555, AP; *ORN*, Ser. 2, III, 221–25, 229–30, 235–37, 278–80, 293–94, 314–15, 325–26; Moran, *Journal*, 870. Hotze arrived in London on January 29, 1862.

11. Sanford to Weed, 18 May 61, WP; Sanford "Confidential" to Seward, 24 Sept 61, Box 140, and Sanford to his uncle, 14 Nov 61, and Sanford to Walker, Nov 61, all in Box 100, SaP.

12. W. M. Walker to Seward, 20 Oct 61, "Miscellaneous letters of the Department of State," RG59, NA.

13. *Ibid*.; Clapp, *Bigelow*, 153.

14. Marsh no. 19 to Seward, 14 Sept 61, NA.

15. C. F. Adams, Jr., "Trent Affair," 79–81, 85–86; Everett to Adams, 24 Nov 61, and Harvey to Adams, 25 Nov 61, both R555, AP; Frothingham, *Everett*, 433–36.

16. Adams to Everett, 27 Nov 61, and Adams to Young, 29 Oct 61, both R166, and Adams to C. F. Adams, Jr., 4 Oct 61, R555, all AP; Gurowski, *Diary*, 110–11, 119.

17. Adams, Diary, 9 Nov 61, R76, and Guildhall Banquet Program, 9 Nov 61, R555, both AP; Moran, *Journal*, 902–903, 1132–35; London *Times*, 11 Nov 61, p. 8.

18. Adams "Confidential" to Seward, 15 Nov 61, R166, and Adams, Diary, 11, 12 and 18 Nov 61, R76, and Harvey to Adams, 25 Nov 61, R555, all AP; London *Times*, 11 Nov 61, p. 6; Seward no. 136 to Adams, 30 Nov 61, NA; *Stanleys of Alderley*, 316. On the evening of Adams's speech to the Lord Mayor's guests, several Confederate emissaries held places of honor at the Fishmonger's banquet near London Bridge, where Southern Commissioner Yancey spoke in favor of Confederate independence and an early reception into the family of nations. See Adams no. 77 to Seward, 23 Nov 61, NA; Parkes to Adams, 23 Nov 61, R555, AP; Moran, *Journal*, 903–904; Huse, *Supplies for the Confederate Army*, 29–30; *Illustrated London News* XXXIX (16 Nov 61), 496; London *Times*, 12 Nov 61, p. 4.

CHAPTER XV: AMERICAN "AMORALITY" AND BRITISH AGGRAVATION

1. Schleiden to Lyons, 10 and 11 Feb 61, both LP; Lyons nos. 56, 65 to Russell, 12 and 18 Feb 61, FO115/251; and Lyons nos. 76, 86, 91, 92, 113, 126 to Russell, 26 Feb and 2, 11, 11, and 25 Mar and 1 Apr 61, respectively, all FO115/252.

2. For a sample of English press sentiment, see editorials in the London *Times*, 22 March 61, p. 9, and 6 Apr 61, p. 8. See also Cobden to Bright, 25 Mar 61, RCP, and "Bright-Sumner Letters," MHSP, XLVI, 99–100.

3. Adams no. 2 to Seward, 21 May 61, NA; Belmont, *A Few Letters and Speeches*, 63–64; John Cowell to Lord Overtone, 9 May 61, attached to Russell to Granville, 5 June 61, PRO30/29/24.

4. *Correspondence of Motley* II, 119–20; Adams to C. F. Adams, Jr., 29 Aug 61, R554, AP; Beverley Tucker to Jefferson Davis, 22 Mar 61, Special Collections, Emory University.

5. *Punch* XLI (17 Aug 61), 66.

6. Seward no. 2 to Sanford, 26 Mar 61, NA.

7. Klingberg, "Harriet Beecher Stowe and Social Reform in England," 543–46.

8. Lincoln's *Works* IV, 263; E. D. Adams, *G.B. & Amer. C.W.* I, 38, 45.

9. Bigelow, *Retrospections* I, 409.

10. Seward no. 2 to Adams, 10 Apr 61, and Seward no. 3 to Dayton, 22 Apr 61, both NA.

11. Sanford to Seward, 12 May 61, and Clay no. 6 to Seward, 17 Aug

61, and Pike no. 17 to Seward, 18 Sept 61, and Schurz no. 18 to Seward, 18 Sept 61, all NA.

12. Seward no. 35 to Schurz, 10 Oct 61, NA; Lincoln's *Works* IV, 317n.

13. Argyll, *Memoirs* II, 173–74.

14. Motley no. 1 to Seward, 20 Sept 61, NA.

15. Russell to Lyons, 26 Oct 61, PRO30/22/96; Gladstone to the duchess of Sutherland, 29 May 61, Add. MS 44,531, BM.

16. Argyll to Gladstone, 23 and 29 Aug 61, Add. MS 44,099, BM; Cobden to Bright, 19 May and 8 Aug 61, and Bright to Cobden, 3 Oct 61, CP.

17. Seward nos. 84, 85 to Adams, both 10 Sept 61, NA.

18. Lyons to Russell, 13 Sept 61, PRO30/22/35.

19. Adams to Russell, 30 Sept and 1 Oct 61, encls. to Adams no. 53 to Seward, 4 Oct 61, and Adams no. 58 to Seward, 11 Oct 61, w/encl. Russell to Adams, 4 Oct 61, and Adams no. 59 to Seward, 17 Oct 61, w/encl. Russell to Adams, 8 Oct 61, all NA.

20. Seward no. 112 to Adams, 29 Oct 61, NA; Lyons nos. 621, 622, 640 to Russell, 4, 4, and 9 Nov 61, FO115/257; Russell no. 423 to Lyons, 22 Nov 61, FO115/248/III.

21. Seward nos. 122, 136 to Adams, 11 and 30 Nov 61, NA.

22. Lyons nos. 216, 545, 577 to Russell, 23 May and 12 and 21 Oct 61, FO115/253, 256, 257; Russell nos. 320, 340 to Lyons, 21 Sept and 4 Oct 61, FO115/246/III, VI; Lyons to Seward w/encl., 11 Oct 61, NA.

23. *ORN*, Ser. 1, IV, 206, and XVI, 534–40, 686; Lyons nos. 592, 775 to Russell, 24 Oct and 18 Dec 61, FO115/257, 259.

24. *ORN*, Ser. 1, V, 659, 684; Lyons nos. 273, 320, 374, 401, 521, 533, 544, 638, 693 to Russell, 13 June, 8 and 29 July, 5 Aug, 28 Sept, 4 and 12 Oct, and 7 Nov 61, FO115/243–48, *passim*, London *Times*, 24 Oct 61, p. 8; Lyons to Seward, 28 Sept 61, NA; Bernath, *Squall Across the Atlantic*, 22–24, 30.

25. Palmerston to Russell, 13 Nov, PRO30/22/21; Palmerston to Newcastle, 12 Nov 61, Add. MS 48,582, BM; Adams "Confidential" to Seward, 15 Nov 61, NA; Adams, Diary, 12 Nov 61, R76, AP.

26. Adams "Confidential" to Seward, 15 Nov 61, NA; Adams, Diary, 12 Nov 61, R76, AP.

27. Seward no. 136 to Adams, 30 Nov 61, NA.

CHAPTER XVI: A HISTORICAL MISUNDERSTANDING

1. *New York Times*, 16 Dec 61, p. 3.
2. Russell to Lyons, 16 Nov 61, PRO30/22/96; Gladstone to Phillimore, 14 Nov 61, Add. MS 44,532, BM; Seward no. 136 to Adams, 30 Nov 61, NA; Tilby, *Russell*, 187.
3. Seward no. 136 to Adams, 30 Nov 61, NA.
4. Lewis to Clarendon, 7 Sept 61, CP.
5. Palmerston to Hammond, 21 Apr 61, FO391/7.
6. Lyons no. 585 to Russell, 21 Oct 61, FO115/257.
7. Chase, *Inside Lincoln's Cabinet*, 56; Lyons to his sister Minna, 28 Feb 60, LP. Harvard College Law Professor Joel Parker remarked at the time of the *Trent* crisis that "the insane violence" of the British "press and people, which drove the government into [extensive warlike preparations] . . . . proved that *it is in a constitutional monarchy that the mob is the ruling power, and not in a republic.*" (Parker, *Case of the Trent*, 63–64.)
8. Gladstone to Lewis, 21 Sept 61, Add. MS 44,236, BM.
9. Among them may be included many historians.
10. Lyons no. 495 to Russell, 16 Sept 61, FO115/256.
11. Monck to Newcastle, 27 Dec 61, and Newcastle to Monck, 4 Jan 62, both NeC; Adams to S. Brooks, 7 Aug 61, R165, AP.
12. Lewis to de Grey, 17 Sept 61, Add. MS 43,533, BM; Buchanan, *Works* XI, 218.
13. Russell, *Recollections and Suggestions*, 286.
14. Russell no. 198 to Lyons, 29 June 61, FO115/243/II; Adams nos. 10, 11 to Seward, 28 and 29 June 61, both NA.
15. Adams to Palfrey, 18 Oct 61, R166, AP.
16. Seward nos. 10, 15, 21, 42 to Adams, 21 May and 8 and 19 June and 21 July 61, all NA.
17. Seward nos. 10, 21, 42 to Adams, 21 May, 19 June, and 21 July 61, all NA.
18. Seward nos. 2, 42 to Adams, 10 Apr and 21 July 61, both NA.
19. Seward nos. 83, 85, 86, 95, 112 to Adams, 7, 10, 11, and 25 Sept and 29 Oct 61, all NA.
20. *Seward at Washington* II, 493; Seward to Weed, 7 Mar 62, WP.
21. *Seward at Washington* II, 35.

Sources

The following compilation of sources includes, with a few exceptions, solely those cited in the Notes above. One who wishes to investigate possibilities for additional reading on topics treated in this book may consult standard bibliographies and the section entitled "Diplomacy" in *Civil War Books, A Critical Bibliography*, ed. by A. Nevins, J. Robertson, Jr., and B. Wiley (Baton Rouge, La., 1967, I, 241–78), and compiled by the author.

Throughout my Notes I have used the shortest possible citations. Certain files of documents located in public archives and various collections of manuscripts have been identified as follows:

ALP.   Papers of Abraham Lincoln, Library of Congress.

AP.   Papers of Adams family, Massachusetts Historical Society, Boston, especially the following rolls from the microfilm edition: R76–77 for C. F. Adams's Diary; R165–67 for C. F. Adams's Letterbooks; R296 for C. F. Adams's Reminiscences; and R554–58 for C. F. Adams's Letters Received and Other Loose Papers.

AT.   Archives of the *Times*, Printing House Square, London, with special thanks to archivist J. Gordon Phillips and William Rees-Mogg, editor.

BM.   British Museum, London. Documents used in writing this book have been cited by manuscript number as follows: 38,987–39,102 for Papers of Sir Austen Henry Layard; 43,386–43,391 for Papers of John Bright; 43,512–43,551 for Papers of George Frederick Samuel Robinson, earl de Grey, and marquis of Ripon; 43,659–43,677 for Papers of Richard Cobden; 44,099–44,938 for Papers of William Ewart Gladstone; and 48,582 for a letterbook of Henry John Temple, 3d viscount Palmerston.

BPCUS, G&B.   Belgian Political Correspondence, United States, General and Bound. Includes dispatches of Belgian minister in Washington. Microfilm copies in National Archives.

CP.   Papers of George William Frederick Villiers, 4th earl of Clarendon, Bodleian Library, Oxford University.

Emory University. Special Collections. Papers of Jefferson Davis, James M. Mason, and John M'Clintock.

Esd. Dispatches of Edouard Stoeckl, Russian minister in Washington. Copies at Library of Congress.

FMAE, AD. Archives of the French Ministry of Foreign Affairs, Paris, including "Archives diplomatiques, Angleterre," vols. 719, 720, and "Archives diplomatiques, Etats-Unis," vols. 124, 125.

FMAE, MD. Archives of the French Ministry of Foreign Affairs, Paris, including "Memoires et Documents, Papiers de Thouvenel," vols. 8, 13.

FO. British Foreign Office records, located in PRO.

Gclp. Papers of Sir George Cornewall Lewis, Harpton Court Collection, National Library of Wales, Aberystwyth. Thanks to Prof. Alan Conway, Dept. of History, University of Canterbury, for assistance in seeing this collection.

Houghton Library, Harvard University, Cambridge, Mass. Papers of Charles Sumner.

HL (or HM). Manuscripts of Charles Sumner, Francis Lieber, and Thomas Dudley, all at Huntington Library, San Marino, California.

Hssp. See SaP.

Hwlp. Papers of Henry W. Longfellow, Craigie House, Cambridge, Mass.

Jbp. Papers of John Bigelow, New York Public Library.

Jmmp. James Murray Mason Papers, Library of Congress.

Jspp. James Shepherd Pike Papers, Library of Congress.

LC. Library of Congress. Manuscript Division has the "Journal" of Benjamin Moran and Papers of Francis Lieber, Abraham Lincoln (alp), James M. Mason (jmmp), James S. Pike (jspp), Rudolf Schleiden (rsd), and Charles D. Wilkes, as well as the so-called Pickett Papers of the Southern Confederacy. Here may also be found diplomatic correspondence pertaining to the United States during 1861 and 1862 of Russia (esd) and England (FO115 and FO5) in either photostat or microfilm form.

LP. Papers of Richard Bickerton Pemell Lyons, 1st earl Lyons, Arundel Castle, England, with the gracious permission of the duke of Norfolk.

Mhsp. Massachusetts Historical Society *Papers*, published at Boston. The society also contains manuscripts of the Adams family, of Governor Andrew, and of Richard Henry Dana, Jr.

Mln. Papers of Sir Alexander Milne, National Maritime Museum,

Greenwich, used with the permission of the trustees of the National Maritime Museum.

NA. National Archives, Washington, D. C. Among the records I have consulted there are (1) dispatches of U. S. ministers at London, Paris, Brussels, Turin, St. Petersburg, The Hague, Madrid, Vienna, Lisbon, and Berlin to Seward, and the secretary of state's instructions to these envoys in Europe, all for the period from Mar. 1861 to Feb. 1862; (2) diplomatic notes exchanged during 1861 by Seward and Lyons; (3) dispatches received by Seward during 1861 from U. S. consuls at Liverpool, London, and Manchester, and at Havana and Nassau; (4) "Correspondence Regarding Prisoners of War, 1861–1862, Parr-Sullivan," Box no. 9, folder nos. 61, 75, 81, "Civil War Papers," and "Instructions to Special Agents," vol. 21, and "Letters Sent Regarding Prisoners of War and Intercepted Messages, Aug. 1861—Feb. 1863," and "Miscellaneous Letters of the Department of State," all in RG59.

NeC. Papers of Henry Pelham Fiennes Pelham Clinton, 5th duke of Newcastle, University of Nottingham, used with the permission of the trustees of the Newcastle estate.

New York Public Library. Horace Greeley papers.

ORA. War of the Rebellion: Official Records of the Union and Confederate Armies.

ORN. Official Records of the Union and Confederate Navies in the War of the Rebellion.

OsC. Papers of John Evelyn Denison, viscount Ossington, University of Nottingham.

PP. Papers of Henry John Temple, 3d viscount Palmerston, consulted at the Historical Manuscripts Commission, Chancery Lane, London, by permission of the trustees of the Broadlands Archives.

Pro. Public Record Office, London, where I have consulted the following records: (1) dispatches exchanged between the Foreign Office and the British legation in Washington which, for the period covered by this book, are found in files FO115/238 through FO115/259 and FO115/283–84; (2) supplementary materials not located in the FO115 files were found in FO5/776 and FO5/906; (3) dispatches exchanged between the Foreign Office and the British Embassy in Paris which I have cited appear in FO27 and in FO519/11; (4) the Russell Papers, as designated by PRO30/22, include not only the private correspondence between Lords Russell and Cowley in PRO30/22/56 (as well as in FO519/228–29), but also private correspondence between Lords Russell and Lyons in PRO30/22/35 and PRO30/22/96, and private correspondence between Lords Russell and Palmerston in PRO30/22/4, PRO30/22/14, PRO30/22/21 and PRO30/22/22; (5) cabinet memoranda which I have cited may be found in PRO30/22/27, while Russell's correspondence with officials like Somerset may be seen in PRO30/22/24; (6) in the Granville Papers, especially PRO30/29/18, PRO30/29/24, PRO30/29/29, and PRO30/29/31, is valuable information ; (7) pertinent records were found in records of the Colonial Office designated as CO42/626–29; (8) memoranda exchanged between the Foreign Office and the crown law officers were discovered in FO83/2212; while (9) in the Hammond Papers, especially FO391/5–7, I found indispensable information.

RCP. Papers of Richard Cobden, West Sussex County and Diocesan Record Office, Chichester, with thanks to Mrs. Patricia Gill, county archivist, for much kind assistance.

RCSA. Records of the Confederate States of America, also called the "Pickett Papers," Library of Congress.

RHDP. Papers of Richard Henry Dana, Jr., Massachusetts Historical Society, Boston.

RSD. Dispatches of Rudolf Schleiden, minister of Bremen at Washington, copies of which are in the Library of Congress.

SaP. Papers of Henry Shelton Sanford, Florida National Bank, Sanford, Fla., with thanks to Mrs. Harriet Owsley for generous assistance in locating them. See especially boxes 99, 100, 132, 139, and 140.

SeP. Papers of William H. Seward, Rush Rhees Library, University of Rochester.

University of Georgia. Special Collections. T. Cobb Papers.

WP. Papers of Thurlow Weed, Rush Rhees Library, University of Rochester.

Unsigned Articles in Newspapers and Magazines

In the Notes to this book I have cited articles (including editorials) published in the following newspapers and magazines, exclusive of those whose authorship was known, in which case they are listed below among other printed sources. *Albany Evening Journal. Charleston Mercury.* Charleston *Courier.* Washington *Daily National Intelligencer.* Washington *Evening Star. Illustrated London News.* London *Morning Post. New York Daily Tribune.* New York *Herald. New York Times. Punch. Quarterly Review. Saturday Review.* London *Times.*

Other sources consulted in writing this book which are cited in the Notes above are listed alphabetically, by author, below. These include Ph.D. dissertations, articles in scholarly journals, monographs, and standard works. Readers who desire critical analyses of these sources will find some appraised in footnotes. Others are characterized in *Civil War Books, A Critical Bibliography*, in the section on "Diplomacy" compiled by the author, whose book, *The* Trent *Affair*, soon to be published, will contain brief characterizations of many of the sources used in this volume.

Adams, Brooks, "The Seizure of the Laird Rams," Mass. Historical Society *Proceedings* XLV (Dec., 1911), 242–333; Adams, Charles F., Jr., "The British Proclamation of May, 1861," Mass. Historical Society *Proceedings* XLVIII (Jan. 1915), 190–241; Adams, Charles F., Jr., *Charles Francis Adams* (Boston, 1900); Adams, Charles F., Jr., *Charles Francis Adams, 1835–1915: An Autobiography* (Boston, 1916); Adams, Charles F., Jr., "The Negotiation of 1861 Relating to the Declaration of Paris of 1856," Mass. Historical Society *Proceedings* XLVI (Oct. 1912), 23–84; Adams, Charles F., Jr., *Richard Henry Dana, A Biography* (Boston, 1890), 2 vols.; Adams, Charles F., Jr., *Studies Military and Diplomatic, 1775–1865* (New York, 1911); Adams, Charles F., Jr., "The Trent Affair," Mass. Historical Society *Proceedings* XLV (Nov. 1911), 35–148; Adams, Ephriam D., *Great Britain and the American Civil War*, reprint (2 vols. in 1) (New York, 1958); Adams, Henry B., "The Declaration of Paris, 1861," *The Great Secession Winter of 1860–61 and Other Essays*, ed. by George Hochfield (New York, 1958), 363–89; Adams, Henry B., *The Education of Henry Adams* (Boston, 1918); Adams, Henry B., *The Letters of Henry Adams, 1858–1891*, ed. by Worthington C. Ford (Boston, 1930); Adams Family, *A Cycle of Adams Letters, 1861–1865*, ed. by Worthington C. Ford (Boston, 1920), 2 vols.; Argyll, George Douglas, 8th duke of, *Autobiography and Memoirs*, ed. by Dowager Duchess of Argyll (London, 1906), 2 vols.; Ashley, Evelyn, *The Life and Correspondence of Henry John Temple, Viscount Palmerston, 1846–1865* (London, 1876), 2 vols.; Atkins, John B., *The Life of Sir William Howard Russell* (New York, 1911), 2 vols.

Baker, George E., *The Life of William H. Seward, With Selections from His Speeches* (New York, 1855); Baker, Philip, "The Confederacy and England: The Editorial Opinion of the Richmond *Examiner*, the *Charleston Mercury*, and the Augusta *Chronicle and Sentinel*," M.A. thesis, Emory Univ., 1955;

Bancroft, Frederic, *The Life of William H. Seward* (Gloucester, Mass., 1967 reprint), 2 vols.; Barnes, Thurlow W., *Memoir of Thurlow Weed* (Boston, 1884); Bates, Edward, *The Diary of Edward Bates, 1859–1866*, ed. by Howard K. Beale as vol. IV of the *Annual Report of the American Historical Association for the Year 1930* (Washington, 1933); Baxter, James P. III, "The British Government and Neutral Rights, 1861–1865," *American Historical Review* XXXIV (Oct., 1928), 9–29; Baxter, James P. III, "Papers Relating to Neutral and Belligerent Rights, 1861–1865," *American Historical Review* XXXIV (Oct. 1928), 77–91; Bell, Herbert C. F., *Lord Palmerston* (London, 1936), 2 vols.; Belmont, August, *A Few Letters and Speeches of the Late Civil War* (New York, 1870); Beresford-Hope, Alexander J. B., *A Popular View of the American Civil War* (London, 1861); Bernath, Stuart L., *Squall Across the Atlantic* (Berkeley, Calif., 1970); Bigelow, John, *Retrospections of An Active Life* (New York, 1909), 3 vols.; Black, Jeremiah S., "Mr. Black to Mr. Adams," *The Galaxy* XVII (Jan. 1874), 107–21; Blumenthal, Henry, *France and the United States, Their Diplomatic Relations, 1789–1914* (New York, 1972); Bourne, Kenneth, *Britain and the Balance of Power in North America, 1815–1908* (Berkeley, Calif., 1967); Bright, John, "Bright-Sumner Letters, 1861–1872," Mass. Historical Society *Proceedings* XLVI (Oct. 1912), 93–164; Broom, Walter W., "An Englishman's Thoughts on the Crimes of the South and the Recompense of the North," *Pamphlets Issued by the Loyal Publication Society*, no. 84 (New York, 1865); Browning, Orville H., *The Diary of Orville Hickman Browning*, ed. by Theodore C. Pease and James G. Randall (Springfield, Ill., 1925), 2 vols.; Buchanan, James, *The Works of James Buchanan, Comprising His Speeches, State Papers, and Private Correspondence*, ed. by John B. Moore (Philadelphia, 1908–11), 12 vols.; Bulloch, James D., *The Secret Service of the Confederate States in Europe* (New York, 1959 reprint), 2 vols.

Cain, Marvin R., *Lincoln's Attorney General, Edward Bates of Missouri* (Columbia, Mo., 1965); Carroll, Daniel B., *Henri Mercier and the American Civil War* (Princeton, N. J., 1971); Case, Lynn M., and Spencer, Warren F., *The United States and France: Civil War Diplomacy* (Philadelphia, 1970); *The Case of Great Britain, As Laid Before the Tribunal of Arbitration Convened at Geneva, Under the Provisions of the Treaty Between the United States of America and Her Majesty the Queen of Great Britain, Concluded at Washington, May 8, 1871* (Washington, D. C., 1872), 3 vols. in 4; Chase, Salmon P., *Inside Lincoln's Cabinet: The Civil War Diaries of Salmon P. Chase*, ed. by David Donald (New York, 1954); Chevalier, M. Michel, *France, Mexico, and the Confederate States* (New York, 1863); Clapp, Margaret, *Forgotten First Citizen: John Bigelow* (Boston, 1947); Coleridge, Ernest H., *Life and Correspondence of John Duke Lord Coleridge, Lord Chief Justice of England* (London, 1904), 2 vols.; *Congressional Globe*, 37 Cong., 1 sess. and 2 sess. (1861); Connell, Brian, *Regina vs. Palmerston* (Garden City, N. Y., 1961); Conway, Moncure D., *Autobiography* (Boston, 1904), 2 vols.; *Correspondence Concerning Claims Against Great Britain, Transmitted to the Senate of the United States, in Answer to the Resolutions of December 4 and 10, 1867, and of May 27, 1868* (Washington, D. C., 1869), 7 vols.; Corti, Count Egon Caesar, *Maximilian and Charlotte of Mexico* (New York, 1929), 2 vols.; Cowley, Henry R. C. Wellesley, 1st earl, *Secrets of the Second Empire* (New York, 1929), also published as *The Paris Embassy During the Second Empire* (London, 1927); Crooks, George R., *Life and Letters of the Rev. John M'Clintock, D.D., LL.D., Late President of Drew Theological Seminary* (New York, 1876).

Dalzell, George W., *The Flight From the Flag: the Continuing Effect of the Civil War upon the American Carrying Trade* (Chapel Hill, N. C., 1940); Dana, Richard H. III, *Hospitable England in the Seventies: the Diary of a Young American, 1875–1876* (Boston, 1921); Donald, David, *Lincoln Reconsidered* (New York, 1961); Dugan, James, *The Great Iron Ship* (New York, 1953).

Fitzmaurice, Edmond, *The Life of Granville George Leveson Gower, Second Earl Granville, K.G., 1815–1891* (London, 1905), 2 vols.; Forbes, John M., *Letters and Recollections of John Murray Forbes*, ed. by Sarah Forbes Hughes (Boston, 1899), 2 vols.; Ford, Worthington C., "Goldwin Smith's Visit to the United States in 1864," Mass. Historical Society *Proceedings* XLIV (Oct. 1910), 3–12; Ford, Worthington C., "Letters to Governor John A. Andrew in March, 1861," Mass. Historical Society *Proceedings* LXII (June 1929), 209–12; Ford, Worthington C., "Sumner-Andrew Letters, 1861," Mass. Historical Society *Proceedings* LX (Apr. 1927), 222–35; Frothingham, Paul R., *Edward Everett, Orator and Statesman* (Boston, 1925).

Guedalla, Philip, *Palmerston, 1784–1865* (New York, 1927); Gurowski, Adam, *Diary From March 4, 1861, to November 12, 1862* (Boston, 1862).

Hale, Edward E., Jr., *William H. Seward* (Philadelphia, 1910); *Hansard's Parliamentary Debates*, 3d Ser. CLXII–CLXIII (London, 1861–62); Harper, Robert S., *Lincoln and the Press* (New York, 1951); Hobson, J. A., *Richard Cobden, The International Man* (New York, 1919); Huse, Caleb, *Supplies for the Confederate Army, How They Were Obtained in Europe and How Paid For. Personal Reminiscences and Unpublished History* (Boston, 1904).

Insurgent Privateers in Foreign Ports, House Exec. Doc. No. *104*, 37 Cong., 2 sess. (Washington, D. C., 1862).

Jordan, Donaldson, and Pratt, Edwin J., *Europe and the American Civil War* (Boston, 1931).

Klingberg, Frank J., "Harriet Beecher Stowe and Social Reform in England," *American Historical Review* XLIII (Apr. 1938), 542–52.

Lewis, George C., *Letters of the Right Hon. Sir George Cornewall Lewis, Bart., To Various Friends*, ed. by Rev. Sir Gilbert F. Lewis (London, 1870); Lincoln, Abraham, *The Collected Works of Abraham Lincoln*, ed. by Roy P. Basler (New Brunswick, N. J., 1953), 9 vols.; Lothrop, Thornton K., *William Henry Seward* (Boston, 1899).

Martineau, John, *The Life of Henry Pelham, Fifth Duke of Newcastle, 1811–1864* (London, 1908); Marx, Karl, and Engels, Frederick, *The Civil War in the United States* (3d ed., New York, 1961); Maxwell, Herbert E., *The Life and Letters of George William Frederick, Fourth Earl of Clarendon* (London, 1913), 2 vols.; Merli, Frank J., *Great Britain and the Confederate Navy, 1861–1865*,(Bloomington, Ind., 1970); *Message of the President of the United States to the Two Houses of Congress at the Commencement of the Second Session of the Thirty-Seventh Congress*, accompanied by *Papers Relating to Foreign Affairs*, Senate Exec. Doc. No. 1, 37 Cong., 2 sess. (Washington, D. C., 1861); Miller, Francis T., ed.-in-chief, *The Photographic History of the Civil War* (New York, 1957 reprint), VI; Monaghan, Jay, *Diplomat in Carpet Slippers, Abraham Lincoln Deals With Foreign Affairs* (Indianapolis, Ind., 1945); Moore, John B., *A Digest of International Law* (Washington, D. C., 1906), 8 vols.; Moran, Benjamin, *The Journal of Benjamin Moran, 1857–1865*, ed. by Sarah A. Wallace and Frances E. Gillespie (Chicago, 1949), 2 vols.; Morley, John, *The Life of Richard Cobden* (Boston, 1881); Morley, John, *The Life of William Ewart Gladstone* (New York, 1903), 3 vols.; Motley, John L., *The Correspondence of John Lothrop Motley*, ed. by George W. Curtis (New York, 1900), 3 vols.; Motley, John L., *John Lothrop Motley and His Family, Further Letters and Records, Edited by His Daughter and Herbert St. John Mildmay* (London, 1910).

Newton, Thomas L. W., *Lord Lyons, A Record of British Diplomacy* (London, 1913), 2 vols.; Nicolay, John G., and Hay, John, *Abraham Lincoln, A History* (New York, 1914), V.

The Official Records of the Union and Confederate Navies in the War of the Rebellion (Washington, 1894–1914), 30 vols.; *ORA*, See *War of the Rebellion*, below; Owsley, Frank L, *King Cotton Diplomacy* (2d ed., Chicago, 1959);

Owsley, Harriet C., "Henry Shelton Sanford and Federal Surveillance Abroad, 1861–1865," *Mississippi Valley Historical Review* XLVIII (Sept. 1961), 211–18.

Park, Joseph H., "English Workingmen and the American Civil War," *Political Science Quarterly* XXXIX, No. 3 (1924), 432–57; Parker, Joel, *International Law: Case of the Trent* (Cambridge, Mass., 1862); Pierce, Edward L., *Memoirs and Letters of Charles Sumner* (Boston, 1877–94), 4 vols.; *The Present Condition of Mexico, House Exec. Doc. No. 100*, 37 Cong., 2 sess. (Washington, D. C., 1862).

Randall, James G., *Lincoln the President* (New York, 1945), 4 vols.; Rice, A. T., "A Famous Diplomatic Despatch," *North American Review* CCCLIII (Apr. 1886), 402–10, plus 13-page facsimile supplement; Rice, A. T., ed., *Reminiscences of Abraham Lincoln by Distinguished Men of His Time* (8th ed., New York, 1889); Ridley, Jasper, *Lord Palmerston* (New York, 1971); Robinson, William M., *The Confederate Privateers* (New Haven, Conn., 1928); Russell, John, *The Later Correspondence of Lord John Russell, 1840–1878*, ed. by G. P. Gooch (London, 1925), 2 vols.; Russell, John, *Recollections and Suggestions, 1813–1873* (London, 1875); Russell, William H., *My Diary North and South* (New York, 1863).

Schmidt, Louis B., "The Influence of Wheat and Cotton on Anglo-American Relations During the Civil War," *Iowa Journal of History and Politics* XVI (July, 1918), 400–39; Sears, Louis M., "The London *Times*' American Correspondent in 1861: Unpublished Letters of William H. Russell in the First Year of the Civil War," *Historical Outlook* XVI (Oct. 1925), 251–57; Seitz, Don C., *The James Gordon Bennetts, Father and Son* (Indianapolis, Ind., 1928); Seward, Frederick W., *Reminiscences of a War-Time Statesman and Diplomat, 1830–1915* (New York, 1916); Seward, Frederick W., *Seward at Washington, As Senator and Secretary of State. A Memoir of His Life, With Selections From His Letters* (New York, 1891), 2 vols.; Seward, William H., *The Works of William H. Seward*, ed. by George E. Baker (Boston, 1884), 5 vols.; Sowle, Patrick, "A Reappraisal of Seward's Memorandum of April 1, 1861, to Lincoln," *Journal of Southern History* XXXIII (May, 1967), 234–39; Stacey, C. P., *Canada and the British Army, 1846–1871, A Study in the Practice of Responsibile Government* (Toronto, 1963); Stanley Family, *The Stanleys of Alderley*, ed. by Nancy Mitford (London, 1939).

Temple, Henry W., "William H. Seward," *The American Secretaries of State and Their Diplomacy*, ed. by Samuel F. Bemis (New York, 1927–29), VII, 3–115; Thouvenel, Edouard A., *Le Secret de l'Empereur* (Paris, 1889); 2

vols.; Tilby, A. Wyatt, *Lord John Russell, A Study in Civil and Religious Liberty* (New York, 1931); Tocqueville, Alexis de, *Democracy in America* (New York, 1955), 2 vols.; Toy, Sidney, *The Castles of Great Britain* (London, 1953); Trescot, William H., "The Confederacy and the Declaration of Paris," *American Historical Review* XXIII (July, 1918), 826–35; Trimble, William, "Historical Aspects of the Surplus Food Production of the United States, 1862–1902," *Annual Report of the American Historical Association for 1918* I, 223–39; Trollope, Anthony, *An Autobiography* (London, 1924); Trollope, Anthony, *North America* (London, 1968); Twisleton, Mrs. Edward, *Letters of the Hon. Mrs. Edward Twisleton, 1852–62* (London, 1928); Tyrner-Tyrnauer, A. R., *Lincoln and the Emperors* (New York, 1962).

Van Deusen, Glyndon G., *William Henry Seward* (New York, 1967); Verner, Willoughby C., *The Military Life of H. R. H. George, Duke of Cambridge* (London, 1905), 2 vols.; Victoria, Queen, *The Letters of Queen Victoria, First Series, A Selection From Her Majesty's Correspondence Between the Years 1837 and 1861*, ed. by A. C. Benson and Viscount Esher (London, 1907), 3 vols.

The War of the Rebellion, A Compilation of the Official Records of the Union and Confederate Armies (Washington, D. C., 1880–1901), 128 vols.; Warren, Gordon H., "Imperial Dreamer: William Henry Seward and American Destiny," *Makers of American Diplomacy*, ed. by Frank Merli and Theodore Wilson (New York, 1974), I, 195–221; Weed, Thurlow, *Autobiography of Thurlow Weed*, ed. by Harriet A. Weed (Boston, 1883); Welles, Gideon, *Diary of Gideon Welles, Secretary of the Navy Under Lincoln and Johnson*, ed. by Howard K. Beale (New York, 1960), 3 vols.; Welles, Gideon, *Lincoln and Seward* (New York, 1874), first published in *The Galaxy* XVI (Oct.-Dec. 1873), 518–30, 687–700, 793–804, as "Mr. Lincoln and Mr. Seward"; West, Richard S., Jr., *Gideon Welles, Lincoln's Navy Department* (Indianapolis, Ind., 1943); Winks, Robin W., *Canada and the United States, The Civil War Years* (Baltimore, 1960); Woldman, Albert A., *Lincoln and the Russians* (Cleveland, 1952).

I finished writing this book in 1972. Since that time I have read a large number of books, articles, and dissertations, most of them published during the 1970s, relating to Civil War diplomatic history during the year 1861. Although many of these writings are important, and some (like several by Thomas Schoonover) deal with topics I have scarcely touched thus far, I have concluded that my narrative, at least for the time being, should stand as written, unaffected by any but the most decisive recent revelations. Most recent publications that have not influenced my story have therefore been omitted from this bibliographic compilation, but I do hope to refer to them in a future work on Civil War diplomatic history.

I would here like to record my gratitude to my daughter Adrienne, who at the age of thirteen proofread the entire manuscript text of this book. I am also grateful to have received a summer stipend in 1970 from the National Endowment for the Humanities and to have obtained from the Faculty Research Fund at Middle Tennessee State University a grant to help defray the expenses of a research trip to England in 1967. Finally, I must record my thanks to my colleague, Professor Robert E. Corlew, for certain indulgences while this book was being prepared for publication, and to Carolyn E. McClain, who typed the final manuscript.

Index

Adams, Charles Francis: arrives in England, 41; and British aid to the South, 171–75, 187–89, 192–93; and Bunch affair, 97, 99–104, 108, 111–15; confers with Lord Russell, 42–44, 52–54, 77–78, 81, 158–63, 203; and danger of British intervention, 126–28, 130–31, 134, 138–43; and Declaration of Paris negotiation, 77–78, 82–84, 94, 228; defends Seward, 56–59, 62–63, 68; disconsolate about quality of leadership in America, 204–205; favorably impresses Lord Russell, 16, 29, 113; meets with Lord Palmerston, 56, 192–93; and Mexican expedition, 157–68; and Morrill tariff act, 180–81; and U. S. propagandists in Europe, 177–79; and Seward's "bold remonstrance," 21–22, 25, 48, 50–52, 57; and slavery question, 183; *mentioned*, 38, 45, 49, 55, 61–62, 71, 87, 89–93, 148
Adams, Charles Francis, Jr., 62
Adams, Henry Brooks, 51, 61, 103
Alabama, the, 174
Anderson, Edward C., 171
Andrew, John A., 67
Antislavery sentiment in England, 15, 33–34
Archibald, Edward, 30, 191
Argyll, 8th duke. *See* Campbell, George John Douglas
Ashmun, George, 67–70, 225–26

Bates, Edward, 148–49
Bedford, duke of, 42
Belmont, August, 235–36
Benjamin, Judah, 133
Bennett, James Gordon, 218
Bermuda, the, 172–74
Bethel, Richard, 1st baron Westbury, 196
Blockade of Southern coast, federal, 4, 7–13, 22, 36–38, 40, 42, 48, 73, 82, 85–90, 93, 98, 105, 123, 126–31, 134, 138–39, 143–46, 148–52, 180–81, 190–92, 197, 204, 213–14, 243
Bonham, Milledge L., 104

Bright, John, 62, 91, 127, 133–34, 154, 181, 187, 198, 220, 235
Buchanan, James, 5–6, 154, 180, 216, 243
Bulloch, James D., 171, 173–74, 204
Bull Run, Battle of, 91–94, 102, 128, 133–34, 238
Bulwer-Lytton, Sir Edward, 131
Bunch, Robert, 35, 39, 74, 80, 90, 96, 98–100, 102–17, 148, 153, 196, 200, 214, 233–34
Bunch affair, 90, 97–115, 117, 171, 192, 196, 200
Burlingame, Anson, 61–62

Campbell, George John Douglas, 8th duke of Argyll, 41, 57, 62, 95–96, 104, 139, 185–87
Canada, 15–18, 24–31, 48, 52–53, 59, 64–70, 90–91, 94–96, 102, 104–105, 136, 192, 200, 202, 206, 219, 240–42
Cardwell, Edward, 1st viscount, 202
Cecil, Robert Arthur Talbot Gascoyne, 3d marquis of Salisbury, 131, 236
Chase, Salmon P., 199
Clarendon, 4th earl of. *See* Villiers, George William Frederick
Clay, Cassius Marcellus, 60–64, 184
Clifford, Charles Cavendish, 236
Clinton, Henry Pelham Fiennes Pelham, 5th duke of Newcastle, 95, 104, 198, 201
Cobden, Richard, 62, 127, 130, 181, 186–87, 198, 202, 220
Confederate commissioners in Europe, 7, 18–19, 21–22, 39–40, 50, 52–53, 128–29, 174–76, 214, 235
Confederate commissioners in Washington, 6
Confederate independence, recognition of, 6–7, 9–10, 18–22, 36–42, 44, 50–51, 59–60, 70–72, 75, 79–80, 84, 100, 102, 105, 110, 112–13, 129–31, 133–35, 143, 149, 153, 164, 193–95
Consuls abroad, American, 5, 174
Consuls in the U. S., British, 35, 39, 74, 86,

261

90, 96–100, 102–16, 118, 123–24, 133, 233
Corwin, Thomas, 156–57, 244
Cotton, importance to European nations of, 4, 10, 13, 24, 33–34, 39–40, 42, 50, 85, 89, 108, 126–30, 134–36, 138–40, 144–52, 171, 185–86, 197, 213–14, 236, 239–40
Cowley, earl of. *See* Wellesley, Henry Richard Charles
Crampton, Sir John, 159
Cuelebrouck, Blondeel von, 19, 214, 218

Dallas, George Mifflin, 7, 18, 38, 44–45
Dana, Richard Henry, Jr., 58, 183
Davis, Jefferson, 37–38, 76, 106, 133, 238
Dayton, William Lewis, 18, 80–82, 143, 150, 167, 183, 228–29
Declaration of Paris, 23, 40, 73–85, 94, 102, 112–13, 163–64, 228
de la Fuente, J. A., 243
Delane, John Thaddeus, 238
Denison, John E., 179
Derby, 14th earl of. *See* Stanley, Edward Geoffrey Smith
Diplomats abroad, American, 5, 60–62, 76
Diplomats in America, foreign, 6–8, 13, 55, 58
Disraeli, Benjamin, 1st earl of Beaconsfield, 28–29

Entente regarding American Civil War, Anglo-French, 10, 13, 16, 18, 22, 24–25, 38, 45–48, 56, 79, 81, 102, 109, 144–45, 221
Everett, Edward, 62–63, 70, 142, 177–78, 217–24

Faulkner, Charles J., 18–19
Fay, Theodore S., 61–62
Fergusson, Sir James, 28, 236
Fingal, the, 173
Florida, the, 174
Forbes, John Murray, 126, 226
Foreign enlistment act, British, 172–73, 204
Forster, William Edward, 41
Forsyth, John, 243
France, 7, 10, 13, 16, 18–22, 24–25, 40–41, 45–48, 61–62, 70, 74, 78–82, 84, 101–102, 106, 109–10, 115, 128–30, 134–36, 138, 140, 142–46, 148–56, 159–60, 162–69, 177, 193, 195, 198, 202, 238, 240–41, 243
Fraser, Trenholm and Co., 171–72

Gerolt, baron von, 45, 71
Gibson, Thomas Milner, 127

Gladiator, the, 175
Gladstone, William Ewart, 35, 49, 95, 104, 141, 186, 200, 221–22
Great Eastern, the, 27–28, 95
Gregory, Sir William H., 36–37, 50
Greville, Charles Cavendish Fulke, 34
Grey, Sir George, 95

Hammond, Edmund, 139
Harvey, James E., 177
Harvey Birch, the, 197
Hay, John, 207, 214
Hiawatha, the, 191–92
Head, Sir Edmund Walker, 26, 30, 64–67, 69, 215
Herbert, Sidney, 1st baron Herbert of Lea, 27
Hicks, Thomas, 70
Holland, Sir Henry, 4th baron, vii
Hotze, Henry, 175, 246
Hughes, John, 177
Huse, Caleb, 171, 173

Illustrated London News, 35, 62
Imprisonment of British subjects in the U. S., 117–25, 200–201
Index, the, 175
Intervention in the American Civil War, foreign, 3, 6–12, 18, 21, 36–37, 47, 126–27, 131, 134–53, 167–69, 213–19, 238, 243
Ironside, Issac, 33

Judd, Norman, 194

Kennedy, John A., 99

Law officers of the British crown, 39–40, 85, 87, 117, 120–21, 173, 188, 191, 203
Layard, Sir Austen Henry, 160
Lewis, Sir George Cornewall, 27, 95, 104, 197, 201
Lincoln, Abraham, vii, 3, 6, 10, 12, 25, 27, 33–34, 37–38, 44, 48, 52, 55, 57, 62, 64–65, 71, 74, 85, 88–90, 94, 101, 109, 118, 121, 123, 133, 155–56, 182–83, 187, 193, 195, 197, 201, 204, 210–11, 214, 217–19, 242
Lindsay, William S., 130, 175
London *Chronicle*, 220
London *Herald*, 122, 137
London *Morning Post*, 138–39
Lyons, Richard Bickerton Pemell, 1st lord: advises that Southern commissioners be welcomed in Europe, 9–11; believes Union

permanently divided, 32, 35; and British aid to Southern Confederacy, 188–89; and British neutrality proclamation, 45–47; and Bunch affair, 97–101, 105–11, 114–15; and Declaration of Paris negotiation, 73–74, 77–82, 84, 228; describes Seward as arrogant and warlike, 8–9, 12–13, 15, 17, 23–26, 29–30, 47–48, 52, 55–57, 60, 64, 66, 70, 78, 81, 86, 92, 94, 101, 109, 147, 180, 192, 196, 200, 212–14, 217–19, 224; and imprisonment of British subjects, 117–24, 200–210, 233; and Mexican expedition, 158, 161, 163–65; on "mob rule" in U. S., 8, 20, 48, 66, 117, 198–99; objects to Morrill tariff, 180; opposes interference with British cotton trade, 7, 9, 11–12, 85–90, 204; and *Peerless* and Ashmun affairs, 64–70; recommends Anglo-French entente, 10, 13, 24–25, 45–46; urges military reinforcements for Canada, 24–25, 27, 29–30, 48, 52, 200, 219, 241–42; warns of impending Anglo-American conflict, 13, 25, 37, 48, 52, 56, 66; *mentioned*, 34, 39–40, 55–56, 58–60, 71, 91–93, 133, 137, 140–41, 145–50, 155, 190–91, 215, 221, 223, 231, 236
Lynn, A. T., 35

McIlvaine, Charles P., 177
Manchester *Examiner*, 139
Mann, Ambrose Dudley, 50
Marcy, William, 76, 80
Marsh, George Preston, 177
Marx, Karl, 239
Mason, James Murray, 194, 201–202
Massachusetts, the, 190
Mediation by European powers, 20, 70–71, 136
Mercier, Edouard Henri, 6, 9, 13, 19–20, 45–48, 78–79, 89, 134–35, 138, 144, 150, 213, 215, 217, 228, 243
Mexican expedition by France, Great Britain, and Spain, 143, 146, 154–71, 192, 197–98, 243–45, 249
Milne, Alexander, 16, 101, 107
Milner Gibson, Thomas. *See* Gibson, Thomas Milner
Monck, Charles S., 201
Monroe Doctrine, 6, 158
Moran, Benjamin, 173
Morrill tariff act, 4, 39, 180–82, 187, 236
Morse, Freeman Harlow, 172, 174

Motley, John Lothrop, 51, 63–64, 134, 160, 181, 185–87, 221
Mure, Robert, 98–99, 117–18, 196, 231, 233
Mure, William, 98, 231

Napier, Lord Francis, 8
Napoleon, Louis, 136, 141–42, 144, 152, 202, 240–41, 245
Nashville, the, 197
Naval reinforcements, British, 25, 38, 69, 90, 96, 101, 104–105, 169
Neutrality proclamation, British, 22, 32, 38–53, 56, 75, 79, 108, 172, 174, 179, 188, 194, 202–205
Newcastle, 5th duke of. *See* Clinton, Henry Pelham Fiennes Pelham
Newspapers, Northern, 6
New York Herald, 31, 67, 218
New York Times, 19, 31, 52, 195

Palmerston, Lord. *See* Temple, Henry John
Parker, Joel, 249
Patrick, William, 118–19, 122
Peerless, the, 64–70, 225–26
Perry, Horatio, 224
Perthshire, the, 190–91
Pickens, Francis W., 80
Pike, James Shepherd, 184, 237
Port-closing bill, 85–90, 93–94
Privateers, Confederate, 22–23, 37–38, 40, 42–43, 49, 64–66, 69–70, 73–78, 80–83, 152, 188–89, 197, 206
Public opinion in England, 15, 18, 35–36, 40, 49, 58–59, 61–64, 91, 131–34, 138–43, 174–79, 181–82, 187, 194–95, 197, 216, 237
Public opinion in the U. S., 29, 39, 52, 109
Punch, 33, 62, 132, 180, 182

Quillan, Purcell M., 98, 117–18

Rahming, John C., 118–19
Ramsden, Sir John, 4
Rost, Pierre, 50
Russell, John, 1st earl: believes Union permanently divided, 34–35, 133–37, 186; and British aid to Southern Confederacy, 172–73, 187–89; on British neutrality proclamation, 37, 39–40; and Bunch affair, 99–106, 110–15, 196, 200; confers with Adams, 42–44, 52–53, 77–78, 81, 158–65; compliments Adams, 16, 29, 113; and cotton shortage, 128–30; and Declaration of

Paris negotiation, 73–75, 77–84, 94; deprecates difficulties with U. S., 29, 31; exhibits anti-American attitude, 16, 198, 226; and imprisonment of British subjects, 117–24; on intervention, 36, 134–38, 150; meets with Southern commissioners, 18–19, 39–40; and Mexican expedition, 157–61, 167–69; and port closing act, 86–88, 90; shows legalistic tendencies, 202–203; threatens British recognition of Confederate government, 7, 18, 21–22, 38; *mentioned*, 15, 17, 33, 45, 47–48, 50, 57, 64, 66–68, 70–71, 91–94, 143, 146–48, 181, 185, 190–92, 221, 243

Russell, William Howard, 10, 133, 196, 210, 212, 236–38

Sanford, Henry Shelton, 19–21, 175, 184, 228, 235

Schleiden, Rudolph, 8, 180, 212

Schurz, Carl, 143, 184

Seward, Anna W. (Mrs. F. W.), 55

Seward, Frances A. (Mrs. W. H.), 55

Seward, Frederick W., 20

Seward, William Henry: advocates naval blockade of Southern coast, 12, 85; and an alleged scheme to invade Canada, 24, 26, 48, 52, 59, 64–67; "bold remonstrance" of, 21–25, 48, 50–52, 57, 217–18; and British aid to Southern Confederacy, 173–74, 187–90, 197, 204, 206; and Bunch affair, 97–102, 104–11, 115–18, 200; criticized, 13, 20, 51, 57–60, 62–63; and Declaration of Paris negotiation, 73, 75–79, 81–84; defended by C. F. Adams, 51, 56–59, 62–63, 68; deprecated by members of British cabinet, 16–17, 26, 31, 56, 101–102, 111, 116; described by Lyons as arrogant and warlike, 8–9, 12–13, 16, 20, 24–26, 29–30, 47–48, 52, 56–57, 64, 66–67, 70, 78, 81, 86, 92, 94, 101, 109, 147, 180, 192, 196, 200, 212–14, 217–19, 224; and fortification circular, 147, 241–42; and imprisonment of British subjects, 117–24, 201, 233; insists that slavery not a foreign policy question, 183–84; and Mexican expedition, 155–57, 159, 162–70; and Morrill tariff, 182; objects to Confederate commissioners being received in Europe, 7, 19, 21; and *Peerless* and Ashmun affairs, 64–70; and port closing bill, 85–86, 88–90, 204; produces "Some Thoughts for the President's Considera-

tion," 10–11; resists foreign intervention, 3, 5, 7–8, 10–11, 13–14, 18–23, 36, 44–49, 51, 59–60, 71, 91, 116, 134, 143–53, 171, 193, 198, 205–207, 213–14, 216–19, 243; seeks to maintain peace with Great Britain, 32, 45, 48–49, 59, 65, 90–93, 179, 194–95; sends propagandists to England, 176–79; and *Trent* affair, 192, 195; *mentioned*, vii, 3, 27, 34, 42, 55, 85, 128, 133, 138, 140, 142, 191, 197, 223

Seymour, Edward Adolphus, 12th duke of Somerset, 95, 104

Slidell, John, 194, 201–202

Somerset, 12th duke. *See* Seymour, Edward Adolphus

Stanley, Edward Geoffrey Smith, 14th earl of Derby, 132, 236

Stoeckl, Edward de, 6, 9, 19–20, 213, 237

Stowe, Harriet B., 186

Sumner, Charles, 9, 13, 23–24, 57–64, 67, 89, 91, 133–34, 154, 181, 186–87, 196, 212–13, 215, 217, 224

Sumter, the, 187–88

Temple, Henry John, 3d viscount Palmerston: and Bunch affair, 101, 104, 110–14, 196, 200; confers with Adams, 56, 192–93; and cotton trade, 126, 129–31; critical of Americans, 15, 27, 179, 198–99; and Declaration of Paris negotiation, 82–83, 94; detests slave trade, 15, 70; favors sending military reinforcements to Canada, 15–18, 26–28, 31, 91, 94–96, 101; and imprisonment of British subjects, 117; and intervention, 36–37, 70–71, 136–39, 232, 240–41; and Mexican expedition, 160–63, 169; opposes Morrill tariff, 4; and port closing act, 87; *mentioned*, 49, 107, 133–34, 142, 174, 192–93, 202–203, 211, 221, 235–36

Thomas Watson, the, 173

Thouvenel, Édouard-Antoine, 18–21, 47, 74, 81, 144–45, 150–52, 229, 244

Times, The (London), 28, 33–35, 52, 60–61, 63, 121, 132, 138–39, 147, 179, 185, 191, 224, 236–38

Toombs, Robert, 128

Trent affair, the, 122, 168, 192, 194–98, 200–202

Victoria, Queen, 27, 49, 162, 204, 232

Villiers, George William Frederick, 4th earl of Clarendon, 186

Walker, Pinckney, 233
Walker, William, 176–77
War, Anglo-American, danger of, 8, 11,
  13–14, 19, 21–30, 48, 50–51, 59, 61, 66–67, ,
  70, 89–90, 94–96, 101–102, 138, 147,
  149–50, 153, 181, 192–97, 202, 205–206,
  217–18, 240–41
Weed, Thurlow, 177
Welles, Gideon, 85–86, 214

Wellesley, Henry Richard Charles, earl of
  Cowley, 40
Wesbury, Lord. *See* Bethel, Richard
Wheat shortage in Great Britain, 140, 239–40
Wilding, Henry, 172
Winthrop, Robert C., 177
Wyke, C. Lennox, 243–44

Yancey, William L., 39, 50, 247

THE UNIVERSITY OF TENNESSEE PRESS
Knoxville

DATE DUE